BEAU BRUMMELL, AGED 27, AT THE HEIGHT OF HIS REIGN IN LONDON
by Robert Dighton

(Reproduced for the first time by kind permission of Sir Kenneth Clark)

THE REIGN
OF
BEAU BRUMMELL

by WILLARD CONNELY

On March 30th, 1840, there died in a French lunatic asylum, obscure, but not forgotten, the greatest dandy, the greatest arbiter of fashion England, and perhaps the world, has ever known: Beau Brummell.

At the height of his power men paid Brummell for the privilege of walking down St. James's Street with him; a note of blame could exclude his unhappy victim from the ranks of fashion; a word of criticism from him was enough to consign a peer's new suit to the dustbin. And his tongue could drip acid if he thought the occasion, or the person deserved it. His boot blacking was sent from Paris, and he had his soles polished as well as

(*Continued on back flap*)

n front flap)

went out to dine,
air picked him up
ssing-room, and, in
should be spotless,
he door of his des-
oot of the staircase.
eneration, he was
e wore three shirts
debtor's prison he
of hot water and
we know them to
shions he set.
tten a brilliant life
ominating figure.
elded new facts to
of this wandering
he chapters on the
h gossip, scandal,
insolence of the
ond part gives an
equally interesting picture of the Beau's exile, his second "reign," and his tragic end.

THE REIGN OF BEAU BRUMMELL

By Willard Connely

SIR RICHARD STEELE
BRAWNY WYCHERLEY

THE REIGN OF
Beau Brummell

BY

WILLARD CONNELY

THE GREYSTONE PRESS
NEW YORK

124946

To
Virginia McKay

CONTENTS

CONTENTS

PREFACE

My INTEREST in Beau Brummell as a character dates from just twenty-five years ago, at which time I was fortunate enough to see that excellent character-actor, the late Arnold Daly, perform the part in the play by Clyde Fitch. Daly "lived" Brummell. Off stage and on, he was almost as original, as eccentric, as conceited, as irresponsible, and as magnetic as Brummell himself. When Daly in the play said "No gentleman is busy. Insects and City people are busy" —when he read that line, it was Brummell who was talking, and the audience were back in Regency days. Fitch wrote *Beau Brummell* for Richard Mansfield, the foremost American actor at the turn of the last century, an actor whose versatility Daly could not encompass. Yet from snuff-box to walking-stick, from white cravat to glistening boots, from pitch of the voice to the grace in his hands, Daly was no mean inheritor of the part which Mansfield created. I saw Mansfield only once. He acted *Dr. Jekyll and Mr. Hyde;* in dreams the green light on Hyde revisits me still. But to have seen Daly as the Beau was to make an everlasting possession of the whole play.

The frontispiece, of which Sir Kenneth Clark is unable to trace the provenance, may call for a word of reservation. Doubt has been cast upon every portrait of Beau Brummell which exists. Owing to the removal of the collection of prints from the British Museum for the duration of the present war, it was not possible to search through their water-colours by Dighton for positive identification of this one. But the intimately detailed description which we have of Brummell from those who knew him seems to fit it. In this picture the pose, the slightly starched elegance of the white cravat which Brummell himself invented, the high forehead, the grey eyes "full of oddity," the very expressive eyebrows and mouth, above all, the broken nose which the Beau as a soldier sustained by a fall from his horse (about eight years before 1805, the date given by Dighton in the lower right corner), may upon the whole be considered too individual to assign to any other character of the period.

With regard to my title, "The Reign of Beau Brummell," I would submit that the life of this man, from his boyhood at Eton to his last days in Caen, was signalized by a kind of sovereignty in character. In his own fashion he ruled London, even after his quarrel with the Prince. Nor did misfortune in exile subdue this regnant personality. He was called the "King of Calais." At Caen, he still held his levées, and though penniless, he maintained almost to the end his sway over the drawing-rooms there both French and English.

The biography of received standard, having now outgrown the abusive epithet "modern," is the study of a personality. "In order that the light of personality may shine through," says Mrs. Virginia Woolf, "facts must be manipulated; some must be brightened; others shaded; yet, in the process, they must never lose their integrity." In attempting a centenary biography of George Brummell I may in some degree, I hope, have achieved this process. More "manipulation" to which I own has been an arrangement of the facts for the first time in chronological sequence, quotation from the letters in essential excerpts only, and the pruning of much extraneous or apocryphal matter.

For example, a good deal of confusion has hitherto obtained in respect of the dates of Brummell's arrival at Eton and his departure therefrom, of his gazetting as a cornet of the Tenth Hussars, and of his admission to Oriel College and his going down. William Jesse, in his biography of Brummell which is the source-book, says that the boy went to Eton in 1790, at the age of twelve. Both the *Dictionary of National Biography,* and L. S. Benjamin ("Lewis Melville") in his later biography, repeat this error. While Jesse evades mention of any duration of the schooldays, other writers have guessed three years. Actually Brummell entered Eton in 1786 (*Eton Lists*), and remained there seven full years. Three years at Eton might not have determined the ruling humour of Brummell as a character; seven years did.

Again, there is a story arising from Gronow, in his *Reminiscences,* that Brummell was presented by his "Aunt Searle" to the Prince, one day in Green Park, and that the Prince said, "George, when you leave Oxford, apply to me.

I will give you a commission in the Tenth Hussars, my regiment." This error is thus expanded by Boutet de Monvel (*Beau Brummell and His Times*). I find, however, that Brummell got his cornetcy on May 17, 1794 (Austen Leigh, *Eton College Registers*), and that he was admitted to Oriel ten days *later*, May 27 (*Oriel College Buttery Books;* also C. L. Shadwell, *Registrum Orielense*, p. 261). Benjamin says (p. 31) that Brummell's father died "later in the year that he (George) went to the university." In fact, the elder Brummell died more than two months before, on March 17. The mother having died still earlier, the boy of sixteen was then under the guardianship of trustees.

Brummell's own word that he met the Prince "on the terrace at Windsor when a boy at Eton" (Jesse, I, 29-30) need not be doubted. This meeting led to the cornetcy. "It was not uncommon for an Eton boy whose friends were connected with the Court to hold a commission in the Guards and draw the regular pay." (Ralph Neville, *Floreat Etona*, p. 28.) An opportunity for further meetings with the Prince fell to Brummell after he quitted Eton at the end of 1793 and went to live in Abingdon Street, London, where he remained for nearly six months before he went up to the university. Jesse mentions these meetings (I, 30), but has no idea of just when they occurred.

To take another instance of material hitherto overlooked, it is pleasant to find, on the word of Charles Greville, and the Duke of Wellington (*Greville Memoirs*, December 5, 1829, ed. Lytton Strachey and Roger Fulford, 1939, Vol. I, p. 341), that King George IV did not utterly abandon his old friend in exile at Calais. Wellington, it appears, "extracted" the consent of the King for an appointment of Brummell to a consulship. The Duke then sent word to Lord Dudley, the Foreign Secretary, and in the heat of a government crisis, gave the matter no further thought. But Dudley, reluctant to act either with or without the consent of the King, neglected Brummell. When the government fell, and Wellington came in as Prime Minister, with Lord Aberdeen Foreign Secretary, Wellington found Aberdeen also opposed to helping Brummell. Aberdeen evidently believed that his own indifference would not be overruled by the King. Then the King died. Wellington, yielding to incessant importunity from Brummell's best friend, Lord Alvanley, disregarded Aberdeen, presented the application to the new King, William IV, and got Brummell named as consul to Caen.

Anyone familiar with another work of Mr. Roger Fulford's, his *George the Fourth,* easily the ablest short life of that King, will be aware that I have followed its authority to an extent only less than that which I have drawn from Jesse on Brummell. To comprehend Brummell it is necessary, I think, to recur to the King as long as the King lived. We have previously known what Brummell did without the King; it is a legitimate curiosity on the part of one who takes a fresh view to inquire what the King did without Brummell.

To Sir David Ross, the Provost of Oriel, I am grateful for his enthusiasm and personal aid in helping me trace the records of Brummell in that college. I would thank

Mr. Claude Elliot, Headmaster of Eton, for his assistance toward a similar end, also Mr. Colin Macmillan, Librarian of the school, for the valuable references which he set before me on the subject of the Eton regime at the end of the eighteenth century.

If I may mention Mrs. Virginia Woolf once more, I would venture to repeat what many must have already affirmed, that her brilliant short essay on Brummell catches the *élan* of the man with extraordinary vividness. She contributes nothing to the facts. But she writes of the Beau almost as if she had known him personally: "flickering, sneering, hovering on the verge of insolence, skimming the edge of nonsense, but always keeping within some curious mean." On Byron's friendship for him, Mrs. Woolf is equally penetrating: "Byron always spoke Beau Brummell's name with mingled respect and jealousy."

When in the course of my reading for this book a year or two ago I saw a performance of *The Mikado,* I was reminded of Brummell as soon as that highly diverting character, Pooh-Bah, said: "I was *born* sneering." By those who sneer as divinely as Pooh-Bah and Beau Brummell let us be amused, for we owe them the applause due to masters.

The Author.

The Athenaeum,
  Pall Mall, S.W.1.
    Brummell Centenary, 1940.

THE REIGN OF BEAU BRUMMELL

PART I

CHAPTER I

THE FAMILY

1734-1785

WHEN IN 1627 Sir John Monson the Lincolnshire baronet married an heiress, he brought the Monsons into the Home Counties. His wife inherited the manor of Broxbourne, Herts. For a century the Monsons of Burton, South Carlton, had represented Lincoln in Parliament; they had figured as well in the Navy and at Court; but now, more easily within reach of London, they strengthened their political hold. By another century, in 1728, just as George II came in, a descendant and namesake of Sir John's was made the first Baron Monson.

In this generation there were four brothers, all of whom had in Queen Anne's day gone up from Broxbourne to Cambridge. The third and the fourth brothers, Charles and Henry, both read law, Charles Monson having in the year of his admission to Pembroke College been admitted also at Gray's Inn, while Henry, scholar of Trinity Hall, proceeded in time to a fellowship. As Henry Monson was a good teacher he remained in Trinity Hall, which was strong in his subject, and soon he became LL.D. In the course of these years Charles had returned to Broxbourne, but established himself equally in town—Spring Gardens, Vauxhall. At the age of thirty-eight, in 1734, he exercised the Monson family prerogative of standing for Lincoln, and was returned M.P. Requiring in this same year a valet, for both town and country, Charles Monson engaged a young man of twenty-five called William Brummell. Of Brummell's immediate relations, nothing is known except that he was one of a family of two sons and a daughter. He had an elder brother, Thomas, and a married sister, called Elizabeth Griffin.

The new valet in his life with the Monsons between Vauxhall and Broxbourne proved to be both capable and diligent. When his master, in the year 1737, was appointed Deputy Paymaster of the Forces, the devotion of Brummell increased with his responsibilities, and the Monsons began to speak of him as "a very excellent servant." Charles Monson continued as paymaster for eight years, until 1745, when his time expired. But to sustain his career there were two things that seemed to embrace no likelihood of ending: his seat for Lincoln in the Commons, and his "very superior valet." By the time Monson's eldest brother Lord Monson died, in 1748, William Brummell had in consequence of strict attention to thrift been able to marry and set up a home of his own. His bride, Jane Garret, three years his junior, was the first-born of three sisters, the others being Margaret, a young woman of rather formidable character, and Sarah. In due time William Brummell

4

in turn begot two sons and a daughter, whom he called "Billy," Benjamin, and Mary. Yet, being so masterly a gentleman's gentleman that he was himself satisfied he could do no better in any other occupation, he continued in the service of the Monsons.

The duties of Brummell in Spring Gardens were not so onerous that they prevented him from undertaking a little business, combined with social enterprise, elsewhere in town. In order to give his family a leg up, he acquired the freehold of a house in Bury Street, St. James's, a neighbourhood not unfashionable, and reserving for the Brummells the ground floor, William turned over to his good wife Jane the letting of the floors above. This venture turned out to be a prosperous one.

When Charles Monson withdrew from Parliament in 1754, after serving twenty years, serving well his country and his family alike, the retirement of the master from public life still made no difference in the plans of the faithful Brummell. Like Shakespeare's Adam, he "sweat for duty, not for meed." One incident only, in these later years, took him out of his usual path between Spring Gardens and Broxbourne. Early in 1757 his master's younger brother Henry, whose gifts as a tutor in Trinity Hall and as a lecturer to the university had won him, not long before, the chair of Regius Professor of Civil Law, fell critically ill. Charles Monson thought the best sort of help he might extend to the stricken man would be to send William Brummell down to attend him. In this emergency Brummell soon showed that he was as painstaking a nurse as he was efficient a valet. Noticing that his patient had difficulty in drinking from the utensils provided, he wrote to London for one of his own, a glass vessel of special design for invalids. "If not in Spring Gardens," Brummell explained to Charles Monson, "it may be found in Bury Street. It was used when Billy was ill." The ailing professor, heartened by such concern for his minor discomforts, might well have been thought to get the better of his major ones. But all the Brummells in London could not have saved him. The malady of Henry Monson took a fatal turn, and on February fifteenth he died, too young, at the age of sixty-one. He was buried at Broxbourne.

After this unhappy interval Brummell returned to Vauxhall and resumed as usual his regular duties. He had more time, now that his master was living in the private way, to visit the "messuage and tenement" in Bury Street. His children were growing up, and Billy, the eldest, was making himself generally useful to the lodgers in the house of Jane Brummell, even as his father continued to typify the perfect valet in Spring Gardens. The surroundings were favourable. The father of the Brummells had as a boy enjoyed nothing of the kind. Bury Street, rich with memories of Dean Swift and Dick Steele who had lived there only a generation or so before, still attracted men of mark, and these men brought with them opportunities. One day, when Billy was about fourteen, Mr. Charles Jenkinson walked past, looking for rooms, and his wandering eye was arrested by the highly accomplished penmanship of a sign "apartments to let," which was fixed to the house of Mrs. Brummell. He went in. Liking what he saw, he engaged quarters. The next thing he found out was that the sign beside the door had been written by Billy, the son of his landlady.

Jenkinson, now at the beginning of a political career, was a young man still under thirty-five, and had been recently returned M.P. for Cockermouth, Cumberland. More important, Lord Bute, the young King's favourite, noticed him, and had him made Under-secretary of State, with the result that the outlook for Jenkinson in both government and Parliament was at the moment a matter of much interested discussion. Perhaps the political position of their new lodger did not concern the Brummells, either mother or son; what did concern them was the comfort of Mr. Jenkinson in their house. There was about the long-faced long-nosed Billy a certain alertness, politeness, eagerness to please. Jenkinson noticed this promising quality, at the same time bearing in mind the skill of the boy in handwriting. Before long, young Brummell had become secretary to the Under-Secretary. When in 1763 George Grenville, Chancellor of the Exchequer, chose Jenkinson—now leader of the "King's friends" in the Commons—as Joint Secretary to the Treasury, Jenkinson found for Billy a clerkship in that office.

In August of the following year Charles Monson died. The Monsons seemed not a very long-lived stock; he was only sixty-eight. William Brummell, having now lost the only master he had known for thirty years, was left feeling somewhat solitary, in spite of his interesting family.

Although he was himself only fifty-five, he could not bear the thought of serving anyone else. All of his children were by this time adequately taken care of. Not only was his elder son safely in the Treasury, but Billy, by the ready influence of Mr. Jenkinson, had found for Benjamin another post in that department. Mary, their sister, was wedded to a certain acceptable Mr. Tombs. The father of the Brummells, noting above all that he had good reason to be grateful to his competent wife Jane for returning a profit from the house in Bury Street, felt justified in retiring. Thus closed the active career of the valet incomparable.

In spite of the serenity in Brummell's domestic circle, it was perhaps not unnatural that the death of Charles Monson should depress with a sort of lingering grief the servant of a generation. No later than February, 1765, barely six months after Monson died, William Brummell set about making his own will. He possessed a substantial estate to bequeath, and he was fond of his entire family. To his wife he devised what she had earned: the freehold house, and an annuity, besides all the plate, linen, and furniture. Not only did he give legacies to each of his children, to his brother, and to his sister, but to both of his sisters-in-law, still maiden ladies, Sarah and the redoubtable Margaret. For executor, in addition to his wife, Brummell astutely named Charles Jenkinson. If the affluent valet himself had laid for his family the foundation to fortune, Jenkinson was the man who was cementing it.

Now living in a not altogether agreeable idleness with his wife and sons, now happy enough, yet melancholy,

Brummell still gained no small satisfaction from increased evidence that his quick-witted Billy was improving his time well at the Treasury, and disclosing a capacity for work quite beyond that of the ordinary staff. Therefore, when in 1767 Jenkinson relinquished his own post in favour of Lord North, the Brummells betrayed no anxiety. Nor need they have done, for Jenkinson on leaving persuaded North to retain Billy, obviously a civil servant of value, as his private secretary. It was thus the luck of young Brummell to fall in with two men who themselves were making their careers. So well did he now answer the expectations of his new master that when in March, 1770, Lord North was named Prime Minister, he kept Billy on.

Here indeed was a triumph for the Brummell family, and it came just in time. On the last day of that month, William Brummell the elder, to whom retirement in Bury Street quite failed to prove a change for the better, gave up the ghost, almost as if he had pined away in mourning for his master. Still, he died no little comforted by the thought that his son, Secretary to the Prime Minister of England, need never be a valet. They buried William Brummell in the courtyard of old St. James's Church, Piccadilly, and on the west wall of that courtyard fixed a plain tablet to commemorate him. Perhaps his ultimate victory was the inscription on his will, as deposited in the public registry: "William Brummell of Bury Street, St. James's; gentleman."

As his son Billy, the new head of the house of Brummell, began at about this time to pick up in Lord North's office any perquisites that might come his way, he grew acquainted with a certain Ann Richardson. She was the youngest daughter of the Keeper of the Lottery Office. Reputed one of the prettiest women of her day, Miss Richardson was a slender graceful figure, with features delicately modelled, and a mass of fair hair to which only Gainsborough could have done justice. Brummell, a person of darker visage, with a long nose almost comic and an underlip slightly undershot, was in breeding no evident match for this young lady. But in understanding of finance he need not have bowed to any of the Richardsons. Billy reckoned that if marriage was a lottery, perhaps one way to diminish the risk of it was to marry the lottery itself. Whereupon, proceeding to win this most eligible daughter of its Keeper, he improved his finances.

The Richardson family were the sort who paid homage to pedigrees. With a monument in Westminster Abbey to the man from whom they claimed descent, Sir Thomas Richardson, Chief Justice under James I, they were not altogether elated to receive a Brummell into their circle. Who *were* the Brummells? Yet within no long period of time the Richardsons themselves were obliged to conclude that this marriage to the Prime Minister's Secretary was not too bad, for of the three elder sisters of young Mrs. Brummell, one gave her hand to an actor, another to a farmer, and the third to a Welshman of whom the utmost that could be said was that he was "a respectable person in the City."

Meanwhile the Brummell family constituency of two

sons and a daughter repeated itself again, as in the case of Billy's father and grandfather. To the present Mr. and Mrs. Brummell were born at short intervals Maria, William, and George Bryan, all in Westminster, and the last, on June 7, 1778, in the parish of St. Margaret's. George Bryan was apparently named in honour of his father's intimate friend and colleague, Bryan Broughton, of the Treasury. Between the infant boys there was only a year. By the time George was exactly two years old the family were privileged to live in Downing Street, where the father as usual was performing his duties with energy, punctuality, and competence.

Although Lord North was having a rather heavy time with his ministry, and the war with the American colonies was plainly going against England, these difficulties, so long as North held office, raised no impediment to the prosperity of Billy Brummell. The Prime Minister even sweetened the labours of his secretary by tendering him a string of the egregious sinecures which were in the gift of Downing Street: Receiver of the Duties on Uninhabited Houses in London and Middlesex; Controller of the Hawkers' and Pedlars' Office; Agent and Paymaster to the Out-Pensioners of Chelsea Hospital. These crushing burdens alone netted Brummell the tidy sum of £2,500 a year. Accordingly, when satirical pamphlets of the day dubbed Lord North the "God of Emolument," Billy Brummell came in for his share of the lashing. It left him supremely indifferent. Upon the resignation of North in 1782, the sagacious secretary was able to retire, and he did so at an age much earlier than that at which his father had retired. During twelve years of successful service for an unsuccessful administration he had plucked the fruits which made him easy for life.

Little George Bryan, then, saw only four years in London before his family carried him away to the country. The Brummells a little later took a pied-à-terre in Charles Street, off Berkeley Square. But they chose Berkshire for the centre of their life henceforth, and they moved into a house of repute in its community. Not so famous itself, this house, which was called The Grove, enjoyed a kind of reflected fame by reason of standing very near Donnington Castle, in which Chaucer had lived, and from which, little over a century before, the King's men had fired their artillery against the forces of Cromwell.

Now Billy Brummell, coming down to the country as a figure of some political standing, decided as a country gentleman to go in for two things: charity and hospitality. On the one hand he began to give bountifully to the infant poor; on the other he started to entertain elaborately the adult well-to-do. To be quite in the swim, he had elaborate portraits of the children done, the boys together by Reynolds and their sister by Gainsborough. William and George were posed in the shade of whitebirch trees, frisking with two small dogs, and William catching his brother by the hair, while George caught one of the dogs likewise. Maria, in a big lace hat with a green bow, and wearing a green sash, was seated tranquilly on a mossy bank, a contented kitten in her arms. The father of this family so early launched into fashion lost no time using his experience in gaining appointments, and was soon made high sheriff for Berkshire. Friends trooped in from the country-side, or down from town, all passing without ceremony through the unlatched door of The Grove, which hung upon great long hinges centuries old.

Over the threshold, before the wondering eyes of little George Bryan, came famous men whom his father knew from Downing Street to Drury Lane. There was Charles James Fox, who seemed to be called "the Opposition," a little fat-faced man, with black eyebrows that arched up, a very small mouth, hair that looked blown both ways by the wind, and always wearing a yellow waistcoat that bulged out a good deal. Mr. Fox often brought with him his "political friend," Mr. Richard Brinsley Sheridan, who knew all about the theatre, had in fact written plays, which were much more important than Parliament. Mr. Sheridan was such a handsome man, too, who walked very proudly and wore fine clothes. He looked serious, but said funny things. And he had a boy called Tom who was nearly grown up, being three years older than George Bryan. Sometimes Mr. Sheridan himself brought a friend, whose name was Harris, and who owned Covent Garden Theatre. George must certainly go there, "a little later on." Then there were baronets and barristers—George had to remember which was which—Sir Joseph Andrews, Sir John Macpherson, and his father's "dear friends," Mr.

Joseph White, of Essex Court, Temple, and Mr. William Chamberlayne, of Lincoln's Inn Fields, not to mention George's own namesake, Mr. Bryan Broughton.

This was the milieu in which the Brummell children emerged from their earlier childhood. Still, the kin of the family, if rather less exciting, were not quite left out. Mrs. Jane Brummell, the worthy grandmother, lived until George was seven; to her, George's father Billy owed no small strain of the character upon which he had wrought his present independence. At her death, the house in Bury Street fell to "Mary Tombs and her husband," George's Aunt Mary. But the relation most feared by the diminutive George Bryan was Great-aunt Margaret, the spinster sister of his grandmother, and a woman with no nonsense about her; the youngest of the Brummells was ever wary to evade Aunt Margaret's disciplinary clutches. On the other side of the family, Aunt Brawn, the Richardson sister who married the farmer, was a visitor to The Grove. Upon occasion the Brummells took coach into Northampton-shire, to Lilbourn, to stay with the Brawns, a journey always memorable to George in view of the fact that his aunt served delicious damson tart. During one visit to the farm the boy created a hubbub at table, crying aloud in rage and shame, because he was quite unable to eat as much of this tart as he had piled upon his plate.

CHAPTER II

ETONIANS

1786–1794

In 1786, when the older of the boys, William, was nine years of age, it was decided by his parents that he should go to Eton, and it was further decided that George might as well proceed thither at the same time. Not that either boy had learnt all the lessons which a local school was able to set. The young Brummells, sad to say, were not what might be called apt pupils. But their father was anxious to secure, by a paternal connection with Eton, his own approach to rarefied society, and he was equally eager that manners, at least, be inculcated in his sons before they grew any less impressionable. On this basis, indeed, the boys might be admitted to the school, although it did not appear from the record of their studies accomplished thus far that their rank at entrance would be very high. Brummell *major* and Brummell *minor* were accepted for the first form, in which few boys at Eton began. William was placed seventh on the list of ten, while George was ninth.

The school costume of the time was distinctly a blue coat and knee breeches. The coat bore a double row of large brass buttons, the top one of which was left open, in order to show a bit of a white waistcoat inside, and a ruffled shirt. The cravat, also white, was tied in a bow, and Brummell *minor* proceeded without delay to wear the wings of his cravat not only longer than his brother's, but more neatly tied, so that it partly overlaid the lapels. At first sight these boys, who were lodged together in Dame Young's, would hardly have been taken for brothers. They both had light brown hair, both were fair of complexion, and both had faces rather long, like their father; but there the resemblance ended. William was the handsomer, George far the livelier. William at this stage bore a languid contemplative look, while George, even at the age of eight, stood upright, self-possessed, a creature of the moment, and alert to respond to the inspiration of the moment. The difference in their character showed in their mouths. William's was soft, almost feminine, a mouth in repose, whereas George's was narrower, with thicker lips held a bit tense, as if with difficulty keeping back impudence. Their very hair, near of a colour as it was, bore out this contrast: George, who had less, wore it like a man, letting it fall in scant locks just below his ears; William had long curls which tumbled down about his shoulders. It was plain that the two Brummells would not beat the same path in Eton College.

Wherever their whims or their duties might lead them, they were not likely to be influenced very much by their Headmaster. This worthy was Jonathan Davies, a learned, pleasant, generous, open-hearted man, but a man of humble birth, and therefore called by the boys "Barber" Davies. He had two drawbacks. He was a loud and voluble talker, and he had "an invincible partiality for the charms of London," whenever his duty did not actually oblige him to be at his lodge. One of the Fellows, describing in rhyme an event as distant and improbable, thus observed:

"Sooner Stentorian Davies cease to talk,
And for his Eton quit his Bond-Street walk."

But the Headmaster when in town never missed a chance to nip in at Carlton House or St. James's Palace, for he found it convenient to justify his absences from the school on the ground that it was essential to sustain the royal patronage of Eton, by sustaining the royal interest in Eton, when the royal family were not in residence at Windsor Castle. Davies, as a man of obscure antecedents, was also perhaps not indifferent to his own social eminence.

But he need have felt no anxiety over any lapse of interest on the part of George III. For twenty-five years the King had kept a weather eye upon this school, and in the streets of Eton he was a familiar personage to the boys. In 1787, only a few months after the Brummells had enrolled, the King said: "I wish from time to time to show a regard for the education of youth, on which most essentially depend my hopes of an advantageous change in the manners of the nation." He was still under fifty, still in his prime, and as he drove through Eton on his way to hunt with the Royal Buckhounds he often stopped to greet any pupils seated on the wall. Flashing a mildly disciplinary look from his rather prominent blue eyes, the King inquired: "What's your name? Who's your tutor? Who's your dame? Very good tutor. Very good dame. Well, well, my boy, when were you flogged last, eh, eh? Your master is very kind to you, is not he? Have you had any rebellions lately, eh, eh? Naughty boys, you know, sometimes. Should not you like to have a holiday if I hear a good character of you, eh, eh? Well, well, we shall see about it. But be good boys!" So George and William Brummell "basked in the sunshine of royalty," as a somewhat jealous old boy of Westminster School remarked, declaring that the vicinity of Windsor Castle was of no benefit to the discipline and good order of Eton.

For more than a year not only Brummell *minor* but his more thoughtful brother as well remained in the first form. This aversion to progress may have been due to their tutor, Dr. Joseph Goodall. While on the side of scholarship and teaching capacity Goodall lacked nothing if his pupils desired to learn, he was a bad disciplinarian. On the other hand his personality immensely impressed, almost hypnotized the Brummells, especially young George Bryan. It was acknowledged by the whole school that Goodall had many of the qualifications of a courtier: with a gracious and polished bearing he combined "a pleasant joyousness which beamed and overflowed in his face," and he was suave, good-natured, witty, and a teller of stories both short and amusing, the supply of which seemed never to run out. Such a man must have seemed to the effervescent younger

Brummell, second from the bottom of the first form, quite the pattern of all that was desirable in life. Awe might overcome diminutive George as at the end of his first year he looked up at his great schoolmates who had gained the heights, George Canning and John Hookham Frere, head boys of the Oppidans, editors of the school weekly, *The Microcosm*. The precocious Canning, on leaving at the end of summer half, thus consoled Eton in that paper: "to have sucked the milk of science, to have contracted for *her* a pious fondness, which will bind me forever to her interests, and perhaps (pardon, kind reader, the licensed vanity of a periodical writer abandoning himself on his death-bed to the fascination of egotism), to have improved by my earnest endeavour, her younger part of the present generation, is to me a source of infinite pride and satisfaction." Little Brummell, possibly admiring at a distance the gigantic intellects of Canning and Frere, may well have caught something of their mental swagger if not of their zeal for learning. But it was Dr. Goodall to whom he could turn for an intimate example, and the influence of this tutor upon Brummell *minor* became a question of the fashioning of a personality.

Not until 1788 did the brothers manage to advance into the second form. This form was ranked in two divisions. William, who had been doing a spot of work, made third place in the upper half, while George, not quite in stride with that company, took first place in the lower. But of all the boys in Dame Young's, none could equal George Brummell in toasting bread and cheese; he it was who gained the honour of toasting the double portion of it allotted each night to the head boy of the house. While this was an accomplishment of no mean distinction amongst the Oppidans, it failed to impress Mr. Brummell senior, of The Grove. He was not satisfied that his younger son, after two years at Eton, should gain a standing no better than the lower half of the second form. Determining that if the school could not administer discipline he would try it himself, he sent his butler over from The Grove with a letter to each son. The one to the elder began: "My dear William." The other letter began: "George." George was to come home at once, was to bring all his clothes, and was not to expect to return to Eton. A schoolmate, entering the room of the Brummells at Dame Young's, found the cheese-toaster in tears, tears streaming down, tears which blurred both of the letters lying before him. Probably not since the heavy day of the damson tart had such eloquent tears issued from the youngest of the Brummells. "George!" exclaimed his friend. "What's the matter?" The boy could not speak, but with agonized face pointed first to "My dear William," and then to the terrifying monosyllable "George." There was nothing to do, but to obey his father.

One mitigating point was that school holidays soon afterwards ensued. Another was that if little George had made no substantial headway in his Latin and his arithmetic, he did bring home, even in his eleventh year, something of the courtliness, the ease, the considerateness for others, which only a mellow Etonian like Dr. Goodall could have inspired him to ape. Few children of the age of George Bryan might in such matters be so impressionable. But he was already harnessing deportment to his animation of spirits. Exposed at The Grove to the metropolitan poise and assurance of such guests as Mr. Fox and Mr. Brinsley Sheridan, he acquitted himself acceptably, and no doubt profited still further from what he observed of their dress, their conversation, even their style of walking. Then, perhaps to his surprise, his father relented, and by next half George reappeared at Eton.

Both brothers achieved the third form in 1789, although not the distinguished end of it. This form was in three divisions, upper Greek, lower Greek, and non-Greek. Listed near the top of the third were the Brummells, able at least to look down upon those few whom they still outranked. Safely within the form, however, George did not allow his studies to interfere with his games. He was well-knit for a boy of his years, and if he had slightly short legs, they were the kind of legs sturdy enough on the playing field. When he put off his brass buttons and white cravat, and got into his thick shoes and striped worsted stockings, he was out to give a good account of himself on the junior football side, and did it. The same was true when summer half brought cricket in. Throughout the session, indeed, Brummell *minor* developed in general to a degree not hitherto discernible. As he courted popularity with his elders, so he reached for it with the boys whom he carefully chose as his intimates: George Leigh and Jack Musters amongst the forty boys in his own house, and Berkeley

Craven at Dr. Foster's. Jack Musters had come to Dame Young's only this year, from Nottingham. Uncommon spirits were these three, and they took a liking to George Brummell because they found laughter in the corners of his small grey eyes, and he was clever, frank, and unsparing in repartee. The end of summer half placed both Brummells not only in the fourth form, but in its upper Greek. William had worked for it; George had done a minimum of work, but had exercised a great deal of charm.

At the end of the year 1791 Jonathan Davies retired as headmaster and was succeeded by Dr. George Heath, senior assistant master. Heath has been described as a strong solid man, but "dim-eyed, and of a melancholy air, without any of the radiance of success." That is, he was somewhat easy-going, and perhaps a bit lazy. One of the best things about him was his eldest daughter Susan, admired at a distance by pupils new and old. His accession, much to the satisfaction of George Brummell, left Dr. Goodall the senior assistant master. To Joseph Goodall, the model of manners, conversation, and wit, this boy now deferred more and more.

Indeed five years of Eton had brought Brummell *minor* to the pitch of making himself something of a personage. When he was dressed for games, he could be as rough-and-tumble as the rest; but now he began to be known at all other times for the elegance of his clothes, as well as for the extreme neatness of them. Before he was fourteen he was called "Buck" Brummell, like other and older schoolmates who affected nicety in dress. With great anxiety he

avoided the muddier streets on a rainy day. With complacent self-assurance he introduced a fashion in neckwear:
a bright gold buckle pinned behind his white stock, an
ornament elusively glittering under the curtain of his light
brown hair. Unambitious for fame in his studies, yet aspiring to distinction as an individual, he began to assert his
personality by cultivating a pose.

One day on the bridge the Buck came upon a small
crowd of his schoolfellows mauling a Windsor bargee. As
a feud always smouldered between bargees and Etonians,
here was a providential opportunity to tip the rascal over
the rail and into the river. Brummell, who would soil
neither his hands nor his clothes in such a vulgar scuffle,
nevertheless became at once the actor, the commanding
figure, the cool remonstrator: "My good fellows," he interposed, "don't send him into the river. The man is evidently
in a high state of perspiration, and it amounts almost to a
certainty that he would catch cold." From anyone else
these phrases would have met with a jeer, and perhaps a
ducking into the bargain. From George Brummell, to such
smoothness had he by this time fetched his affectation, they
evoked good-natured laughter, approval, and assent. The
bargee was hustled along the road instead, and let go.

Pranks of this kind were not suppressed under the reign
of George Heath. The sleepy old Headmaster was a bit
lax, and the boys were quick to sense it. Not a few of them
shirked their books if they felt so inclined, for the penalties appeared to be eased up. Under the last year of Davies,
the Brummells, for example, had applied themselves stead-

ily enough to gain the upper Greek of the fourth form, whereas now, in 1792-3, although promoted to the fifth form, they both slumped to the lower division, and their names were next to each other. George Brummell, then, in restraining his comrades on the bridge, was by no means frowning upon horse-play. He was merely parading his egotism. It was a fascinating talent, he thought. Dr. Goodall had helped him discover it. But the Buck was as ready as anyone to sally forth upon adventures, as when of a spring evening in this half he and two friends put on outlandish costumes with intent to serenade the winsome Susan, daughter of the Headmaster. Halting beneath her window, they made a great hubbub upon a triangle, a hurdy-gurdy, and a French horn. Brummell played the horn. He was not flogged. Dr. Heath was too fond of him. "He was never flogged," said an old Etonian years afterward, "and a man is not worth a damn, sir, who was never flogged through the school." While it need not be added that the father of Buck Brummell would hardly have approved of this moonlight serenade to Miss Susan Heath, the mild regime of the present Headmaster suffered young Oppidans to do many things of which their parents would have disapproved.

All was thus going reasonably well with young George at Eton, his manner if not his intellect taking the mould which he personally designed for it, when in the middle of March of his seventh year at the school, 1793, his mother, still a young woman in her forties, died without warning. For a good ten years Mrs. Brummell had been at The

Grove a capable, untiring, and resourceful hostess. She had so excelled in the art of entertaining that she made her house almost a landmark, which steadily attracted from London the sort of guests whom she and her husband wished their children to know and admire. Her work with these children was left unfinished. But she had seen Maria, William, and George through some of their most critical years, and whatever she had been able to give them of that "Richardson tradition" so revered by her own family, they took in, and profited by, let the discipline come as it might from the Brummell side.

When George went back to Eton for summer half he did not give way to his sorrow, but put on his cricket togs and played hard. It was of course a show of prowess on the playing field that gained him a following amongst the heartier boys like Jack Musters and Berkeley Craven; if there had been nothing to Buck Brummell but precious utterance, he could never have restrained a crowd of his fellows from pitching a bargee into the river. They knew that in games, when dirt and sweat befitted the occasion, Brummell took his share. This term his cricket was good enough to put him into the Eton side. In mid-season, on the day the Etonians played against the Oldfield Club, a neighboring team from Berkshire, he scored naught not out and twelve, besides making three catches in his opponents' second innings.

It was at about this time, according to his own recital of the matter, that the first great event in the life of George Brummell occurred. On Sunday afternoons, it was the custom of the royal family to walk upon the terrace at Windsor Castle. Etonians were in the habit of going there in full dress, dress which must be imperatively tidy, complete, and correct. (If the black stockings had holes, the boys inked their legs; but Brummell *minor* was never of those afflicted with holes.) Often the King—as when the boys were sitting on the wall in front of the school—stopped and chaffed the young promenaders, in particular about being out of bounds, for while the terrace itself was in bounds, the way to it was not. Sometimes the King invited into the Castle a number of the pupils to entertainment and supper, and "remembered to forget" to invite the masters. In the case of Buck Brummell, therefore, visits to Windsor, familiarity with the Castle, and an occasional "basking in the sunshine of royalty" were by the end of his seventh year at Eton nothing new.

But it was not the King alone who was fond of the school. Old Jonathan Davies, in the eighteen years of his headmastership, had seen to that, in the course of his frequent calls at Carlton House upon the Prince of Wales. The Prince was now thirty-one. Since the very year of his birth, he knew, his father had made repeated and minute inspections of Eton; accordingly the Prince was willing enough to "inspect" any dignitaries of the school who might come to town. Davies not only made the most of the hospitality of Carlton House, but sometimes made too much of its wine-cellars. When one evening the Prince in deference to his learned guests spoke of Homer, the Headmaster demanded, "What do you know about Homer?

I'd bet you don't know a line of the Iliad." Whereat the Prince, showing that he had at least got through the first book of it, flashed back in Greek the words of Achilles to Agamemnon: "Thou wine-bibber! thou with face of dog and heart of deer——" That was enough for Davies. But he and the Prince continued very good friends, and when Dr. Heath succeeded Davies, the Prince remained no less a patron of the school. Upon his visits to Windsor he found like his father his own measure of fun with the boys.

For nearly eight years the Prince had been morganatically married to Mrs. Fitzherbert. If his constancy to her was one laudable thing about him, his debts—now amounting to £400,000, what with improvements to Carlton House and building a Pavilion and cottage for the lady at Brighton—were a thing not so much to be approved. "Newmarket," the Lord Chancellor commented, "and other extravagances more referable to profusion than essential to dignity." But not even the Lord Chancellor would say that the visits of the Prince to Windsor lacked either dignity or sobriety. At a glance, George was a great person; and he made sure that his dress emphasized the fact. As Knight of the Garter, he liked to wear his star; he wore it when he rode his horse at Windsor; when he put on the uniform of a grenadier; even when he walked in ordinary day clothes, on the terrace. In those times when men arranged their hair almost like women, combed out at the sides, and on top brushed back high in the manner of a pompadour, the Prince took pains with his headdress, and protected it on either side by the great black hat then in fashion, with a broad brim, high crown, and a buckle in front. About his neck the collar of his coat stood high, too, and opened to small triangular lapels, the whole enclosing a white stock. But at a glance, also, the Prince was a Hanoverian; he had the Teutonic blue eye and full cheek, the Teutonic slant of nose and forehead, while his expression, if regal enough, gave no sign of any very likely play of wit.

Now upon the terrace at Windsor this Sunday afternoon, the Prince of Wales, meeting a number of young gentlemen from Eton, gave "some slight notice" to George Bryan Brummell. A boy half the age of the heir to the throne arrested the royal eye. Was it a question of dress, or manner, or both? The things that bred curiosity in the King about his Etonians—tutors, dames, floggings, holidays—were no special concern of his son. But the coat and the white muslin of young Buck Brummell—perhaps he wore them noticeably well. Now fifteen, Brummell *minor,* to a degree not attained by his older brother William, had caught that worldly air which Eton peculiarly bestows. He was precociously aware of himself. His principal study had for some time been the study of his own appearance. As Tacitus put it, he enjoyed his own fame. If the Prince took notice, this notice was not lost upon the favoured schoolboy, there on the gravel walks, before the grey battlements of Windsor, and overlooking the school distinguished by royal largesse.

Not long thereafter, by the end of this year 1793, the father of the Brummells came to the decision that it was

time for his sons to leave Eton, where in seven years they
had managed to progress through only five forms. After
the Christmas break they did not return to the school.
William may have regretted it; not so George. He was
growing up a little. He had won popularity. He had met
the Prince. One thing at Eton irked him: a certain rev-
erend tutor, a master in Lower School, was given to the
repellant habit of sending to The Grove a "true and particular account" of the delinquencies of Brummell *minor*.
Why should a young gentleman of the world indefinitely
put up with that? Perhaps his father concluded that he
himself need be no longer afflicted with these reports.
George had made his way in cricket if not in construing.
There was also a question of the boys going on to Oxford, and to get ready for that new chapter in their lives
they might do better under the parental eye.

Whereupon Billy Brummell took his sons to live with
him at the house in London, in the surroundings of which
they could meet more of the men upon whom their future
might depend. It was well for the fate of these boys that
they were introduced in town no later, and that they enjoyed an opportunity of strengthening their acquaintance
with men of the stamp of Sheridan, and of Charles Fox.
Suddenly, as early as the month of March (1794) the
father of the Brummells untimely died, leaving his three
children now complete orphans. Just a year and a day
after his wife had been taken to the family vault in St.
Martin's-in-the-Fields, Billy Brummell was also buried
there.

CHAPTER III

ORIEL COLLEGE

1794

BILLY BRUMMELL had survived his master Lord North by only two years, but of course had died a much younger man, being still under fifty. Having accumulated a fortune which enabled him to retire at the age of thirty-five or thereabouts, Brummell did not live more than twelve years after his retirement. Under North, he had learned both how to save and how to realize on his savings; the inside knowledge of finance to which the Prime Minister had access, and upon which he speculated to advantage in the funds, was not lost upon his observant secretary. The resulting assets reached no small total. At The Grove this retired young capitalist lived on a scale which only a generous income could support, and yet at his death he left £65,000, to be divided in equal portions between Maria, William, and George Bryan as soon as they should come of age. To secure the legacy first payable, the sister had not long to wait; William had longer; but Buck Brummell faced five full years before he could gain his financial liberty.

The trustees to whom the father had for the interim confided the control of his estate approved the plan that the sons, young as they were, should proceed to Oxford. It was perhaps natural that the Buck, for his part, should choose Oriel, that college which just two and a quarter centuries before had admitted Sir Walter Raleigh. Whilst this debonair young Etonian remained for the moment with his brother in London to make arrangements with the trustees and to prepare for his new scene of life, he remembered that he had friends at Court. No small part of his heritage were those friends whom his father had collected both in London and at The Grove, and had handed on. There were still those great men, Fox and Sheridan. Strictly speaking, Fox was by no means "at Court"; the King detested him as a gambler and a rake; but he had served as a junior Lord of the Admiralty under Lord North, at which time Billy Brummell had been useful to him, and Fox did not forget the sons of Billy. If now at the age of forty-five he was unpopular for having quarrelled with Burke, had been deserted by most of the Whigs, and was in political eclipse, Fox was still the man for whom the beautiful Duchess of Devonshire, in order to win a vote for him, had kissed a shoemaker. Therein, for Buck Brummell, lay the value of the influence of his father's friend. Sheridan was less the complete politician. Although in politics the ally of Fox, he was now an "independent member," and was more famous for his speeches in the trial of Warren Hastings than for any defence of the waning Whigs in the House. Here again, the entourage of Sheridan in society was the thing that attracted the young man down from Eton.

Whether by the sponsorship of Sheridan and Fox, or indirectly by some of their acquaintance, the Buck soon found himself in the company of intimates of the Prince of Wales. In George Bryan they discovered wit, style, magnetism, and a sense of dress, indeed a character reminiscent of that of another Etonian, George Augustus Selwyn, who had lately died and was much lamented. (Selwyn had been also an acquaintance of Billy Brummell's.) If this young Buck should prove a second Selwyn, as it appeared he might well be, he ought to be gathered into the circle of the Prince.

When the companions of the royal heir communicated their news, the Prince did recall that "slight notice" which a certain smart young Etonian had drawn from him a year or two before. He said he would like to see Brummell again. The consequence was that the Buck at the height of a London season was invited to a party. With all his equipoise, so consciously trimmed during his last years at school, George Bryan demeaned himself in the eyes of the Prince with such ingratiating manners that on the spot he was enlisted not merely for the royal amusement, but proposed for a cornetcy in the Tenth Hussars, the Prince's own command. Only two months after his father's funeral, to a day, May 17, 1794, George Brummell was gazetted.

Yet it was thought wise that both he and his brother, since they were only sixteen and seventeen, should go on to the university for a time. It was not uncommon for an Eton boy—even whilst he was still at school—whose friends were connected with the Court, not only to hold a commission in the Guards but to draw the regular pay. Accordingly, only ten days later, on May 27, George and William were admitted commoners at Oriel College, paying £15 caution money each. On the following day they both matriculated. George gave his address as "Abingdon Street, Westminster."

Oriel, though founded by so remote a king as Edward II, had freshly made a stir in the university by building in the back quadrangle a new library, grim and gaunt, but rich within. It was built to hold a bequest of all the books of Lord Leigh—an Oriel man who had been High Steward of the university—and with the arrangement of it the college entrusted a Fellow himself grim and gaunt, Henry Beeke, reputed inventor of the income-tax. But the Provost, John Eveleigh, was the man to whom the credit of the library went. He made its opening the first important event of his reign.

With this good man Buck Brummell must have felt at once congenial, for Eveleigh by nature was not unlike the beloved Joseph Goodall, courteous, fine-mannered, with Goodall's "pleasant joyousness," and no idolator of discipline. The Provost came of a Devonian family, a family celebrated for one idiosyncrasy, which was a perpetual fondness for light blue. They were nearly all as blonde as angels. Eveleigh himself was fair-haired and fair of skin, and true to the disposition of many of his family he was "mild, inoffensive, and unambitious." Sang a waggish undergraduate of the day, "Here comes fair Eveleigh with his blue hose." Even at formal college meetings the Provost could never dispense with the family colour. But in the words of a later colleague, he was "a man to bring down a blessing on any society of which he was a member." The Fellows of the 1790's must themselves have felt reasonably well blest, for they were living loosely and luxuriously, dined early and drank late, and over their cards of an evening played high.

Here was an atmosphere not inimical to the ends which Buck Brummell held in view. To one intent upon shaping his own ego, such a setting might even contribute. George began modestly enough, his battels for the first week running only to the sum of 9s. 8d., whereas the sober William exceeded that amount by a shilling. In the following week the expenditures of William were three shillings greater than those of his brother; but in the third week the Buck "found himself" and went ahead of William by half a crown. The boys had entered in the tenth week of term, the term known as "Act." As this term ended on June 13, the accounts in the buttery books were then made up in totals for each item. Again, under one suggestive heading, William Brummell had proved the greater libertine: his fines for "knocking in at the gate" after closing hour were 1s. 9d., whereas those of the Buck were only 1s. 1d. That this behaviour was not altogether riotous on the part of either one, may be gauged from the fact that another undergraduate, called Lowther, who had been up not much longer, was fined for the same offence 7s. 6d. But under a second item, "knives, forks, and clothes," Buck Brummell revealed somewhat his propensity: his charges for those things were 4s. 2½d.; William's were 2s. 10½d. Perhaps it was the heading "letters" which told a story most indicative: hereunder the claim against William was 2s. 2d., while against George it stood: one penny. That appeared to be a College record.

Trinity term continued immediately after Act, without any recess. By this time the Buck had made some start in selecting his acquaintance. He sought out those whose knowledge was unique, not profound; usable, not worthy; and before long he fastened upon a student unrivalled in the university for droll anecdotes and comic songs. This was learning indeed. George took pains to get by heart the ballads as well as the yarns. Then, at wine-parties, he so cleverly entertained a widening cluster of undergraduates with them that instead of depressing his tutor with derivative essays he took to delighting his friends with original jingles. In this term, the position of the brothers Brummell in respect of "knocking in at the gate" was rather more than reversed. The fines against William were ten-pence; against the Buck, twice as much.

Soon the Oxford reputation of George Brummell for wit exceeded that of the man from whom he had borrowed it. Quips fathered upon Brummell himself took wing round the college. "Did you hear what Buck Brummell said about that?" "Do you know Buck Brummell's very latest one?" "That sounds just like Brummell." It was said that satirical squibs posted up in the Lodge were by him. A certain horse, always ordered at hall-time, was Brummell's. Buck Brummell put down in the quadrangle a tame jackdaw, with bands on, to mimic the dear old Provost.

Throughout the month of June, however, the battels of George and William Brummell remained about even, roughly in the same sum as in their first week of residence at Oriel, with the Buck on the shorter side. In July, only a negligible charge was recorded opposite the names of both: the amount against George was only five shillings, and against William no more than one shilling. Probably the brothers were dining out every night. In the case of the Buck at least there was a significant reason for this sharp drop: fed up with Oxford, he was going down; the pull was too strong; he wanted to "join his regiment." It is of course quite possible that good John Eveleigh, no longer amused by jackdaws and satire, refrained from discouraging the departure of Brummell the younger. After July 4 no battels were debited to this undergraduate in the buttery books.

The name of George Brummell, which at the beginning of the next Michaelmas term was still carried on the college list, although he was not present, was in November taken off the books of Oriel for all time. In actual residence his Oxford education had extended through a period of just five weeks and two days. But had he not put in seven years at Eton? There he had cultivated some taste for French and English literature, for painting, and for drawing, and he was content to "face the world" with that. No more Brummells of the elder generations survived to bid him do otherwise, neither his parents, nor his father's parents. As for the trustees, they were not to interfere with the plans of the Buck.

His brother William returned alone to Oriel in October, for Michaelmas term. Not a very serious student, though with a reasonably acceptable record in deportment, he remained in residence until near the Christmas recess.

CHAPTER IV

THE SOLDIER

1794-1798

THE TENTH Hussars was a regiment of the sons of dukes and earls: there were Lord Edward Somerset, son of the Duke of Beaufort; Lord Charles Ker, son of the Duke of Roxburgh; Lords Charles and Robert Manners, sons of the Duke of Rutland; and for good measure, young Bligh and young Lumley, sons of the Earl of Darnley and the Earl of Scarborough. Here was worshipful society, ready-made for the valet's grandson who had so rapidly, yet so serenely, stepped across the threshold of London. As it happened, his retreat from Oxford was most opportune. In this very summer the Prince was in need of the kind of diversion with which a young and original wit could furnish him. The royal heir, after ten years of infatuated devotion to Maria Fitzherbert, had just broken off with her. Buck Brummell, gay but placid, merry but correct, fresh yet oddly mature, strolled into the breach.

The Prince had not fallen out of love with his plighted

mistress, although by her he had no child. It was in another quarter that childlessness was a serious matter: none of his brothers had begotten any offspring, and the succession was in danger. For that reason he must marry, and old George III had repeatedly made it plain that unless the Prince did marry, none of his debts, now swollen to a figure quite beyond the power of the debtor to remedy, would be paid. Again, the Prince had developed an intimacy with Lady Jersey, daughter of an Irish bishop, a bewitching little woman, notwithstanding she was ten years older than himself; she played the harp to him, and (anything to get him away from Maria) induced him to believe that he ought to marry a Princess. The harried heir finally gave in; he did not care who the bride might he, he would take the first German frump that a boat could deliver. All this the King settled with no more ado. "His wish is," said George III, "that my niece, the Princess of Brunswick, may be the person."

Meanwhile the Tenth Hussars cavorted about on their usual excursions, either from London to Brighton, or from Brighton to London, according to where their Colonel-in-Chief, the Prince, might choose to sojourn. Very fond of his "military camps" at Brighton, he had made the town a fashion since he had first known Mrs. Fitzherbert. When he built his first Pavilion there, its centre a circular room with a bulge of Corinthian pillars outside, and its dining-room in a wing so close to its kitchen that his guests dined steaming, he also built an Adam house in the grounds for Mrs. Fitzherbert, with an ale cellar, a small beer cellar, a wine in casks cellar, and a wine in bottles cellar. But there were cellars in the Pavilion as well. Old maids left town when the Prince and his officers arrived. "The military" brought their blood horses, their curricles, and their girls. George Brummell early distinguished himself at a review by being thrown from his horse and breaking his nose. After parade, at one o'clock, the Hussars drank until five, dined, and at eight trooped to the theatre. "Vivent l'Amour et Bacchus," said a newspaper of the day.

Early in the spring (1795) Brummell accompanied his fellow-officer, Lord Edward Somerset, with the escort to fetch Princess Caroline from Greenwich to London for her wedding. She was twenty-eight, five years younger than her bridegroom; she was short, but rather attractive, and she had an abundance of fair hair. The young cornet in his rich uniform, impressed by his errand as never before, found enthusiasm for the Princess. "A very handsome and desirable-looking woman," was his comment. Upon the arrival of the party in London the Prince, first meeting the lady, unfortunately did not appear to be so full of admiration. Turning to Malmesbury, who had brought Caroline from Germany, he said, "Harris, I am not well; pray get me a glass of brandy."

But from Buck Brummell this contretemps remained hidden. To him, all was well. In his boyish exaltation over the great event, and the part which he was so excitedly playing in it, the poise, the restraint, even the percipience which he had for several years studied to cultivate over lesser matters, these things naturally enough failed to operate. When on April 8 the wedding took place in the Chapel Royal, Brummell as *chevalier d'honneur* was in personal attendance upon the Prince. Not to his ear had come the first comment of the Princess upon her husband-to-be: "I find him very fat." (The Prince weighed about seventeen stone.) Nor was it evident to Brummell, in the church, as it seemed to others, that the bridegroom "looked like Death . . . as if he wished to hide himself from the looks of the whole world." Caroline, whatever her true feelings, walked in "the highest spirits . . . smiling and nodding to everyone." And the young *chevalier,* through rose-coloured glasses, amply satisfied with himself and with life, later remarked, "The young couple appeared perfectly satisfied with each other, particularly the Princess."

Brummell went down with them to Windsor for the first few days of the honeymoon. His duty was to report to the Prince each morning, whilst his master was still at his elaborate and fastidious toilet, to take the orders for the day. Then he accompanied them, and his regiment, to Brighton for the summer. It was here that his Oxford education, that is to say, his collection of stories and songs, served Buck Brummell well, for whether he was with the Prince in the morning, or at the officers' mess for lunch, or dancing with the ladies at night, he played Boccaccio to them all. Excuse for absence from duty, or from tardiness at parade, was perhaps too easy: he was with the Prince. Late for drill, he galloped up to the colonel with an excuse half impudent, half apologetic, but wholly original, and by the very humour of it he was ordinarily let off. So seldom with the Hussars, he was hardly acquainted with his own troop. But, when he came along ten minutes late, he had a way of finding it: there was in the company a Bardolph, with a great blue nose; Brummell rode down the line until he arrived at the nose, then took his place to the front or rear as necessary.

Back in London for the autumn season with Edward Somerset, Charles Ker, and the Manners brothers, Brummell soon took with them "a course through the town." Without seeking, he was sought after by all the ladies of fashion, who were not only attracted by the royal favour which the Buck enjoyed, but were fascinated by his oddity, charmed by his gallantry, and enslaved by his wit. One evening a great law Lord who lived in a big house near Russell Square gave a ball. The belle of this ball sat through dance after dance and declined all offers. Late in the course of the party the footman announced Cornet Brummell, and scarcely had this sensational arrival made his bow to the belle when she arose, gave him her hand, and was whirling into the midst of those whom she had refused. It was too good not to have been prearranged. As Brummell and his partner brushed against one of the discarded, the Buck inquired of him, "Who might be that ugly man, near the chimney-piece?" "Surely you know him," was the answer: "That's the master of the house." "No," replied Brummell, "how should I? I was not invited."

On January 7, 1796, the date being no later than the law allows, a princess was born at Carlton House to the Prince and Princess of Wales. She was named after his mother, Charlotte. But as between the parents of this child no affection had developed from the day they had met, even the birth of the infant failed to engender any change of feeling. Caroline was as frivolous as George was fickle; they bored each other, and they seldom met. In March the Prince left his wife to go to Windsor. At the end of April he wrote to her to say that neither should "be held answerable to the other because nature had not made them suitable to each other." He proposed that their future intercourse be restricted to "tranquil and comfortable society"; he only wanted peace. The Princess complied. In this adjustment of domestic maladjustment Buck Brummell of course played no part. But only a month thereafter, on June 1st, almost as if in celebration of the event, the Prince approved the promotion of Cornet Brummell to a captaincy in the Hussars.

He had hardly sought for this promotion. Higher rank, what with its higher pay, was convenient, and an honour, yet carried with it some increase of military duties and consequently a curtailment of his independence. His tall spare figure was attractive to the ladies, and Captain Brummell yielded willingly enough to their invitations. One of those who fell in love with him at Hampton Court was Julia Storer, daughter of a maid of honour to the Queen, and a niece of Lord Carysfort, a girl shy and reserved enough, exquisitely mannered, but with arms and hands rather more engaging than her features, which were not regular; Julia played the harp, very gracefully, in a perfumed room with a lamp lit low. Another of his admirers was Lady Sarah Savile, who was so fond of the Buck that she worked for him a green portfolio. Daughter of the Earl of Mexborough, Lady Sarah was among the most captivating young women at Court, and was accounted of "surpassing beauty." One summer afternoon she included Brummell in a picnic party to Gypsy Hill, Upper Norwood. A gypsy woman there encamped came forward, took the hand of Lady Sarah, and read its lines; she predicted marriage to a nobleman, and described him, prophesied his death, and a second marriage, but did not characterize the second husband.

In these little adventures with the ladies lay more amusement for the Buck than any number of parades, manœuvres, and debauches with the Tenth Hussars. True enough, he had got into fashionable company in London by reason of his membership in the Prince's own regiment; yet it was fashion which now appealed to him more than a uniform. Fashion, for example, had now decreed that hair must no longer be either tied or powdered. Under the leadership of Lord Jersey, husband of the Prince's new favourite who had been made a lady-in-waiting to Caroline, a number of noblemen had concocted an anti-pigtail plot. Brummell as a captain in the army chafed because all officers were still required to powder their hair, indeed to use upon it a pound of flour a week. Must he be unfashionable?

How was he to withdraw from the Hussars and still maintain his valuable friendship with the Prince? He could hardly come right out and say he objected to powdering. But it happened that upon a certain day when the troops were quartered in Brighton a sudden order came to them to march to Manchester, where mill-hands were rioting. To Brummell the thought of Manchester even without a riot was unbearable. Early on the morning after the order arrived he made his way to the Prince.

"I really could not go," said Brummell after apologies, "*think*, Sir, *Manchester!* Besides, *you* would not be there."

The tactful word struck home, as the Buck was quick to observe. "I have therefore determined, Sir," he continued, "with your permission, to sell out."

"Oh, by all means, Brummell," said the Prince, "do as you please, do as you please."

It was now 1798, and the Captain was twenty, and the heir to the throne was thirty-six. At the moment the Prince happened to be in no state of mind to argue with his young follower. Lady Jersey, who had been for about four years the royal mistress, was not quite so enchanting now that she had dwindled into the later forties. The Prince was alone in Brighton; it was too awkward for him to bring Lady Jersey there after he had separated from Caroline. With Lady Jersey he had put in an autumn at Bognor; with her again he had tried a winter in Dorset; and now it was plain to everyone except herself that he was done.

In this year the Prince gave the lady her *congé*, although

she tried hard to think he would retract if only she gave him time. She was wrong. There was only one thought in the head of George the Fat, and that was, for his peace, for his solace, for his very life in nearly all that counted with him, he must rejoin Maria Fitzherbert.

CHAPTER V

CHESTERFIELD STREET

1799–1803

AT THE supposedly responsible age of twenty-one, it is no
small undertaking for a man to make a solemn determination to be a successful do-nothing. Only one with supreme
faith in himself as a character will calmly dedicate his life
to being simply the architect of that character. But Brummell, having for four years tasted of the success which can
arise from a well-directed study of self, reckoned that if he
could go thus far with no money at all, he might as a man
of independent means encounter hardly any limits to his
personal triumph. The army had tidily bridged him
across his minority. Within a few months after he quitted
the Hussars he got his inheritance. It amounted, including interest, to £30,000. As he came into this patrimony,
he embarked upon his new scheme of life, less gregarious,
more individual, less confined, more varied; modified,
regulated, dictated, by himself alone. This was no mere
scheme of elaborated idleness; rather, it entailed a hard

enquiry into leisure, a very elusive subject. The inquiry involved, at least to begin with, bachelorhood, no easy state for a wealthy young man already old in experience, and already petted by young ladies of the stamp of Sarah Savile.

To carry out his plan he took lodgings in Mayfair. The address was Chesterfield Street, No. 4. In that street Selwyn had lived. Conscious that he had been likened to him, and by no means disdaining the heritage of wit which Selwyn had left, Brummell may well have fancied being identified with "the street where George Selwyn used to live." First it was essential to employ a manservant skilled in cookery; this done, he designed to make the reputation of his bachelor quarters by little dinners richly served. Next, though he hated exercise of any kind, Brummell knew that for the sake of the figure he wished to cut he must do a bit of hacking in the Park; he bought two horses. Third, in order to confirm and expand his already assured start in society, he determined to be the best-dressed man in London.

The art of dress may be said to have been made easier for Brummell by birth. To the very tips of his fingers the dimensions and proportions of the man were remarkable, and not needing to become a model for an artist, he became an artist in outfitting himself as a model. With no inclination to excess in either food or drink, he could by scarcely any effort keep his figure to lines which might well set a fashion, lines which would not belie the head and features that lent them all the more distinction. While

48

his head was well shaped, his face was long, and neither plain nor handsome; he retained the fair complexion and light brown hair of his boyhood, the hair, now that pigtails and perruques were abolished, growing full about the ears and curling halfway down his high forehead. Upon meeting Brummell, one had to observe not so much his steady grey eyes, but the play of expression round his mouth and his eyebrows; to a word politely spoken the eyebrows might give the twist of sarcasm, impishness, or doubt. To set off these features he chose for the morning either Hessians and pantaloons or topboots and buckskins, with a blue coat and a buff waistcoat; of an evening, the waistcoat white, with blue coat, and black pantaloons buttoned tight to the ankle over stockings of striped silk. This was the style which Brummell affected at the outset of his career in Chesterfield Street. His aim was to make the fit of his clothes the admiration of London, and since his measurements were almost the tailor's ideal, he found himself at the age of twenty-one more than half onward to his goal.

In this question of dress, Brummell as a friend of the Prince adroitly played the game of the Prince, who fancied his own achievements in costume second to none in the kingdom. The withdrawal of Captain Brummell from the regiment made no alteration in their friendship, except that when the Prince left London for a visit in the country Brummell perhaps oftener than before was a member of the party. In January, 1799, they went down to Leicestershire, to celebrate at Belvoir Castle the coming of age of the Duke of Rutland. Others in the company were the Duke of Argyll, the Marquis of Lorne, and young Lord Villiers, to whom, although he was the son of Lady Jersey, the Prince did not object. Magnificently upon the summit of a hill stood the castle; in its quadrangle, for the festivities, a bullock was roasted whole; in front of the castle there were fireworks in bizarre designs, hours of screaming splendour in yellow; and at the bottom of the hill another bullock turned on the spit. For three weeks this party went on, whilst the October ale never ceased flowing. One morning Brummell was cheered as he went down the hill in a pelisse of fur to skate upon the ice; the tenants thought he was the Prince. One night he was not cheered by the guests; he rang the great firebell, and all who had gone to bed came rushing out in their nightgowns; Brummell, appearing on an upper balcony, said his valet had forgotten his hot water.

This valet Robinson he made seem sometimes his villain and sometimes his master. Not long after the party at Belvoir, Brummell was driving through Kent with a carriage and four. It was his habit, whenever he drew anywhere near the quarters of the old Tenth Hussars, to pop in and pay them a visit; indeed, so often did he visit them that the officers were now saying they knew him much better than when he belonged to the regiment. Into the barrack-yard at Canterbury he drove this day. "Hello, George!" called a friend from the mess-room window; "When did you take to four horses?" "Only since my valet gave me warning," came the swift reply, "for making him travel with a pair."

But the country held little lasting charm for him, and as Brummell in town fashioned himself into a character, Robinson, that indispensable right wing at the dressing of his master, could hardly avoid developing a character of his own. One day an acquaintance in the course of a morning call in Chesterfield Street, a man just down from the Lake country, rapturously described his travels, dwelt at length upon the scenery, and with rather tedious persistence interrogated Brummell as to which of the lakes *he* liked best. "Robinson," Brummell implored his valet, "which of the lakes do I admire?" Quickly came the rescue from Robinson, "Windermere, sir." "Ah, yes—Windermere," repeated Brummell, "so it is—Windermere." If on the other hand the Prince called, to watch his young friend being skilfully attired by Robinson, the talk was not of lakes, but of clothes, a subject upon which not even the most fashionable woman of the day ever expended so much worry, invention, and fastidiousness as did the heir to the throne. Brummell was willing. Was he not in process of making himself arbiter? Sometimes the Prince sent away his horses, and stayed on. Sometimes, lost in fine points about the cut of a coat or the decoration upon a snuffbox, he stayed to dinner, at which the wine ran late and free.

It was this extreme attention to taste in dress that soon won for Brummell the title of Beau. If Beau Wilson was a duellist, Beau Nash a martinet, and Beau Fielding a sot, Brummell was none of these; he made the resolution to be a Beau in his own way. This scheme embraced correctness in dress without ostentation, cleanliness in habits without use of scent, originality in character without caprice, and superiority in manner without undue seriousness. Nor, to sustain his emergence into individuality, did he depend upon the Prince. A Prince, by absorbing time no end, must not overshadow a Beau. In April of this year (1799) Brummell joined Brooks's Club, being both proposed and seconded by his elder friend, Sir Edward Fawkener, Ambassador to Turkey. While Brooks's was one of the two leading clubs, the Beau took little interest in it as a club, but rather in the fact that it gave him an excuse to walk down St. James's Street; again, it was perhaps a swift escape from unpleasant country houses. When upon his return after a day in a certain house in the country a friend asked Brummell what sort of people he had been staying with, Brummell groaned, "Don't ask me. In my bedroom I actually found a cobweb in my pot." He was therefore acquiring a travelling one, in a folding mahogany case covered with carpet.

Yet life in the country was to be a part of his life, and while he took no thought of maintaining a country house of his own, he gave exceeding care to the selection of those which he visited. When the Beau did leave London, he liked to get far enough away to exercise his horses, not only to Leicestershire, but to Derbyshire, where, at Chatsworth, he pursued his acquaintance with the true leader of society, Georgiana, Duchess of Devonshire. Already as welcome in Devonshire House, Piccadilly, as in Carlton House with the Prince, Brummell lost no time in making his presence at Chatsworth an event. The Duchess was now forty-three. Fourth in descent from Sarah, the great Duchess of Marlborough, she looked rather like her in distinctness of personality, her hair tinged with red, the play of her features alert and animated, her manners irresistible. Poets of the day, as well as many who were no poets, showered her with stanzas; one wrote verses in honour of her petticoat. When Gainsborough painted Georgiana with her arm resting upon a ledge of marble, two curls hanging forward a bit dishevelled about her neck, and looking pensive, he did not paint quite true unless he caught her just after she had lost heavily at faro; that was her worst vice. But her virtue was that she nursed her own children, in order to discourage the common practice of sending them away from home in charge of ignorant nurses. The Duchess herself thought the highest compliment she ever got was from a coalheaver, who said to her, "I could light my pipe at your eyes." At the turn of the century it was the eyes of Georgiana, after all was said, that drew Beau Brummell and his friends, the Prince included, to Chatsworth.

Others in the company were the royal Dukes of York and Cambridge; the Dukes of Beaufort, Manchester, Dorset, and Argyll; the Earls of Westmoreland and Chatham; the Lords Alvanley, Apsley, Frederick Bentinck, Forester, Willoughby d'Eresby, and Brummell's old friends in the Tenth, Charles and Robert Manners, as well as Generals Grosvenor and Upton. The Beau was not the only guest without a title; but those not so ornamented were like himself at Chatsworth because of personal distinction, as for example Chig Chester, a notable whist-player, a sportsman, and a good fellow. Sometimes they all moved on to Belvoir, or to Cleveley, another seat of the Rutlands, for the hunting and shooting, both of which sports Brummell hated. The best he could do with his gun at Cleveley, after the others had enjoyed a day's bag of 150 brace, was to bring down two tame pet pigeons off a chimney. At Belvoir he kept a stud of horses; but if the meet was distant, even the efficient Robinson could never get his master up in time to join the hounds; if the meet was near, and they found quickly, the Beau after riding a few fields made haste to the nearest farmhouse to do something he really liked: gorge bread and cheese. "I cannot bear," said he, "to have my tops and leathers splashed by the greasy galloping farmers." The tops were his especial care, for they were white tops, which he himself invented and made the fashion.

Much more to the taste of Brummell was it to return at two o'clock to lunch with the fair young Duchess of Rutland and the other ladies. The Duchess was a charming girl, young enough to be a daughter of the Duchess of Devonshire; she had a head of brown ringlets which fell upon her shoulders like a perruque of Queen Anne's time, and she was fond of a headdress of feathers and silk. One thing that attracted the Duchess to Brummell was a talent for drawing which he had in common with her; but while she did landscapes—a tendency which grew out of her love of landscape gardening—the Beau sketched heads. He made a pencil drawing of the Duchess of Rutland, a water-colour of the Duchess of Beaufort, and a sketch of the Duchess of Devonshire from her portrait by Reynolds. This work of his was at least good enough to be asked for. "I am quite unhappy," he wrote in this year (1800) to an intimate, "that I have not any more drawings to send you, and I have equally to regret my inability to plead any better excuse for the poverty of my *portefeuille* than my natural idleness and the depredations of my friends."

It was elegance in manner that made the Beau everywhere welcome, whether in country or in town. This quality he was bred up to; now, in his early twenties, he had no need to study it, although the company which he frequented would have done much to remedy any defects if he had possessed them. On the other hand, when he observed vulgarity of manner in those whom he considered ought to know better, the discovery gave him almost physical pain, and he shot his arrows of sarcasm at the offender. If he was impudent, his impudence was peculiar to him; amongst those with whom he mingled, it was not only permitted but expected; in this Brummell was as privileged as a court jester. Upon occasion, he thought, he might best attack with impudence what he took to be vulgarity. Dining at a certain country house, he found the champagne very bad; at a pause in the conversation he raised his glass and said loudly, "John, give me some more

of that cider." Even at Belvoir the Beau spoke his mind.
He was a connoisseur of snuffboxes, and had one with
him, at about this time, which only he could open, and
containing snuff which only he could get. Another guest,
desiring a pinch of it, tried to open the box with a knife.
"Confound the fellow!" exclaimed Brummell. "He takes
my snuffbox for an oyster." At a dinner one day with the
Prince in the Pavilion at Brighton, Brummell casually laid
a fine enamelled snuffbox upon the table. Next him was
sitting the Bishop of Winchester, who reached over and
took a pinch from the box. Brummell called his servant,
and ordered him to throw the rest of the snuff into the fire.

But this expertness in snuffboxes was due to no passion
in the Beau for tobacco; it was a phase of his elegance. He
liked to carry a box because he was well aware of the peculiar grace with which he could take snuff, always holding
the box with the left hand, and with the right, give elegance to a gesture which only a thin line separated from
vulgarity. If he was to the manner born, he was to the
collecting habit inspired, not only by his friends, but by
the great houses which they frequented. The Beau grew
to admire whatever was elegant, and made no secret of his
admiration. In Chesterfield Street he filled his rooms—not
too full—with beautiful things. He saw beauty and value
in walking-sticks, and collected them; he collected buhl,
china, plate, and books in French and Italian. A sedan he
considered the only vehicle fit for a gentleman, and his
own chair he lined with white satin quilted, put down-
squabs in it, and a white sheepskin rug on its floor. He

always ordered this chair brought to the door of his dressing-room, which was on the street floor; from there he was borne to the foot of the staircase of the house which he deigned to visit, thus preserving himself immaculate from the streets whether wet or dusty.

But in the country, as in the old days at Eton when he played games, the Beau was, humanly, not always spotless. When in 1803 England was resting upon an uncertain peace with Napoleon, but still resting, a number of individual leaders in various counties undertook to give the nation a warlike hue by recruiting companies of their own against an emergency. Among those so inspired was Brummell's young friend and host the Duke of Rutland. The Duke set up the Belvoir Volunteers. Remembering that Brummell had been a captain in the Prince's Own, Rutland, by offering to make the Beau a major, prevailed upon his guest to become Commanding Officer of the troop. Duly the Volunteers got into uniform, and drilled, drummed, marched, and trained. Then they invited official inspection, naming a time and place, to which the Horse Guards responded by agreeing to send down a General Officer.

It happened that upon the chilly day set, there was a meet close by of the Belvoir hounds, and Major Brummell, mildly desirous of giving his white tops an airing, left the castle with the pack. The morning wore on, the Volunteers assembled and drew up, the drums and colour took their place, and the General arrived, punctually, upon a punctual horse. Where was the Major? Nobody knew.

As they waited, the junior officers perspired with anxiety. The General snorted; his horse pawed; his patience ebbed. At length he began his inspection of the headless regiment. When he had nearly finished his review, someone descried, moving upon a distant hill, a pink coat. Faster it came, then slower, then faster again as it reached the flat, and in a minute the Beau raced up, not innocent of mud, cap in hand to the General, who suddenly halted the line. In short breaths the Commanding Officer most apologetically explained that he fully thought to have been home in time—meet so near by—favourite horse failed—landed him in a ditch—dreadfully shaken, lay there an hour! "See the state of my pink!"

"Sir!" sputtered the General. "This conduct is wholly inexcusable. I tell you, sir, I should be wanting in a proper zeal for the honour of the service if I did not report this disgraceful neglect, sir, to the Commander-in-Chief, as well as the state in which you present yourself in front of your regiment. And this shall be done, sir. You may retire, sir."

Brummell bowed in silence, and did retire. But scarcely five paces had he walked his horse when he wheeled about, and in lowered voice again addressed the General: "Sir, excuse me, but I forgot to deliver a message which the Duke of Rutland desired me to give you when I left Belvoir this morning; it was to request the honour of your company at dinner."

The General coughed. "Ah! why, really I feel, and am, very much obliged to His Grace . . . I shall be most happy, and . . . Major Brummell, as to this little affair" (the Beau had already turned his horse towards Belvoir), "I am sure no man can regret it more than you do. Assure His Grace that I shall have great pleasure. . . ."

But Brummell was in a hurry. He had to post for his life to the Castle in order to acquaint the Duke of the imminent appearance of a visitor unexpected.

The favourite horse, which "failed" him, was no doubt Stiletto, in charge of his groom James Ell, for when the Beau returned to town in the summer, having dispensed with the services of Ell, he received from his friend Lady Hester Stanhope an inquiry about the groom. Lady Hester, daughter of Earl Stanhope, was only two years older than Brummell, and very like him in originality, in satirical bent, and in tartness of repartee. Like her mother, who was a Pitt, Hester was a plain young woman, and she was nearly six feet tall; but she fascinated those who crossed her path by the imperious freshness of her manner. Disliking her father's temper, she had fled from her home at Chevening in Kent, three years before, to her grandmother's house at Burton Pynsent, Somerset. In the course of her wanderings round country houses Hester often fell in with Brummell, with whom she was much taken by their very kinship of spirit. "Why," she one day asked him, "does not so clever a person as you are devote his talents to a higher purpose?" Replied the Beau, "My dear Lady Hester, I know human nature well. I have adopted the only course which can place me in a prominent light, and separate me from the society of the herd. If I were to do as you advise, do you think I could stand in the middle of the pit at the opera, and beckon to Lorne on one side, and Villiers on the other, *and see them come to me?*" Indeed Hester Stanhope herself craved distinction, and not finding it at Burton Pynsent, she had sought it abroad.

Now, she had returned to England to be chatelaine of Walmer Castle for her uncle William Pitt, who was Warden of the Cinque Ports; and for the retinue of the fortress Hester required a groom. From Cheltenham, writing on August 30 to George Brummell, she said: "If you are as conceited as formerly, I shall stand accused of taking your groom to give me an opportunity of writing to you for his character. All the inquiry I wish to make upon this subject is, to be informed whether you were as well satisfied with James Ell when you parted with him, as when he had Stiletto under his care. If so, I shall dispatch him at the end of next week, with my new purchases, to Walmer . . . I am not a little happy in having it in my power to scamper upon British ground . . . I saw a good deal of your friend (Sir Bladen) Capel at Naples; if he fights the battles of his country by sea as well as he fights yours by land, he certainly is one of our first commanders . . . he was as yet unsuccessful in the important search after a perfect snuffbox when I left Italy . . . Capel on his return will of course be made Admiral of the *White* (White's Club) for the signal services he has rendered to coxcombality. I met with a rival of yours, in affectation, upon the Continent, William Hill! I fear it will be long ere this country will again witness his airs, as he is now a prisoner—this, perhaps, you are glad of, as the society of statues and pictures has infinitely improved him . . . and therefore rendered him a still more formidable competitor."

Whatever Brummell replied to Lady Hester in respect of James Ell, he did not defend himself against her insinuations of conceit, coxcombry, affectation, or devotion to snuffboxes. He accepted the implied homage of Hester. But he was too much like her to dispute with her. In a London summer, the only season in which his heart thawed, he preferred to reserve his badinage for either married women or widows, because of their wider knowledge of what is called the world. When the widow of a certain peer left for Brighton to pass the summer, the Beau sent from Chesterfield Street a letter in pursuit, seeking not only to make her keep thinking of him, but advising her how to get rid of one rival, and how he dealt with another: "I am almost inclined to believe that you have forgotten me in the protracted space of five days, and that you have amused your leisure hours with something or somebody more interesting to you. You are too overtly severe with Lord L; he has effrontery enough to persuade himself that you are piqued with him, and he will interpret that into a latent interest for him: what can it possibly be to you whether he goes to Brighthelmstone or not? Affront him, but with dexterity, and his own consummate and mistaken vanity will be his speediest drawback . . . Attar-Gul . . . has not perceptibly touched a bristle of his raven crown since you saw, or rather turned away your eyes from, him. In submission to your desire I have minutely scrutinized his head. He had the effrontery the other day to be irritated because I asked him to lend me his brush of a sconce to assist at the morning toilette of my boots! The Monster! Do not forget your parasol in this inflammatory weather."

Boots in that morning toilette were a critical consideration, for the brilliancy of their polish was the envy of all St. James's. When an aspiring young emulator begged for its recipe, Brummell responded, "Blacking, my dear sir? Well, you know, for blacking I never use anything but the froth of champagne." Thus he turned aside, as a triviality, every question about his apparel. "Hairdresser? I have three; the first for my temples, the second for the front of my head, and the third for the back." Likewise he had a pair of perfect gloves, cut by two glovers, one of whom made only the thumbs. For designing the ties of his cravats, he engaged the ablest portrait painter in London, whose pictures only since then had become the rage. But his distinctive contribution at this time to the dress of men was that he made a neckcloth out of what had always looked like a bandage.

When the Beau came to study these swathes of muslin which passed for fashionable adornment of the neck he determined that improvement in this detail was imperative because, whatever other part of men's costume might be left attractively *negligé,* the neck, being almost as certainly as the face that part observed of all observers, must be trim and orderly as well as clean. The French Revolution, with its cry of "equality," had wrought in dress a slovenliness which was only too well reaffirmed by the passing of powdered wigs. Against this rebellion Brummell rebelled. As he looked at the neckcloth he saw that it bagged out in front, rucked up to the chin, and rather suggested chronic sore throat. He invented the simple device of slightly starching it, and the transformation was done.

At the same time, by making himself the arbiter of its creases, the Beau set a style which at once challenged emulation and defied betterment. With this new fashion he took infinite pains. What was the morning good for, if not to afford opportunity to encompass perfection in dressing? If he at first did not tie properly this stiffened neckcloth, he tossed it aside, took up others—all of them a foot high—and standing intently before his glass, fastened and folded down one of them until he was satisfied. For the success of this very serious process Brummell pronounced the formula: "Clean linen, plenty of it, and country washing."

CHAPTER VI

THE ALBUM

1804–1805

IF IN all his seven years at Eton the Beau had cultivated manners at the expense of intellect, he did on the intellectual side pick up an interest in poetry. He was now neither student nor critic of it; but he felt an inclination to write it, and to be the cause of it in others. As the old century gave way to the new, poetry of course was in the air, and although the French Revolution had done a disservice in England to the dress of men, it had under the inspiring leadership of Wordsworth and Coleridge revitalized their poetical thought. Brummell did not really write much himself. To such few hours of solitude as he withheld from society he might well have devoted the fashioning of satirical or humorous verse, in line with his own bent; instead, he became that extraordinary thing, a collector of verse of any kind, original poetry written by his friends.

Not that he carried with him to assemblies and country-houses an autograph-book, requesting signatures and

spontaneous verses; but he did encourage the lords and
ladies, the public men and the authors, either to give him
during the course of the party or to send him by post a few
stanzas upon any subject they chose. Nor did Brummell
care primarily for the actual manuscripts. What he did,
when he got these loose scraps of paper, or notes in the
mail, was to copy them with scrupulous neatness in an
album. He bought a thick quarto in plain vellum, had it
bound in dark blue velvet, and corners and clasps made for
it of massive embossed silver gilt, like a medieval missal.
When he came to transcribing he did his best, without
crowding, to confine each poem to a page. It was another
expression of his collector's proclivity: the Beau collected
poetry as he collected snuffboxes, walking-sticks, or china,
although the degree of craftsmanship in the verses was not
always so high as that in his objects of art.

Naturally one of his first contributors was the well-read
Duchess of Devonshire, from whom Brummell had
achieved no little of his own taste for French and Italian
literature. Educated well beyond the level of women of
her time, Georgiana wrote poetry because she was artistic
in many ways, if talented only in few; she composed verses
just as she composed harmonies for her lyre. When the
Beau went to Chatsworth, he wrote poetry with the
Duchess in the same spirit that at Belvoir led him to
sketch and paint with the Duchess of Rutland. These *vers
de societé* often took the form of an elegy on the death of a
friend. In 1804 Georgiana gave Brummell for his album
five quatrains prompted by the passing of a great favourite,

James Hare, whose wit, she said, "beamed in vivid flashes from his eye," and who "threw keen darts of matchless satire." It was true that at the Opera a bow from Hare, who was an intimate of Charles Fox, was considered a greater compliment than from the Prince of Wales. But when Fox himself came to contribute to Brummell's album he took a lighter line; he preferred to do a jingle on the Hon. Mrs. Bouverie, who was a daughter of Sir Edward Fawkener, the man who proposed the Beau for Brooks's. Mrs. Bouverie, although wife of the Hon. E. Bouverie, had been for twenty years the faithful and devoted mistress of Lord Robert Spencer. Fox said that she and Lord Robert "made adultery respectable," and for Brummell's collection the amiable Charles thus paid tribute to the lady:

"She loves truth, though she lies till she's black in the face;
She loves virtue, though none in her conduct you trace;
Her delicate feelings all wickedness shocks,
Though her lover's Lord Robert, and her friend's Charles Fox."

Yet Georgiana Devonshire herself was versatile enough to swing into comic vein when the occasion suited, and at about this time she seized such a chance to have a bit of fun with Lord Boringdon, heir to Lord Morley, and a strong supporter of Fox's rival William Pitt—Pitt himself being none of the company at Chatsworth. To this mock-heroic for Brummell's album, faintly suggestive in theme of Coleridge's "Christabel" which had been read by everyone since its appearance two or three years before, the

Duchess in honour of Boringdon gave the title "Borino the Brave":

> "A baron so bold, and of parentage fair,
>   Was riding beside the green sea;
> His vizor was up, and his forehead was bare,
>   His face it was comely, and long was his hair,
> And tall, and full portly, was he. . . .
>
> A Bedlamite Duchess was bathing hard by,
>   When she saw the young Paladin pass;
> He bewilder'd her brain, and he dazzled her eye,
>   Her guides could not stop her, she strove to rush by,
> And swore that she would, 'by the mass!'
>
> The baron was frighten'd, with reason and truth,
>   For her love and her frenzy were strong;
> She turn'd as he turn'd, and with gesture uncouth,
>   Her arms she elongated straight at the youth,
> And they seem'd to be half a mile long. . . ."

In two more stanzas the baron screamed, fell into the water, and woke up from a dream. But it was "a very good story to tell," and he told it every night, and forgot that it had ever been told.

Then the Duchess would turn her hand to lyrics quite lovely, as "I've known all the beauties of sight," or "Here in the bower of beauty newly shorn." For her, Fox wrote in turn a sonnet "On the Death of Faddle," her favourite spaniel, and this too Brummell gathered in. In 1805 George Canning, now Treasurer of the Navy in Pitt's ministry, contributed to the album about twenty lines of amusing doggerel on Whitbread's speech at the impeachment of Lord Melville, a rather silly trial of which the judge said that although he had heard of "impeachment of waste," these proceedings were a waste of impeachment. Canning in his verses made Whitbread sing his own praises, and as the enemies of Canning were fond of scoffing at *his* mother as a strolling player, Canning did not spare Whitbread an allusion to beer:

"My Lords, while the beams of this hall shall support
The roof which o'ershades this respectable court,
(Where Hastings was tried for oppressing the Hindoos,)
While the beams of the sun shall shine in at the windows,
My name shall shine bright, as my father's now shines,
Emblazon'd on Journals, as his is on Signs."

During all this time that the Beau was collecting immortal verse for his blue-velvet book, his friendship with the Prince (who wrote him no poems) though perhaps not so intimate remained firm, even if Brummell found it a bit difficult to keep up with the royal amours. Having been part and parcel of the royal wedding, and of the entourage for some time thereafter, and having actually witnessed only the happier side of the Princess, such as it was, the Beau could not be altogether serene about the estrangement. The Prince had gone back to Maria Fitzherbert indeed, back to her winning eyes, her quiet smile, and her very white bosom. One evening he made bold to appear with her at the Opera when Caroline was present in another part of the house. Maria, having obtained permission from the Pope, consented to return, while the Prince, as if to seal the reunion, presented her with a painting of his right eye in a locket.

But in 1805 Mrs. Fitzherbert herself was the means of throwing the Prince in the way of a lady who bore for him the same fatal distinction as Lady Jersey: she was a grandmother. This lady was the Marchioness of Hertford. It happened that "Minnie" Seymour, a child of seven whose parents had died, and who since that time had been adopted by Mrs. Fitzherbert, was about to be taken away from Maria because the executors of the child's father did not wish Minnie brought up a Catholic. Lord Hertford then announced as head of the Seymour family that he would undertake to act as guardian; securing custody of Minnie, he proceeded to appoint Mrs. Fitzherbert to act for him. The Prince, very assiduous in these arrangements himself, saw much of the Marquess, and still more of Lady Hertford. As she was icy, dignified, and in her middle forties, he besought her love.

But Brummell was too sufficiently occupied with ladies of his own to devote his waking hours to anxiety over the fluctuations of the royal heart. One country house the Beau had to leave because he fell in love with its lady, a countess, and she with him. Almost boyishly outspoken, his vanity overcome by honesty, Brummell on an early day of a month's visit explained the position to the earl, who hitherto had not known his wife to be susceptible, though he had seen many guests enchanted by *her*. Brummell with the earl's approval decamped. It was at about this time, upon his return to town, that he fell in love again, with one Lady Jane of Harley Street. She, though not encumbered with a husband, unhappily could fetch from her heart only a meagre response to the Beau. At a party he begged from her a miniature of herself which she was carrying; she answered by hurling her glove at him. Baffled, he restored it on the next day with a note: "My dear Lady Jane——

"With the miniature it seems I am not to be trusted, even for two pitiful hours; my own memory must be, then, my only disconsolate expedient to obtain a resemblance. As I am unwilling to merit the imputation of committing myself, by too flagrant a liberty, in retaining your glove which you charitably sent at my head yesterday . . . I restore it . . . I have too much regard and respect for you, and too little practical vanity myself . . . to defraud you of it. You are angry, perhaps irreparably incensed against me, for this petty larceny. I have no defense . . . but that of frenzy . . . you are an angel visiting these sublunary spheres, and therefore your first quality should be that of mercy; yet you are sometimes wayward and volatile . . . though you have no wings, still you have weapons; and these are resentment and estrangement against me . . . always your miserable slave."

But he could recover quickly from his wretchedness. It was now his period of speculation in courtship; if at the end of one of his adventures matrimony awaited him, good; if he found no prospect of honey in a flower, he was a diligent bee, and knew how to look elsewhere. In the case of a certain Lady Mary, Brummell now discovered no more hope than he had with Lady Jane. Yet when a friend rallied him about this fruitless episode, the Beau had his rejoinder ready: "Why, what could I do, my good fellow, but cut the connexion? I discovered that Lady Mary actually ate cabbage!" Again, one night he laid all his plans to elope, though not with a lady of title, from a ball in a house near Grosvenor Square. The stage-setting for the first act was perfect: the gay ballroom, the unsuspecting hostess, the stealthy departure unobserved. But a servant, faithless, unromantic, and meddling, "told all" to the mother of the girl, and at the corner of the next street the pair were overtaken and caught.

As Brummell did encounter these little reverses amongst his women friends, that sex could not complain if he occasionally took revenge, especially if ever they were so bold as to hint sarcasm. At Ascot one day, as the Beau walked his horse up to a lady's carriage, the lady begged him not to throw away his time on her, nor risk being seen with so unfashionable a person. "Pray don't mention it," replied Brummell, "there is no one near us." In a drawing-room upon a certain evening he went so far as to request a duchess to walk out of the room backwards, because he could not bear looking at her back. Why take anything in serious vein? What was life, if it had to be serious? When he wished to escape the pretences of London, he could quickly enough find a way. "Come to Brighton, my dear fellow," he said to Cecil Jenkinson, son of his father's old patron Lord Liverpool. "Let us be off tomorrow; we shall eat currant-tart, and live in chintz and salt-water." On his way up to town again from Brighton he caught a bad cold. "The landlord," explained the Beau to a solicitous friend, "put me in a room with a damp stranger." When a club-mate met him limping in Bond Street, and sympathized, Brummell added, "The worst of it is, it is my favourite leg." Asked if he had ever seen such a cold summer, he quickly responded, "Yes, last winter." It was dangerous to ask him a question unless the interrogator was prepared to invite a reply which he could only repeat, round London, as a *mot* of Brummell's. "Won't you dine with me one evening in Bloomsbury?" a secretary of the Admiralty begged him. "Bloomsbury?" repeated Brummell. "Yes, if you tell me where I am to change horses."

After midnight, if amusement at the club palled, the Beau gathered a few of his friends and, not unlike the merry ones of Restoration days, set forth upon pranks. There was a certain staid and scientific Fellow of the Royal Society who needed attention, for his name seemed to be Snodgrass. At about three o'clock on a frosty morning, Brummell and his assistant conspirators knocked loudly upon the door of this savant. Thinking the house afire the sober Fellow, in a nightcap, put his head out of an upper window in no little agitation. "Sir," demanded Brummell, "is your name Snodgrass?" "Yes, sir," came the anxious reply, "my name is Snodgrass." "Snodgrass—Snodgrass," repeated the Beau. "A very odd name that, upon my soul; a very odd name indeed! But, sir, is your name *really*

Snodgrass?" The sleepy scientist, having by this time developed a rage, threatened to call the watch. "Good morning to you, Mr. Snodgrass," cried Brummell in his politest tones, bowing himself away.

Upon another evening he would leave the club to go to a party at Harriette Wilson's. Harriette was a dark-haired young courtesan, Mayfair-born and bred, smart, saucy, with good eyes, and the "manner of a wild schoolboy," who before she was twenty had been successively mistress to the Earl of Craven, the Hon. Frederick Lamb, and now, to Brummell's close friend, the Marquis of Lorne. She and her sisters Amy and Fanny played a brisk game of ensnaring the younger nobility amongst whom Brummell circulated. To this end an alluring trap of theirs was a box which they took for the season at the opera, and Brummell, who often borrowed the Duke of Bedford's box, near Harriette's, had been surprised one night to see in the company of Harriette his old friend of Hampton Court days, Julia Storer.

The history of Julia, since the idyllic hours which the Beau had passed with her, was somewhat out of the common: with Colonel Cotton, her host at Hampton—a fellow-officer of Brummell's in the Hussars—she had fallen into a romantic passion, although the Colonel was a married man with nine children. This had made no difference to Julia. She proceeded to bear him five more children herself. Now, after eight years, she was living with her brood on a small legacy from one of the Storer family in a cottage near Harriette's lodgings, and having casually made acquaintance with Miss Wilson she was out for a new adventure of the Wilson kind. Brummell, seeing Julia for the first time after all these years, entered the box, and according to Harriette, "addressing himself to Julia, expressed his surprise, joy and astonishment at meeting with her."

The sequel was that the Beau soon took to frequenting the gilded rooms of the Wilson girls for suppers of cold chicken and champagne. "It appeared plain and evident to me," commented Harriette later, "that his attention to Julia was no longer the effect of love. Piqued at the idea of having been refused marriage by a woman with whom Cotton had so easily succeeded *sans cérémonie,* he determined in his own mind soon to be even with his late brother officer." On Harriette's unsupported evidence, it is doubtful whether Brummell felt anything of the sort, and equally doubtful whether he ever designed marrying the concupiscent Julia. When Julia had her first child by Cotton, the Beau, a little heart-stricken by memories of their juvenile meetings, did send her half a dozen consolatory stanzas, which began:

> "Unhappy child of indiscretion,
>   Poor slumberer on a breast forlorn!
> Pledge and reproof of past transgression,
>   Dear, though unwelcome to be born. . . ."

But since Julia Storer had gone on and had four more children by the same man, Brummell perhaps concluded that she was no more forlorn than the children were unwelcome. As for "being even" with Colonel Cotton, that state of mind, however commonly it may have possessed Harriette herself, had not yet afflicted the Beau.

At the Saturday-nights of Amy Wilson he nevertheless got fun enough out of his renewed dalliance with Julia, although the guests in the Wilson drawing-room proved occasionally a bit mixed. One evening when he got there with his fat little clubmate Lord Alvanley they discovered in one corner young Lord Palmerston, and in another a certain John Mitchel, who was a wealthy grocer. The conversation, as noted by Harriette Wilson, took this turn: "Fanny," observed Brummell to Harriette's sister, "you will make a point of cutting the grocer, I hope?" "Do, pray, Fanny," said Harriette, "cut your Mitchels. I vote for cutting all the grocers and valets who intrude themselves into good society." Brummell was well enough aware that his grandfather had been a servant; but instead of trying to hide the fact he let Harriette's remark come a generation nearer. "My father," he quickly retorted, "was a very superior valet, and kept his place all his life, and that is more than Palmerston will do."

In the autumn of this year (1805) for a change he travelled north to Nottingham, to stay for a week near there with a party at Colwick, a country house. It was the house of a couple who had been married only a few months, Mr. and Mrs. Jack Musters, or, as the bride preferred for the moment to keep her own name, Mr. Musters and Mrs. Chaworth. All that could be said for Musters apart from his having been a boyhood friend of Beau Brummell at Eton, was that he was one of a species: a country gentleman, and a great horseman, whose talk was of horses and the country. Not long before his marriage, Mary Chaworth had jilted Byron for him, Byron being still a schoolboy at Harrow, but blindly in love with her. She had led Byron on; but one night in her own house at Annesley he had overheard Mary say to her maid, "Do you think I could care anything for that lame boy?" Mary had got what she wanted. She was an attractive-looking young woman, two years older than Byron, and she had graceful features, thoughtful eyes, and hair parted down the middle and held in place by a band. But she was perhaps not always graceful enough to feel quite sure of herself. Beau Brummell had a week in which to take the measure of Mary Chaworth. He called her *la petite dame blanche.* "She appeared to me," said he, "to be always vigilant for admiration, coarse in her manners."

The manners of any woman, to a man whose standard was bound to be the manners of the Duchess of Devonshire, may well have seemed coarse. But now a bitterly unhappy circumstance was to compel the Beau to look elsewhere for a living example: no later than the end of March (1806) this Duchess, Georgiana Devonshire, aged only forty-nine, died of an incurable organic ailment. His beloved friend and sponsor in society had lived too well. Brummell was poignantly sensible of all that he owed to the gifted and lovely Duchess from the very start of his acquaintance in great houses. By virtue of her favour, more than by that of any other person, he had developed his friendliness with the Prince into outright companionship, for to the Prince, Devonshire House, to which the Beau had been constantly invited, was Carlton House all over again. "We have lost," said the Prince when the Duchess died, "the best-bred woman in England." He well knew that he had derived much of his own high-bred manner from the incomparable Georgiana.

Not many months afterward, in the autumn, there appeared in the *Gentleman's Magazine* a fantasy in verse for children, called "The Butterfly's Ball." It was by William Roscoe, the historian, famous for his biographies of Lorenzo de' Medici and of Leo X. These verses charmed thousands, and were by order of the King and Queen set to music for the Princess Mary. To Brummell, who upon occasion renewed his own excursions into verse, "The Butterfly's Ball" was an inspiration, and he resolved to attempt a companion-piece to Roscoe's work, a piece to be called "The Butterfly's Funeral." Although he meant this poem to appeal to children as well, it is quite possible that the Beau was still grieving over the loss of Georgiana Devonshire, and fashioned his lines to fit her as the Butterfly, and himself as a Grasshopper, the chief mourner. At all events the opening stanzas suggested both the character and the life of the Duchess, while the second stanza might well have reflected the mood of George Brummell at her death:

"Oh ye! who so lately were blithesome and gay,
    At the Butterfly's banquet carousing away;
Your feasts and your revels of pleasure are fled,
    For the soul of the banquet, the Butterfly's dead!

No longer the Flies and the Emmets advance,
 To join with their friends in the Grasshopper's dance;
For see his thin form o'er the favourite bend,
 And the Grasshopper mourns for the loss of his friend."

The scenes bore the colour, the reminiscence, of gatherings at Chatsworth and at Devonshire House. After describing in five more quatrains the mourners—bee, beetle, mole, dormouse, gnat, moth, silkworm, hornet, spider, glowworm, and grub—Brummell ended with this epitaph, which could equally well have applied to the Duchess and himself:

"At this solemn spot where the green rushes wave
 Here sadly we bent o'er the Butterfly's grave;
 'Twas here we to beauty our obsequies paid,
 And hallow'd the mound which her ashes had made.

And here shall the daisy and violet blow,
 And the lily discover her bosom of snow,
 While under the leaf in the evenings of spring,
 Still mourning his friend shall the Grasshopper sing."

It was no better, but not much worse, than many of the rhymes he had copied into his blue-velvet book. Sentimental as it was, it reflected an association which was far more than that. By John Wallis, the publisher, three thousand copies were sold, and not all of them to children.

CHAPTER VII

THE REGENT

1806–1811

AFTER THE death of Charles Fox in 1806, the food as well as the company at Brooks's, of which Fox was perhaps the most eminent member, seemed to lose its savour. Sir Thomas Stapley, another member, complained to the Prince. "The eternal joint and beefsteaks, the boiled fowl with oyster sauce, and an apple tart. That is what we have, sir, and very monotonous fare it is." The Prince came to the rescue. He asked his chef, Watier, to set up a new club, and to see that the cooking in it would do justice to Carlton House itself. In Piccadilly, at the corner of Bolton Row, Watier found a house just vacated by a musical society, secured it, staffed it with the Prince's page Madison as manager and the Prince's cook Labourier as chef, and opened its doors in 1807, giving it the name of Watier's.

Under the patronage of the Prince's popular brother the Duke of York, and under the presidency of Beau Brummell himself, Watier's almost at once became the fashion.

The Duke was remarkable among the sons of George III for being the only one, according to report, who had the feelings of a gentleman; whatever might be alleged against a friend, the Duke was never known to desert him. In the country the Duke occupied himself with racing, and in town with cards. Cards and Watier's were to be synonymous. To this club Brummell drew in also his friends Alvanley, Sir Henry Mildmay, and Henry Pierrepoint, preferring town members, for the boots of most country gentlemen "stank of horse-dung and bad blacking."

Soon the dinners at Watier's were so much talked about that the high play in the games seemed a secondary consideration. All the young men of fortune aspired to join. Since thousands of pounds changed hands nightly, the charges for the luxurious dinners seemed a bagatelle. The income of Brummell was only between two and three thousand; he began by playing cautiously, though at times deep in the pocket. Macao was the favourite game, being both simple and adaptable to varying stakes, and the luck of the Beau on the chances he took was remarked. One night early in the life of Watier's, Tom Sheridan, only son of the dramatist, came in; like Cassio, Tom was "a fellow almost damned in a fair wife," for Caroline Callander was described as "more beautiful than anybody but her daughters," three children at this time under ten years of age, yet giving promise of superlative loveliness. This handicap of being overshadowed both by the charm of his family and by the fame of his father made the lot of Tom Sheridan not an easy one; he took to poetry, as well as he could. But he knew even less about gambling. He laid £10 at macao. From the Opera, along came Beau Brummell to the table, and suggested that he take Tom's place, promising him half of any winnings. The Beau added £200 to the stakes of Sheridan, and in ten minutes had won £1,500. "There, Tom," said he, handing his friend £750, "go home and give your wife and brats a supper, and never play again."

Upon another night, later, the story was not so serene. Brummell lost, and the sum was more than he could afford. Putting on a tragic face, he affected to be at the end of his tether. He called to the waiter: "Bring me a flat candlestick and a pistol." In this little farce the surrounding members joined, themselves not averse to a bit of play-acting upon occasion. Brummell's late fellow-officer in the Hussars, Bligh, the son of the Earl of Darnley, had a pistol on him, and handing it to the Beau, observed, "I am extremely happy to offer you the means without troubling the waiter." Play at macao proceeded. Perhaps Brummell departed for a change to Lincolnshire, for his horses were standing (1807) at Grantham, conveniently over the county line from Belvoir.

He was by this time also a member of White's, in St. James's Street opposite Brooks's. In gambling, the difference between White's and Watier's was that White's was the centre of play at whist. The walk between these clubs, down Piccadilly, became as fashionable for the beaux, as well as for their ladies, as the walk down St. James's Street itself. To gamble at either club was to win or lose with distinction, since the money always changed hands between gentlemen themselves distinguished. One might lose a good deal, but was not supposed to be cheated, whereas in a common dive given over to similar games, one might risk little, but was cheated a good deal. A certain nobleman happened to accuse Brummell of luring his son to a gambling loss in a place that was disreputable, a place with which the Beau really had nothing to do. It was in fact a question whether the nobleman minded the disrepute quite as much as the loss of the money, although association with Brummell, who acknowledged his patronage of the son, may possibly have incited in the young man a desire to gamble somewhere. The Beau denied responsibility, claiming on the contrary the performance of a favour. "Really," said he, "I did my best for the young man; I once gave him my arm all the way from White's to Watier's."

Brummell was right. If the sprig of the nobleman had had any wits, he would have known how to make the most of the acquaintance which the first gentleman of Watier's bestowed upon him. It was a time when the very cut of a man's coat depended not so much upon the cloth, but upon the line of it which Brummell dictated. Of an expensively dressed person who was mentioned in company, the Beau was able to observe, "Yes, his tailor makes him; now I, I make my tailor." The tailors so blest by Brummell, men whom he sought for until he found those who would follow his instructions to the last stitch, were two; Meyer, in Conduit Street, and Schweitzer and Davidson, in Cork Street. Naturally both firms got the Prince for a customer; Meyer, who dressed in the livery of a page, often went to Carlton House on the night of a reception to lift the Prince into his clothes. When Brummell invented a trouser which opened at the side of the bottom of the leg, and was closed by buttons and buttonholes (of which the modern spats are a survival), Meyer made a fortune out of it, for the Beau, being the first to wear the new style, was at once copied by all the other men of fashion. At Schweitzer's the story was the same. A baronet, who had been at Eton with Brummell, was choosing cloth one morning and asked Schweitzer which kind he advised. Came the answer, "Why, sir, the Prince wears superfine, and Mr. Brummell the Bath coating. . . . Suppose, sir, we say the Bath coating—I think Mr. Brummell has a trifle the preference." Again, one day at White's the Beau was asked about his brother. The position was that William Brummell, upon coming into his legacy, had married Anne Daniell (daughter of James Daniell, Governor of Bombay) moved into the house of her family, Wivenhoe, near Colchester, Essex, and settled there as a contented country gentleman. "Brummell," said the member of White's to the Beau, "your brother William is in town; is he not coming here?" "Yes, in a day or two," was the prompt reply. "But I have recommended him to walk the back streets till his new clothes came home."

This was not an exaggerated liberty which George Brummell took merely with his own relations. As one afternoon he was strolling with a certain lord up St. James's Street to the club he stopped abruptly, looked down, and asked the lord what he called those things on his feet. When the abashed peer attempted the simple and only answer, Brummell, stooping a little, remarked doubtfully, "Shoes, are they? I thought they were slippers." Not long afterward the Duke of Bedford, to whom the Beau was continually indebted for the loan of the ducal box at the Opera, asked Brummell for an opinion of a new coat just put on. The Beau inspected the Duke from top to toe; he might have been the old General who had come down from the Horse Guards on that awful day to inspect the Belvoir Volunteers. Delicately, with thumb and finger, Brummell felt the lapel. "Bedford," said he earnestly, "do you call this thing a coat?"

Neither dukes nor the sons of dukes did he spare. One day, in the drawing-room of the engaging Harriette Wilson, Brummell repeated nearly the same admonition for the benefit of Frederick Bentinck. The Beau had lately encountered some difficulty in finding Harriette at home. In fact they were a pair of make-believes; she made believe to avoid Brummell; he made believe that he was weeping his heart out for her; both were playing a game purely for their own amusement. Harriette said that Brummell sent her notes "full of nonsensical vows and professions." According to her, he wrote, "When, beautiful Harriette, will you admit me into your house? Why so obstinately refuse my visits? Tell me, I do entreat you, when I may but throw myself at your feet without fear of derision from a public homage on the pavement, or dislocation from the passing hackney coaches." She told him when, well

84

enough, nor did she keep him out of doors on the pavement. The Beau had not been long with Harriette when Fred Bentinck called, wearing a new pair of leather breeches with which he appeared elaborately pleased. "Made by a man in the Haymarket," he beamed. Brummell walked critically round him. "My dear fellow," exclaimed the arch-censor, "take 'em off directly!" At this, Harriette, with a rebirth of modesty, voiced a strident protest. "What's the matter with 'em?" wailed Bentinck. "Bad knees, my good fellow," Brummell quietly remarked. "Bad knees."

In the question of snuff he held equal primacy. It followed naturally that a connoisseur of snuffboxes should be an authority on their contents as well. The finest quality of snuff being difficult to come by, shipments of it were sometimes bespoken even before it arrived, and this was the case with a hogshead of Martinique imported on one occasion by Fribourg and Treyer, then and now in the Haymarket. Rather carelessly the Beau had neglected to put his name on the list of applicants for this prize hogshead. But he took good care to be in the tobacconist's, with some friends, upon the day on which the snuff was to be opened up. Brummell took a few pinches; those standing about waited in awe. "Detestable compound!" cried the arbiter. "Not at all the style of thing that any man with the slightest pretensions to correct taste could patronize." His friends left the shop, to spread the unhappy word, whilst Brummell lingered to discuss the matter with the stricken dealers. Then he confessed to his stratagem. "By some oversight I did not put my name down on your Martinique list, and I must have allowed the thing to have been disposed of to others, who know not its value as I do. Since the hogshead has been condemned, you will not object to my having three jars full of it: that fact once known, there is little doubt that the remainder will find a speedy demand." It did.

The wonder was that Brummell could hold this supremacy and still be reminded of the nearness of the humble beginnings of his family. Late in October (1807) his old friend Lady Sarah Savile, Mexborough's daughter, with whom the Beau used to go upon picnics to Gypsy Hill, Lady Sarah the "surpassing beauty" who for ten years had put off many a suitor, so far fulfilled the prophesy of the gypsy as to marry a nobleman, and became Lady Monson. It was Monson's uncle, Charles, to whom old Brummell, the grandfather of the Beau, had been for thirty years a valet. George Brummell could perhaps not too comfortably take notice of the Monson family, not even of Lady Sarah any longer, now that she was a member of it. But there was no embarrassment for him, from persons who counted; among them, Harriette Wilson, who had attempted to twit him about valets and grocers, was hardly to be included.

All this time the polygynous Prince of Wales, without quite abandoning Maria Fitzherbert, was pursuing the elderly Marchioness of Hertford. Mrs. Fitzherbert was described by a contemporary as "very fat but with a charming countenance; her features are beautiful, except her mouth, which is ugly, having a set of not good false teeth; but her person is too fat, and she makes a great display of a very white but not prettily formed bosom, which I often long to throw a handkerchief over. Her manners are good-humoured . . . unaffected and pleasing." More seductive to the Prince was Lady Hertford, who was not so fat, and much haughtier. She lived with her dangling husband in Hertford House, Manchester Square (now the Wallace Collection). A delicate touch of the Prince, as he pressed his passion, was to give to Lady Hertford a portrait of his old love of a generation before, "Perdita" Robinson, by Reynolds, although the significance of this gift, really, was that it signalled on the part of the Prince his desire to encourage the Hertfords—with their £150,000 a year—in collecting beautiful objects of art. To smooth the path of this liaison with Lady Hertford, as the corpulent lover thought, he expected at every dinner-party he gave for her that Mrs. Fitzherbert would attend. Maria began to fret a bit.

But what was to be looked for in a Prince who insisted that the only one of his ancestors amongst the English kings fit to be lived with as a gentleman was Charles II? The difference in their ladies, which the Prince failed to recollect, was that Charles did retain the decency to pick them young. Lady Hertford scarcely managed to keep her front place very long. Soon the Prince was out hunting for still another grandmother. He found one in the Countess of Bessborough, and pitched upon her; like Lady Hertford, Lady Bessborough was also one of the great hostesses of London, and the Prince had known her for thirty years. But within the last ten, although a grandmother, she had inspired Lord John Townshend, writing for the album of Beau Brummell, to these poetic lines upon her charms:

> "Think in my breast what wild despair,
> What rash tumultuous passions rise!
> Think of your glossy auburn hair,
> Your pearly teeth, your hazel eyes!!"

Perhaps the royal libertine still saw her with all the ardency of Lord John. With due strategy he stalked his prey. Since the weak spot of Lady Bessborough was George Canning, who by this time had risen to be Foreign Secretary, the Prince, calling upon the good lady and sitting tight up to her on a couch, swore that if she would but yield to his love he not only would dismiss both Lady Hertford and Mrs. Fitzherbert, but would make Canning the Prime Minister. He rolled about, half on the couch, half on the floor, and every time he said "Canning" he reached for the startled lady. But the grandmother with the glossy auburn hair demurred. Still the Prince sat on, hour after hour, tempering his passion with politics.

These antics George Brummell might not have minded so much if in this same year (1809) his very good friend and colleague in Watier's, the Duke of York, favourite son of the King, had not run into trouble over one of his own mistresses, whereas the Prince in his escapades never suffered any check. The Duke was in command of the army; Mrs. Clarke, his mistress, was publicly accused of traffick-

ing in military titles. True, none of the "grandmothers"
ever brought herself into the position of having to face so
awkward a charge; but whatever they did, and whatever
the Prince chose to do in their company outdoors or in, no
curtailment of either political power or prestige befell the
heir to the throne. This was perhaps as it should have been.
But the Duke of York was compelled to resign his command, and the pre-eminence of Watier's as a club of royal
patronage was put in jeopardy. Between the liberty allowed
to the Prince and the penalty inflicted on the Duke, Brummell felt his sympathies tending to split.

He now gave up his rooms in Chesterfield Street to move
into more spacious quarters a few blocks away between
Grosvenor Square and Park Lane. The new address was
24, South Street. This street was similarly celebrated for
its famous men; as George Selwyn had lived in the old
neighbourhood, so in South Street stood the house of the
lamented Charles James Fox, who spent his last years there,
although dying in a house of the Duke of Devonshire's in
Chiswick. But in quitting the familiar lodgings in Chesterfield Street the Beau was leaving within their walls memories of certain ones who had known him there, memories
at times perhaps too shaking to be continually reminded
of. There was Georgiana Devonshire of course. But after
her, the lovably impudent Hester Stanhope, who, no sooner
than Brummell had settled in South Street left England
forever. He knew she was going; her departure had nothing to do with him; but the period of merry passages of
wit between them was the period of his life in Chesterfield

Street; and now, it was done with. Lady Hester had been in love with General Sir John Moore, a man fifteen years her senior; he fell in Spain, fighting the French at the Battle of Corunna, and he died with the name of Hester Stanhope on his lips. Early in 1810 she went away from England in deep mourning.

If the death of Moore deprived Brummell of the bracing society of Lady Hester, the death of the King's youngest daughter, the Princess Amelia, from consumption in the autumn of this year, led to a change which was to touch the Beau critically. George III, to whom his child sent a last message, "Remember me," suffered a recurrence of his madness, which began with his familiar incessant chatter to his attendants, and continued to the pronouncement of such disconcerting delusions as that all marriages were dissolved. Within a month (December) the question of a Regency engrossed the politicians of all parties. Within three months a Bill was passed, and in February (1811) the Prince became Regent, being sworn in on the 5th of the month at Carlton House, whilst the band of the Grenadier Guards played martial airs from noon to tea-time.

At this turn of events the reputation of Beau Brummell was approaching its height, and it almost seemed as if the elevation of the Prince to power carried Brummell simultaneously upward. For instance, in process of certain structural alterations at White's, a bow window was built out over the entrance. No sooner was the last carpenter dispensed with than the Beau took possession of the window; moreover, he alone invited those who were to sit there with him, men strictly within the inner circle of the club. Everyone in the "Bow Window," as plainly as if they were in a broad shop-window, could be seen by all who passed on the pavement of St. James's Street; but the first rule made by Brummell for his associate Beaux was that from this window no greeting should be given to anyone outdoors. George Drummond, a banker, came into White's, and took a hand of whist. He had never played there before. One of the players at his table happened to be Brummell; whether Drummond, the hard-headed financier from the City, was abashed by his distinguished opposition, whether he miscalculated and staked recklessly, or whether his case was plain bad luck, he lost to the Beau at a single sitting £20,000.

In the arena at Almack's, Brummell was equally supreme. This club, built in King Street back of Pall Mall forty-five years before, by William Macall, a Scot, and named by reversing his own name, was the ironclad citadel of the select; to Almack's, three-fourths of the nobility were denied admission. Macall made the gilded arena, or great room—with its double chandeliers, its massive mirrors, its orchestra in a basket-balcony—an assembly for cotillons, while he put the gambling in rooms roundabout. No one was permitted to enter the club after eleven at night. It was an oligarchy of "lady patronesses," among the most powerful being Lady Jersey (her consolation after being discarded by the Prince); Lady Castlereagh, wife of the War Minister whose life was beginning to be English history in the making; and Lady Willoughby d'Eresby, wife

of Brummell's old fellow-officer in the Hussars. One evening when the Beau was in the arena, quietly elegant in
his blue coat, white waistcoat, and black pantaloons, a certain Duchess had fetched her daughter to Almack's for
the first time. Said this seasoned chaperone to her little
Lady Louisa, "Do you see that gentleman near the door?"
"Yes . . . who is he?" "A person, my dear, who will probably come and speak to us; and if he enters into conversation, be careful to give him a favourable impression of you,
for," she whispered, "he is the celebrated Mr. Brummell."

It was perhaps not too fortunate for the Beau that he
should be perfectly aware of this idolatry, and should distil
his impudence from it; but his friends at Watier's, in fact,
baited him just to hear that impudence, to them the flower
of wit. Near this time a member at the club said, "Brummell, you were not here yesterday. Where did you dine?"
"Dine! Why, with a person of the name of R——s. I believe he wishes me to notice him, hence the dinner; but,
to give him his due, he desired that I would make up the
party myself, so I asked Alvanley, Mills, Pierrepoint, and
a few others . . . there was every delicacy, in or out of season; the Sillery (champagne) was perfect . . . but, my dear
fellow, conceive my astonishment when I tell you that Mr.
R——s had the assurance to sit down and dine with us!"

If it was bad enough to be seen with such a host inside
the host's own house, it was much worse to be caught in
the man's company outdoors. At another dinner of the
sort, Brummell, shortly before leaving it, asked the guests
which one was to have the honour of taking him to Lady

Jersey's (probably Almack's) that evening. "I will," piped up the host, delighted. "Wait till my guests are gone, and my carriage is quite at your service." "Thank you," replied the Beau, pretending to take the offer literally. "Very kind . . . but, pray, how are you to go? You surely would not like to get up behind?"

For anyone taken up by the Prince of Wales, singled out, favoured and flattered, deferred to, even at times obeyed by the Prince, it was after a long course of years very difficult not to make game of ordinary beings from dukes down to dustmen. Brummell had grown so sure of himself that he no longer thought he needed to make sure actually of that Prince. In the view of the Beau, the figure of the Prince and the figure of Mr. Brummell, the two beacons which lighted up the new Regency, were not sovereign and subject, nor Regent and subject, nor master and man; they were one gentleman to another. Only recently the Prince, looking over Brummell's superb collection of snuffboxes—unrivalled since that of Beau Nash in Bath—had taken such a fancy to one of them that he ejaculated: "Brummell, this box must be mine; go to Gray's, and order any box you like in lieu of it." The Beau suggested that he might have one made with the Prince's miniature upon it, to which the Regent assented. Designing the pattern and form himself, Brummell set round the portrait with diamonds—perhaps a fair exchange for another box so captivating that a royal appropriator saw fit to make off with it. But the Prince raised no manner of objection. On the contrary, when the miniature partly filled in was submitted to him, he took the liveliest interest, suggested an improvement here and an alteration there, and let the work proceed.

It was on the strength of such episodes that Brummell reckoned he held even the Regent of England in the hollow of his hand. If he, George Brummell, disapproved of the Prince's mistresses, for example, why should he not say so? Did not his original loyalty, dating many years back, belong to the Princess of Wales? Mrs. Fitzherbert knew this well, and knew that the Beau always disliked her for being the first of the women to draw the Prince away from his consort, disappointing, unattractive, and misbehaving though that consort may in many ways have been. But if Maria Fitzherbert was long-suffering from rivals amongst the women—Lady Jersey, Lady Hertford, Lady Bessborough—need she allow men to be added to their number? No longer a strong first in the affections of the Prince, she still exercised an odd influence over him, not unlike the influence of Queen Caroline upon George II. Maria may have been a "scandal-blanket" at the Prince's parties, whilst he fondled another woman in a corner of the room; but by day she supervised his correspondence, and he was now the Regent. She dropped a hint that George Brummell laughed at him behind his back.

One evening at a ball given by Lady Jersey—discarded but still a friend—the Beau took it upon himself to call the carriage of Mrs. Fitzherbert. What he cried out, and the call was clarion, was *"Mistress* Fitzherbert!" It was loud enough, later if not at the moment, to reach the ears of the Prince. Again, there was at Carlton House a most regal hall-porter, both fat and tall, known to everyone as Big Ben. As the Prince himself was now much fatter than he ought to be, though so extremely sensitive about his contour that he designed his great-coats to hide it, Brummell thought he might serve a needful warning upon the Regent by transferring to him the epithet of the hall-porter. Nor did he spare Mrs. Fitzherbert, now grown fat beyond recall. Her he dubbed Benina.

The combination of "Ben and Benina," with all the changes which puns might ring upon it, was too good to be kept long from overspreading the town. Many of the Prince's intimates laughed; some chuckled; a few remained silent. When shortly afterward Charles Ellis, heir to Lord Seaford, gave a party at Claremont, in Surrey, historic house of the great Duke of Newcastle, and to this party invited the Prince, Brummell received no invitation. But he never allowed any such trifle to keep him away from any assembly which he took a notion to honour by attending. Did not the Prince often invite himself to dine with friends, and even take a dozen guests along with him? To Claremont in a post-chaise went the Beau, as a matter of course.

It was a Vanbrugh house, bedecked; an E-shaped house with domes on pillars atop every corner, and two clock-towers in the middle. There were statues, fountains, arches, temples; even the garden wall gloried in bastions. Through this wilderness of stone-masons' dementia one gained the great house only to be admitted to another wilderness inside, a house indeed to get lost in rather than to find one's way out of. But Brummell found no wandering to do. Almost at the threshold he brought up squarely against the man whom he had made free to call Big Ben.

The Prince was extraordinarily polite, but said that the presence of Mr. Brummell was offensive to Mrs. Fitzherbert. "Unless you return to London," he added, in a tone which the Beau had never before heard, "the party will be destroyed."

The post-chaise reappeared at the door. Brummell got in, and obliged his royal patron by vanishing.

CHAPTER VIII

THE FINAL BREAK

1811–1813

NOT CHAGRIN, but a slight sense of irritation, a vestige of annoyance, was the feeling with which the Beau retreated from Claremont. Surely, as Big Ben had expanded in girth he had shrivelled in humour. Had the man no gratitude? "I have made him," said Brummell, "and I can unmake him." Meantime he thought he might as well go to Gray's and pick up that snuffbox; a picture of anyone could be tolerated if it was encircled with diamonds. But upon inquiry at the shop a few days later the Beau was told somewhat to his further exasperation that the Prince of Wales had ordered work on the snuffbox to cease, that it was not to be delivered. And yet, Brummell's own prize snuffbox, which the Prince had so cavalierly carried away from South Street, was not returned.

Under these circumstances, however, George Brummell was the last man in England to consider himself stranded. Long had he found more agreeable the society of the Duke and Duchess of York, and indeed the Duchess, since the death of the Duchess of Devonshire, had come nearer than any other woman to assume primacy in his fondness, his affection, his devotion. Frederica, Duchess of York and Princess Royal of Prussia, being twelve years older than Brummell, was now forty-five, and after a marriage of twenty years remained childless. Like many German princesses, she was rather showily given to jewellery, and even in informal dress wore bracelets, rings, earrings, and a necklace of pearls in three or four loops. When she played hostess her additional adornment of headdress, compounded of ribbons, muslin, and feathers, added about a foot to her height. No little bookish, the Duchess liked to pick up a book at a table and discourse upon it before her guests. Her features, small and even, were without blemish, and if, desiring to be taken seriously, she rarely smiled, she was affable, charitable, knowledgeable, and in most respects a woman of sense and judgment.

But there were two things in the life of Frederica to which she assigned the utmost importance: manners and animals. It happened that on both of these scores Beau Brummell won her golden esteem. When in 1791 the Princess had married the Duke, she found him surrounded by rakes grievously lacking in their courtesy to women; now, in her own time she had seen manners in England improve to a striking degree, and the credit for it she bestowed largely upon the example set by Brummell himself. As for her absorption in animals, it was simply the tendency often exhibited by women who have no children to look after. The Duchess surrounded herself with troops of dogs, parrots, and monkeys. Oatlands Park, near Walton-on-Thames in Surrey, was the scene of this menagerie, at a house built by the Earl of Lincoln, who had included in the grounds a remarkable grotto of stalactite rock and shells. At one time the Duchess kept as many as a hundred dogs on the place, and whenever her favourite ones died she buried them round a fountain in front of this grotto, and erected monuments to them. Often she sat beside the fountain with her work or a book. Brummell, always considerate, was thoughtful enough to present his friend upon her birthday with another dog, making the number a hundred and one. "This pretty little dog," the Duchess thanked him effusively, "is the emblem of Fidelity; I love to flatter myself that it will be also of the continuation of our friendship, to which I assure you I attach the greatest value. . . . Your most affectionate friend and servant, 'F.' "

These birthdays of hers Frederica sometimes celebrated at Oatlands with great splendour, for the date, which fell in May, saw the gardens at their opulent best. In 1811 the party, in which Brummell serenely and prominently joined, was notable because the King and the Princesses all went down from Windsor. The old King, now seventy-three, amazed everyone but the Prince, whom he vexed, by recovering his sanity and actually walking about, so that the Prince had to keep postponing his fête at Carlton House by which he was to confirm with no small display his accession to power. But George III, rambling round Oatlands in honour of his daughter-in-law, enjoying the music, the games, the dancing, the fireworks, was not in the least disturbed over all this fuss about a Regency. The tone was touched by Brinsley Sheridan, who wrote a pastoral dialogue (for Brummell's album) beginning:

"Where Oatlands' lofty bank, in sylvan pride,
Looks o'er the Thames and the fair prospect wide . . ."

Even the tenants and labourers in the neighborhood, as at Belvoir when young Rutland came of age, all joined the romping, and feasted at tables specially laid for them, each table fortified with six quarts of punch. At nine o'clock a gay dance called the "Labyrinth" began, in which the Duchess led off with Colonel Upton. Of these festal scenes George Brummell was great part. "If the Prince does not behave himself," he was heard to say, "I shall bring the old King again into fashion."

But in June the Prince opened the doors of Carlton House to two thousand guests, "in the costume of the manufacture of the country." He himself made his grand entry in a Field Marshal's uniform, said by a wit to have cost and weighed two hundred pounds. Mrs. Fitzherbert was not allowed in; the Princess of Wales was not invited in. But the party was enlivened by a cluster of Bourbons, from the Comte de Lille (later Louis XVIII) to the Duchesse d'Angoulême, only surviving child of Louis XVI. On the other hand, notably absent on the English side were Queen Charlotte and her daughters, the Queen objecting to the whole business because of the latent infirmities of George III.

This time there was no doubt. Only a month later the King collapsed, beset with delusions crazier than ever, in consequence of which everyone foresaw that the restricted Regency which hampered the Prince would veritably end as soon as the stipulated twelve-month ran out in the coming February (1812). Thenceforth the Prince would in all essential respects be King. With this turn of events, the jest of Beau Brummell lost its edge, although his proposal to manipulate to his purposes the tottering figure of George III was too good to be forgotten.

If during the rest of this year of 1811 the contributions to Brummell's album could be taken as any indication of his own state of mind, one might gather that he was depressed indeed. The first poem, in September, was by Lord John Townshend, on the death of his daughter "Bella," who had just come of age, twenty lines of lamentation that would shame a church-full of epitaphs. The second, in December, from the pen of Tom Sheridan, still a better gambler than poet, was eleven stanzas on the loss of the *Saldanha,* a naval frigate, in which 300 men were drowned in a hurricane off the coast of Ireland. But there is at a given time hardly any certain connection between Brummell's choice of manuscripts for his album and his personal feelings. He could only be amused, as the year turned into 1812, at the report of an indignant letter which the Prince wrote about him to the Duke of York, in February, as if to inaugurate the independent Regency. Tom Moore, the poet (one of two or three whom Watier's condescended to ad-

mit to membership) got wind of this letter, possibly from
the Duke, his fellow-member in the club; Moore made a
parody of it in verse, and had the Prince say:

> "Neither have I resentments, nor wish there should come ill
> To mortal, except, now I think on't, Beau Brummell;
> Who threatened last year, in a superfine passion,
> To cut me, and bring the old King into fashion."

Nor was the Beau yet ready to believe, after his years of
intimacy, companionship, even joviality, with the Prince,
that this man meant to remain indefinitely estranged over
a bit of a joke at the expense of a waning mistress. Was it
not Mrs. Fitzherbert who was feeding the Prince's ani-
mosity? Did she not persist in the preposterous vanity of
identifying herself with the Crown of England? This
woman, a commoner, was overbold, presumptuous, absurd,
to think herself entitled to share the throne. But upon a
certain morning Brummell and his friend Alvanley, the
dapper peer from Watier's, were taking a walk down
Bond Street. Alvanley, since the inception of that club, had
grown more and more the companion of the Beau, to
whom, in witticisms, he ranked a close second. Two things
distinguished him from Brummell: Alvanley had a slight
lisp, which always seemed to heighten the humour of what
he said; and he had cultivated nearly to perfection *l'esprit
français,* which gave point to the charm of his manner, his
repartee, and his good nature. As he and the Beau this
morning strolled on, along came the Prince, toward them,

leaning on the arm of Lord Moira. Brummell knew that a moment which would indicate a fair test of his position had come; he was used to thinking quickly, and he was ready for it.

The Prince stopped and spoke with due cordiality to Alvanley. Of Brummell he took no notice. But the Beau, with imperturbable calm, greeted Moira, asked after his health, discussed the weather; with Moira he had often sat over a bottle in Carlton House with their host. By a contemporary it was said of Brummell that he "could assume that calm but wandering gaze, which veers as if unconsciously round the proscribed individual, neither fixing nor being fixed; that indefinable look which excuses you, perhaps, to the person *cut,* and at any rate prevents him from accosting you." If the Beau had taught anything of that trick to the Prince—as he taught him no little about the question of dress—the Prince was now not only executing it, but was perhaps bettering the instruction. However, as the Regent and Lord Moira turned to continue their promenade, Brummell, quite as if he had never before in his life set eyes upon the Prince, stared slightly round, raised slightly his voice, and exclaimed, "Alvanley, who's your fat friend?"

The test was taken. Brummell saw that the Prince was still intransigent. But he resolved to give this man as good as he sent. Was not Beau Brummell still the idol of London? Was it not of more worth to him that the Duchess of York should be his "affectionate friend" than that Maria

Fitzherbert should? True it was that Lady Granville, wife of the statesman and first earl, said this year (1812) that "Mr. Brummell makes himself rather expected than desired." Yet her acquaintance with the Beau was meagre. It would have been more accurate—on behalf of some people—to say that it was his presence of mind, his instant wit, his repartee, that was rather expected than desired. When on one occasion Brummell borrowed some money of a man in the City, and in return gave that man his patronage, he grew indignant at the lender for asking to be repaid. "Do you know what has happened?" the Beau complained to a friend. "There's that fellow Tomkins, who lent me five hundred pounds, has had the face to ask me for it; and yet I have called the dog 'Tom', and let myself dine with him." If he paid back such loans, how could he expect to have any money for himself, or even for beggars who asked him for alms? There was one beggar during these days who besought him for help, even if it was only a halfpenny. "Poor fellow," said the Beau. "I have heard of such a coin, but never possessed one. There's a shilling for you."

But the difficulty encountered by the Prince in trying to avoid Brummell was that everywhere he wanted to go, Brummell was sure to be. If he walked down St. James's, there was the Beau, in company equally eminent; if he drove in the Park, there was the Beau, driving just a bit smarter; if he went to the Opera, there was the Beau, barring his path, and always threatening to have the last word. One evening after the Opera, as the Regent was leaving, he noticed an individual in a blue cloak, leaning with his back to him upon the checktaker's bar, quite as if blocking the exit on purpose. The Prince stopped in his tracks, nonplussed; the other man stood yawning at the bar. Up came a third man, known to both, and tapped the blue cloak on the shoulder. Brummell condescended to turn his head, eyeing the Prince, whilst the Prince eyed him, and very slowly the Beau moved away from the exit, but never took his eyes off the Prince, who in turn never desisted from glaring at him, until the crowd swirled them apart.

Why miss an opportunity of teasing the Fat Friend? Unless chafed, he might never mend his ways. On another day, when the Prince was driving to the Picture Gallery in Pall Mall, Brummell was walking with a friend in the same direction. As the royal carriage, which was low and dark red, drew up at the door of the Exhibition, the Beau happened to have come exactly as far as that space on the pavement between the carriage and the entrance to the building. Two sentinels at the door presented arms. Brummell, with an air of superb acknowledgment and dignity, raised his hat, just as if the salute had been to him, and at the same time he turned his head graciously toward the sentinels, and his back to the carriage window. Anyone who at the moment had peeped within the carriage would have discerned upon the Prince a face of thunder, but would have heard no thunderclap. That was the misfortune of the Prince; he never quite knew what to say.

In taking this line in respect of personal behaviour toward a ruler who had proved somewhat unforgiving, vindictive, and deficient in humour, Brummell was not without sympathizers. At the club he even won away from the Prince some of his old friends, such as Sir Henry Mildmay and Tom Moore, the poet. Moore, who had fittingly dedicated a translation of Anacreon's ribaldries to the Prince, had been unwelcome at Carlton House since he circulated that parody about "bringing the old King into fashion." The defection of Mildmay was perhaps still more keenly felt by the Regent, for Mildmay had a handsome and accomplished wife, who, wherever she went, was a sensation. When, characteristically, but without either malice or undue earnestness, Brummell remarked that "he had made the Prince, and could unmake him," and the words fell upon the the ear of Colonel MacMahon, an Irish hanger-on at Carlton House, only to be repeated to the Regent, this was the Regent's retort: "He is only fit to make the reputation of a tailor." But the public did not believe that; and it was in Brummell that public favour still resided.

A large share of this favour was reserved for the Beau at Oatlands, where he was joining a merry party to spend the Christmas holiday. Indeed, to exchange Carlton House for Oatlands was no very conspicious loss; at Oatlands one could be surer of one's company; the monstrosities—at least the macaws, eagles, ostriches, and kangaroos—were confined in cages in the Duchess's zoo. Christmas with Frederica was rather an experience. She turned her great dining-room into a German fair. Along each side ranged booths festooned with knick-knacks; in the centre stood a

tree which scraped the ceiling and was hung with sweet-
meats and cakes; at one end, on a table, lay spread out the
presents for the guests; at the other end there was a table
piled with presents which the guests had brought to the
Duchess. At one Christmas she gave to Tom Raikes, a
member of Watier's whom Brummell occasionally permitted to lend money to him, a morocco pocketbook, embroidered in gold by herself, with a gold pencil-case and
amethyst seal. But the Duchess always requested that the
presents brought to her should be inexpensive. Notwithstanding this, the Beau once laid upon her table a lace
gown from Brussels, for which he had paid 150 guineas.

The hostess at Oatlands accommodated herself to the
waking habits of every guest, for she rarely went to bed.
If she desired a few hours' sleep, she took it sitting dressed
on a couch or in a chair, now in one room, now in another.
She delighted in solitary walks at dead of night. After
breakfast, which she took at three o'clock in the morning,
she went for a long walk either in her own park or in the
village, followed by at least forty of her dogs. So it came
about that no ceremony was observed at Oatlands, and
each guest was free to be as eclectic as the Duchess herself.
In the party this Christmas, besides Brummell, were Colonel James Armstrong, aide-de-camp of the Duke; William
Spencer, the "poet of Society," who had just dedicated
a volume to Lady Jersey; "Monk" Lewis, nicknamed for
his salacious novel, *The Monk;* General "Kangaroo"
Cooke, another aide of the Duke's, who had once let loose

a cageful of kangaroos; Charles Culling Smith and his
wife, Lady Anne Culling Smith, together with Anne Fitz-
roy, a daughter of Lady Anne by an earlier marriage; De
Lancey Barclay, still another aide to the Duke, and very
popular in the army; Chevalier Cainea, an Italian amateur
singer; Mercer, another singer; and Lord Erskine, who
elected himself the poet of the party.

Of these guests, the oddest was Monk Lewis, a small
ugly man, with "queer projecting eyes like those of some
insect." Many thought him a fop; others a bore; none
denied his gift for epigram, which won him the hospitality of the Duchess. One day after dinner she whispered
something to Lewis. His eyes filled with tears. Asked what
was the matter, he replied, "Oh, the Duchess spoke so *very*
kindly to me!" "My dear fellow," put in Armstrong the
aide, "pray don't cry; I daresay she didn't mean it." But
it was Lewis, when Erskine across a dinner-table said that
"a wife was nothing but a tin canister tied to a man's tail,"
it was Lewis who wrote the best verses refuting him.

As for the rhymes of Erskine, 125 lines which he ground
out in commemoration of the dinner on this New Year's
Eve, lines describing each guest, his tribute to Brummell
was one of the aptest:

"By this Colonel sat one in gay circles well known,
  Yet, who see him in rounds of amusement alone,
  Know little about him—they see him at ease,
  A high man of fashion, with talents to please;
  But believe me, in London to rise to the top,

Like Brummell (since London discarded the fop),
You must know all that's known to the highest in place,
And possess the rare gift to give knowledge a grace.
But why should the muse, *his* acquirements to show,
Fly to commonplace truths which the vulgar well know?
Since the brighter the emerald the Duchess now wears,
The higher of course is the polish it bears."

If the place of the Beau in London was still as secure as
Erskine suggested, he need have had no fear in returning
to town from Oatlands. Soon after he got back, he made
a new acquaintance in the person of a new member of
Watier's, Lord Byron. It was a curious meeting for Brummell, to meet the man whom his old intimate at Eton, Jack
Musters, had so easily vanquished in the rivalry for the
affections of Mary Chaworth. Byron was riding high upon
the fame of "Childe Harold," a fifth edition of which had
been published just before Christmas; Lady Oxford and
Lady Caroline Lamb were fighting for possession of him;
the great hostesses, Lady Bessborough, Lady Heathcote,
Lady Jersey, had thrown wide their doors to him; "Byron
Fever" was at its peak. His escape was Watier's.

Brummell and Byron struck up almost instant mutual
liking. Of the members in the club, Byron called Brummell, Alvanley, Mildmay, and Pierrepoint "the four
chiefs," although his intellectual interests naturally lay
closer to those of the only two other literary members,
Tom Moore and William Spencer—Brummell's late fel-
low-guests at Oatlands. (The club would have none of

Monk Lewis; indeed, they "persecuted and mystified" him). In explaining how he happened to get on with Brummell and the rest, the "Dandy Club," as he called it, Byron later observed: "though I gave up the business early, I had a tinge of dandyism in my minority, and probably retained enough of it to conciliate the great ones, at five-and-twenty. I had gamed and drunk, and taken my degrees in most dissipations, and having no pedantry, and not being overbearing, we ran on quietly together."

Other literary lights fared less well under the stern scrutiny of the Beau. In the spring turned up Anne Louise, Madame de Stael, aged forty-six, leading her eldest son, her daughter Albertine, and her unacknowledged second husband M. de Rocca, who was exactly half her age. She was famous not only as the author of *Corinne,* but as having been banished by Napoleon. If her reception was brilliant, from those who went in for lionizing, she made rather less impression upon Brummell and the Dandies, including Byron, all of whom met Madame when dining out. For she was a coarse-featured woman, with "two irregularly prominent teeth," and she did not talk; she declaimed. Brinsley Sheridan, who was accustomed to taking upon himself a fair slice of the conversation, made fun of her, mimicked her. When Brummell clearly saw that one of the objects of Madame in London was to make a rich match for the child Albertine, he and Mildmay got the poor lady in a corner and confided to her that Alvanley (who was head over heels in debt) was worth £100,000 a year. The eyes of Anne Louise nearly started from her head. Losing no time, she made a set at Alvanley, who in spite of his rare grace and charm was downright ugly to look at, and to his very face she praised him for his beauty.

Only later did Madame de Stael reach the melancholy awakening that she had failed to please Beau Brummell. All along she had been haunted by a dread of his disapprobation, like everyone from Lady Louisa the Duchess's daughter down to Schweitzer the tailor. "Malheur," was the word of Madame de Stael for this miscue, the greatest, she considered, that had been visited upon her during her stay in London. Only second in gravity was the fact that the Prince of Wales neglected to call upon her.

The question of the Prince, incidentally, came up in July, when the Dandies, in order to celebrate a remarkable run of luck in Watier's at hazard, decided to give a masquerade ball at the Argyle Rooms. Should the Regent be invited? Amongst the four, he had quarrelled with Brummell and was offended at Mildmay for espousing Brummell's side; but he was nursing no grievances against either Alvanley or Pierrepoint. In fact, Henry Pierrepoint was in excellent standing at Carlton House. Brummell generously enough laid aside his own militant feelings. It was thought by all that the Prince might like to court public favour by attending, since in the eye of the populace he had suffered a lapse, beneath the combined onslaughts upon his character by the Princess and the Whigs; when in April he had visited St. George's Chapel at Windsor to witness the opening of the tomb of Charles I (to make sure of its location) who was buried near Henry VIII,

Byron, his favourite poet, had scorched the Prince with these lines:

> "Charles to his people, Henry to his wife,
> In him the double tyrant starts to life: . . .
> Ah, what can tombs avail! since these disgorge
> The blood and dust of both to mould a George.

Surely, agreed the Dandies in council, it would be an act of charity to ask the hard-driven Regent to the Ball; it might "bring old friends together." Accordingly Pierrepoint was deputed to sound the Prince, as to whether he would care to receive an invitation. He proceeded to Carlton House. The effect of their interview was that the Prince did not only voice his desire to attend but showed a certain alacrity at the prospect. Then the four, to make sure that he would know beforehand the identity of his hosts, despatched to the Regent an invitation in the names of them all.

On the night of the Masque the great man arrived at the Argyle Rooms in good season. At the door stood the Dandies, each with a torch, to welcome him into the hall of sparkling chandeliers and bizarre costumes. The Regent bowed majestically to Alvanley, and to Henry Pierrepoint, showing evident heartiness as he shook hands with both. Of Mildmay he took no notice, except a faint mutter. Of Beau Brummell he took no notice whatever. A slight frost fell upon the surrounding assembly. Then the ball right merrily went on.

When the time came for the Prince to leave, Brummell did not attend him to his carriage.

Byron, oblivious of all this, was inside, busily weaving about with the ladies. "Our masquerade," he later said, "was a grand one."

On the next day the Prince commented upon the parting incident, which hurt him perhaps more than he had intended to hurt the others. "Had Brummell," he said, "taken the cut I gave him good-humouredly, I would have renewed my intimacy with him."

CHAPTER IX

FLIGHT

1814–1816

As THE acquaintance of George Brummell and Lord Byron deepened to the point of mutual confidences it was inevitable that the Beau should allude to his erstwhile friend and schoolmate Jack Musters, and that Byron should recur to the subject of the woman whom Musters had deprived him of: Mary Chaworth. There was Byron with all the women of London at his feet. Yet Brummell "frequently heard him romanticize for hours" about Mary. The Beau could not understand this "never-dying attachment," for to him Mary Chaworth, with what he called her coarse manners and her vanity, was "far from resembling what he should have conceived the *beau ideal* of Byron." But when he asked Byron (as was sure to happen) for a contribution to the Album, the poet turned out twenty lines to a nameless lady, including these four:

"But never again shalt thou be to my heart
What thou wert—what I fear for a moment thou art:

To see thee—to love thee—what heart could do more?
To love thee—to lose thee, 'twere vain to deplore!" ...

Brummell asked for a second contribution, and got a manuscript of eight lines more; though this poem may well have concerned a different lady (or indeed no lady in particular), the same reminiscence, applicable to Mary, now eight years married, emerged from it. It was called "To One Who Promised on a Lock of Hair":

"Vow not at all, but if thou must,
     Oh! be it by some slender token:
Since pious pledge, and plighted trust,
     And holiest ties, too oft are broken.
Then by this dearest trifle swear,
     And if thou lov'st as I would have thee,
This votive ringlet's tenderest hair
     Will bind thy heart to that I give thee."

It was at Watier's that Brummell was most often thrown with Byron, apart from meeting him continually at evening parties given by the "great hostesses" in their own homes. If with him the Beau had talked poetry more, and stood at the green gaming-table less, the outcome for Brummell would have been happier. But before this year 1813 was out, the Beau had won £26,000, almost doubling his capital, and twenty times his income. He conjured up the idea that he could not lose. Sweet was the temptation to extravagance, and he indulged it, whilst those who knew him best, fearing a sudden reverse, knowing how small his means really were, begged him to buy an annuity with his winnings, and if he must continue gambling, to reduce the scale of his stakes. Brummell gave them no heed.

Nor did the excitement of the new year, in particular after the Allies occupied Paris and Napoleon abdicated in April, tend to produce an atmosphere in the clubs which might cause the fever of gambling to abate. No sooner had Louis XVIII departed from England to claim his dominions than the Czar Alexander and the King of Prussia arrived in London to celebrate the victory. In the wake of the visiting monarchs came foreigners galore, army and navy, generals and admirals, together with innumerable British guardsmen spoiling to risk all their back pay on the jingling tables of the clubs. Sometimes they won, too. While Brummell began the season a winner, he soon lost all his takings of the year before, and in addition, what he called "an unfortunate ten thousand pounds." Even at White's, where in a happier day he had raked in double that sum from the banker Drummond, he could make nothing out of whist. For five nights running the Beau lost and lost. "I have lost every shilling," he exclaimed. "I only wish someone would bind me never to play again." His friend Pemberton Mills from Watier's, standing by, anxious for him, piped up, "I will." Mills handed Brummell a ten-pound note, on condition that he should forfeit a thousand if he played again at White's within a month. The Beau took it.

He stayed away from White's for some days, perhaps taking advantage of the respite to pull himself together and to sound his true position. He could still borrow money on the strength of having spoken in public to one individual, or of having been seen in public in the company of another individual; one might call these sums "recognition loan," or "associative loan." The Beau now got money from Tom Raikes, that idolator of the great, for letting himself dine with Raikes, who wanted to be able to say that Brummell and he were dining the other day etcetera, that Brummell, you know, was an excellent fellow, etcetera. Another man at this juncture was permitted the honour of lending the Beau £500, since the Beau, standing in the window at White's, had gone so far as to break the rule of the club and say to the man as he passed by outside, "Ah, how do you do, Jemmy?" Again, Brummell was careful, while abstaining for the moment from White's, he put in appearance elsewhere, and to look prosperous. He saved something on his household account by dining—if not in the house of one of the great ladies of London—at Brooks's:

> "Liberal Brooks, whose speculative skill
> Was hasty credit, and a distant bill."

Or he strolled down King street to Almack's, and deigned to be seen talking to the Duke of Wellington, the hero of the season. The Duke could nearly always get in at Almack's, being turned away only once because he was seven minutes past the hour, and only once because he was wearing trousers, "God damme!" and not knee-breeches, "By God!" But Brummell and the Duke understood each other, and were fond of each other; however many victories the Duke had won on the battlefield, he was big enough a man to appreciate that Brummell had won still more in the drawing-room.

But after a fortnight, not a month, the Beau ineluctably eddied back to White's. Doubtless he thought he had borrowed enough to make big winnings a possibility. Worse luck, Pemberton Mills strayed in, and discovered his friend hard at the cards. Brummell must now forfeit a thousand. But Mills let that go. Touching the Beau gently on the shoulder, he said, "Well, Brummell, you may at least give me back the ten pounds."

It was at about the time of this profitless evening that he lost a certain silver sixpence with a hole in it, a coin given him years before, perhaps by the gypsy on Gypsy Hill, with the injunction that he should take good care of it, for everything would go well with him as long as he did. By mistake, in an evil hour, the Beau gave this sixpence to a hackney coachman. Frantically he advertised for the lost treasure. Twenty people came with sixpences having holes in them; his was not amongst the lot. "No doubt," said he, "that rascal Rothschild, or some of his set, got hold of it."

Though not unduly depressed by superstition, Brummell did sense the advisability of moving from his semi-palatial house in South Street to quarters more in keeping with such resources as he still possessed. An acquaintance, one Hart, steward to the Duke of Gloucester (who had married one of the five royal princesses) owned a little house

near Park Lane—in Chapel Street, No. 13. It was next a
mews. There was a time when the Beau could not even
bear to be in the same club with men from the country,
lest they be redolent of the stables. But now, should a good
horseman like himself object to a few neighbourly horses?
They might be unobjectionable horses, belonging to the
Duke. Brummell dismissed his cook—the man who for
years had made his dinners a social event, relished even by
the Prince—packed up his furniture, and moved into
Chapel Street.

A removal is a good time to take stock of one's chattels.
Many of the things, which would have been an adornment
to Carlton House itself, might have been quietly sold, and
the sum raised would in no small degree have relieved
his wants. But the Beau was not the sort of man to do
that; he loved being surrounded by rare, artistic, and beautiful objects, which were almost a part of his life, like
friends; besides, in Chapel Street he had both a drawing-
room and a back drawing-room to fill up, not to mention a
dining-room. What would his guests say—he must still
contrive to give occasional little dinners—if they did not
see his Sèvres china, his silver tea-kettle (embossed and
chased), his nine wine coolers, above all, his cheval dress-
ing-glass, with its brass arms for candles? Perhaps he
might have disposed of a few of the wine coolers; but these
were heavy-drinking days, and he still had twenty-six
dozen of port, claret and burgundy, which had lain in the
cellar since the Duchess of Devonshire died.

Into his new drawing-room Brummell put his chimney-glass, with its carved ebony frame; his chintz furniture, and a stout Brussels carpet. The walls took portraits of the old King, and of the benefactor of the Brummells, Lord North; here the Beau also hung up portraits of Nelson and of Pitt, and one of his own friend the young Duke of Rutland. Prints by Cipriani and by Bartolozzi formed a suitable minor decoration. Then of the back drawing-room he made a library. It was a curious collection of books, a collection in character, not the choice of either a scholar or a booklover. Side by side with Shakespeare stood the *Edinburgh Review*, bound; beside the *Memoirs of Grammont*, a volume in raised calf, called *Specimens of Early English Metrical Romances*. He had neither Homer nor Aeschylus themselves, but copies of Flaxman's designs for them. There were many French and Italian books, the bindings of which were works of art. Of odd volumes, one could see Berrington's *Abelard and Eloisa,* and Bürger's *Leonora*; but the characteristic book of the lot, perhaps, was Chesterfield's *Letters.* For the rest, shelf after shelf of ephemeral novels, almost as if the Beau had been a book reviewer.

Little need be said of his dressing-room, which was of course dominated by the cheval-glass in its mahogany frame. But Brummell had near it a ewer and basin which was a sight to see. It was in gold and mazarine blue, richly ornamented with birds and exotics painted in compartments, with the name of each bird lettered in; the handle of the ewer was silver gilt. To this man, washing was a ritual. He could risk, he thought, living next to a mews.

Here was enough of his old luxury, perhaps too much, to enable him to accommodate himself to his humbler quarters; this brave setting of the stage must perforce impress friends from whom he could still borrow, must sway moneylenders who would cast a covetous eye upon such furnishings and regalia. But as the year 1815 wore on, and all London was rejoicing on the one hand over Waterloo and on the other over the betrothal of the young Princess to Prince Leopold, affairs did not prosper for Brummell. Alvanley, who was in continual money difficulties almost as bad as the Beau's, periodically skipped off to the Continent just as the Jews were about to pounce upon him; but Brummell stayed on; he seemed to have more faith in gambling, or at least was more blindly addicted to it. "He is the only Dandy-lion," said Alvanley of his friend, "that flourishes year after year in the hotbed of fashion; he has taken root; lions are only annual; but he is perennial."

If Brummell at Watier's or at White's did have a run of luck, as happened upon one or two forlorn occasions, he paid back none of his loans, but only dreamed of recovering his entire fortune; then he lost again. Lord Robert Manners, for the sake of old times in the Tenth Hussars, came handsomely to the rescue of the Beau more than once; other lords, with at least one marquess, did likewise. However, the spare funds of these friends had limits, and as the number of such rescuers dwindled, the number of moneylenders, with their extortionate rates of interest, and their relentless demands for repayment, grew ominously. Neither the brother nor the sister of this beleaguered man appeared inclined to offer a helping hand. William Brummell, the country gentleman who wore bad clothes, kept his discreet distance in Essex, while Maria the sister, who had married a Captain Blackshaw, remained out of touch in Berkshire, living in a cottage near The Grove, the scene of her childhood.

At long last the Beau was driven to the desperate expedient of attempting to raise a large sum—said to be £30,000 —on the joint security of himself and Alvanley, backed by the Marquess of Worcester. The recital of this transaction, in its details, is confused, tinctured with malice, and not wholly credible, coming as it did from Harriette Wilson; but it was corroborated in some degree by Byron. It appears that Worcester knew one Richard Meyler, a wealthy sugar-baker, who perhaps like John Mitchel the grocer was a frequenter of Harriette's drawing-room, and who at all events had the entrée to White's. On account of Worcester, Meyler lent Brummell £7,000. But the guarantor of the entire sum, £30,000, was to be the Duke of Beaufort. The Duke, however, upon inquiry was informed that Brummell was already so deeply embarrassed that there was small likelihood of his ever being able to pay a guinea of interest upon any loan. The state of Alvanley's affairs, though not hopeless, hardly promised much more.

When Meyler heard this news, he was furious. According to Harriette Wilson he declared he would cut Alvanley wherever he met him, "notwithstanding no man delights more in his amusing qualities than I do." Toward Brummell, Meyler was still more venomous: "I would forgive him," he said grandly, "the seven thousand pounds he has robbed me of; but on Worcester's account I shall expose him tomorrow at White's!"

On the next morning Meyler waylaid every member who entered the club, unburdened himself of this tangled story to each, with plentiful mention of his friend the Marquess of Worcester, and touched his top note by calling Brummell a "disgrace to society," and "unfit to remain a member of that club." Tom Raikes, who got caught in this fusillade, recounted the matter to Brummell. But the Beau did not take the trouble to argue it out with Meyler, who, on the word of Byron, earned for his pains the slightly contemptuous name of "Dick the Dandy-killer."

Nevertheless Brummell at this contretemps took serious thought of turning his back upon London. If only he could go like Byron, who in April of this year (1816) was setting forth to Ostend, and leaving no liabilities behind except women! Byron still spoke of Brummell with admiration and envy, though the poet managed to be ecstatic enough to applaud himself in the same breath. "There are but three great men," said Byron, "in the nineteenth century: Brummell, Napoleon, and myself."

As for the circumstances closing in upon the Beau, and tempting him to depart in the same general direction, it was doubtless a melancholy reflection to him that the Duke of Beaufort had failed him so summarily. Sharp was the present contrast with the day when George Brummell had been a guest of the Beauforts in the country, applauded, flattered, made much of, the day when he had honoured the Duchess by drawing her portrait in water-colours. If now the Duke, in putting his questions about the financial standing of Brummell, had only taken the trouble to press those inquiries far enough, he might have discovered that the security attested by the Beau was not a myth, that "a considerable sum of money," ultimately to become his, was vested in the Court of Chancery. It was true that stern measures would have had to be taken to compel Brummell to stop gambling; yet it might have been done. As things turned out, Richard Meyler, worshipping the first word of a Duke just as he grovelled in his "friendship" with a Marquess, saw fit to give way to panic, and unhappily there were a number of members of White's who were impressed by the histrionics of a sugar-baker, because he was rich. Alvanley laughed Meyler off as "a damned methodistical grocer." To Brummell, no such way out was visible, for he was caught further in the meshes of one Solomon, a moneylender, who was threatening him with arrest.

The Beau now saw clearly enough that if he desired to continue a free man, he could do so only outside England. In May he resolved to go. This committing of patriotic suicide he set about with all his habitual composure and deliberation, making sure of each arrangement just as he studied each crease of his cravat. It was of course difficult to collect enough money to make a stylish escape. But his friends were many; and the majority of those few of whom he asked donations—except Scrope Davies, like himself a hard-pressed gambler, who refused him £200—

the majority contributed something. On May 16, a Thursday, Brummell sent his own carriage and four a short distance away from town, to wait for him, having packed in it very quietly such movable belongings as it would take, including the blue-velvet Album of Poetry. Dressed for the Opera as usual, in his familiar blue coat and white waistcoat, black pantaloons and striped stockings, Beau Brummell, in his own lodgings in Chapel Street, dined with Beau Brummell, like Lucullus with Lucullus. While the fare was only a cold fowl, sent in from Watier's, and a bottle of his own claret, the service and the Sèvres were as perfect as anything Rome ever knew. And then the Beau took a last look round, at his portraits, his prints, his books, his inlaid buhl furniture, with perhaps a parting glance at that ewer and basin, and certainly a moment, fond though sombre, before the cheval-glass.

Only one little detail remained to be attended to. At the Opera, he arranged with a friend, a nobleman, to have a chaise drawn up for him, to be standing near the door. Inside, Brummell looked idly on from his box; he was seen; he appeared to both friend and foe quite unconcerned. But he left early, stepped into the chaise, and vanished. Joining his own carriage at an hour agreed on, he drove all night, as fast as post-horses could take him down the Dover Road, and before dawn he was at the sea. Immediately he hired a small vessel, drew his carriage on board, and made sail for Calais.

The West End of London looked about rather early for Brummell on the morning of May 17th, his tradesmen, his creditors, his moneylenders, his enemies, even a few friends. The wolves among them were hungry, vociferous, relentless. In a matter of actual hours they had engaged James Christie, the auctioneer, to draw up a catalogue of sale of every stick that the Beau had left behind in Chapel Street. Christie advertised the sale—to be held only five days later, May 22, and the day following—as "the genuine property of a Man of Fashion, gone to the Continent."

In the blessed phrases of the auctioneer, the property included "a Library of Books," "three capital double-barrelled Fowling Pieces," and "The admired drawing of the Refractory Schoolboy." But there were other things that friends of Brummell, so often and so exquisitely entertained by him, came to bid upon. Though the Duke of York was not there, he gave orders for some of the Sèvres, perhaps the green oval vases, with flowers, fruit, and mouldings of burnished gold, which sold for nineteen guineas; or for a small cup and cover in the same pattern, which fetched almost as much. Other friends who attended were Lord Bessborough, Lord Yarmouth, Lady Warburton, Pemberton Mills, and even Colonel Cotton, the patriarchal lover of Julia Storer. Those who had dined with the Beau were not surprised to see 78 meat-plates, 62 wine-glasses, and 20 soup-plates. Those who knew his cellar were not slow to offer five guineas a dozen for his claret, and nearly the same for his champagne and port. Those who had come to his levée could hardly have wondered at his 16 pairs of sheets and 40 huckaback towels. Only the bidders for silverware were disappointed, for

Brummell had left behind but half a dozen spoons and four forks—a memento, no doubt, of his last dinner.

The high moment of the sale came when Christie picked up a very handsome snuffbox, and before asking offers for it, opened the lid. A piece of paper fell out. On this paper was written, in the handwriting of Beau Brummell: "This snuffbox was intended for the Prince Regent, if he had conducted himself with more propriety toward me."

PART II

CHAPTER X

LELEUX ET LEVEUX

1816–1819

THE HIGH tower of the church of Notre Dame in Calais was the landmark for sailors—for the captain of the little vessel which was bearing Beau Brummell to his refuge. As the boat passed into the outer harbour and neared the channel, the forts, batteries, and ramparts of the old town emerged sharply from the grey haze of the morning. Under the shadow of these walls Brummell was not sorry to disembark. Once inside them, he perhaps thought, he could stand a siege rather longer than the English garrison from whom the Duke of Guise, in the time of Bloody Mary, wrested Calais after seven days. The Beau passed at once to the centre of town, the Place d'Armes, and made his way to the bourn of all Englishmen, Dessein's, an hotel then in charge of M. Quillacq. To this landlord, with very little ado, he sold his carriage; he would have no more need of that.

But his first anxiety, within twenty-four hours of his

arrival, was to write to those friends of his earliest days in the Hussars, Charles and Robert Manners, who to the end had lent him all they had to give: "Persecuted to the worst extent," he told them, "by those to whom I was indebted, without resource or even the hope to evade . . . menaces which I was well assured would have instantly been enforced against my personal liberty, I have been driven to the only alternative . . . that of quitting my country forever. . . . In acknowledging my obligations to you . . . I still feel anxious in the wish to realize the promised power of future remuneration. . . . The last remaining hope of my broken fortunes consists in a considerable sum of money now vested in the Court of Chancery. . . . The reversion I abandon legally and willingly to you . . . to show that though unfortunate . . . I am not destitute of strong feeling and gratitude toward those who have been so seriously my friends . . . I can look forward to no means of subsistence beyond the year—yet I feel some remote satisfaction in the idea that the slight reparation I am offering is everything that is left to your former friend."

Added satisfaction, perhaps not so remote, the Beau might find in the compatriots he was to encounter in Calais, some of them there for the same purpose as himself, others passing through. A fellow-member of Watier's —who was also a friend of Byron—in Calais at the moment was the Earl of Blessington, a man with tastes almost as extravagant as Brummell's, and with him the Beau exchanged greetings well understood. Sir William Bellingham, the Irish baronet and man of fashion, was another guest in Dessein's to whom Brummell spoke. But the newly-arrived fugitive was hardly prepared to see such a close friend of the Regent as Prince Paul Esterhazy, the man who by express desire of the Regent had lately been named Austrian Ambassador to England. Esterhazy, who was on his way to London, came bounding into Brummell's room at the hotel quite unexpected. The Beau gave him a few letters to take back to friends at home, friends from whom he had been unhappy to part.

Within a very few days (May 22) he sent a word of cheer to his faithful satellite Tom Raikes: "Here I am *restant* for the present, and God knows solitary enough in my existence . . . I should not complain, for I can always employ resources within myself, was there not a worm that will not sleep, called *conscience,* which all my endeavours to distract, all the strength of coffee with which I constantly fumigate my unhappy brains, and all the native gaiety of the fellow who brings it to me, cannot lull to indifference . . . I am punctually off the pillow at half-past seven in the morning. My first object—melancholy indeed it may be in its nature—is to walk to the pier-head and take my distant look at England. This you may call weakness; but I am not yet sufficiently master of those feelings which may be called indigenous to resist the impulse. The rest of my day is filled with strolling an hour or two round the ramparts of this dismal town, in reading, and the study of that language which must hereafter be my own, for nevermore shall I set foot in my own country. I dine at five, and my evenings have as yet been occupied in writing letters. . . .

"As to the alteration in my looks, you will laugh when I tell you your own head of hair is but a scanty possession in comparison with that which now crowns my pristine baldness; a convenient, comely scalp, that has divested me of my former respectability of appearance (for what right have I now to such an outward sign?) and if the care and distress of mind which I have lately undergone had not impressed more ravages haggard and lean than my years might justify upon my unfortunate phiz, I should certainly pass at a little distance for *five-and-twenty*."

He was just thirty-eight. It was a tender age for a man of eminence to go into exile. To Brummell, the Regency and the decade preceding it had been like the Age of Augustus to Ovid in Rome; but Ovid, when he was banished, had turned fifty, and he had seen perhaps ten years more of life in the capital than the Beau had enjoyed in London. Ovid, well past middle age, could take his punishment upon a richer cushion of memories; but how far supportable would be a town like Calais to a man who had hardly emerged from his youth? The gossip-mongers of London, neglecting to think of this side of the case, vouchsafed to Brummell scant pity. Even as the Beau was writing to Raikes, a diarist in St. James's (May 21) had only this to say: "The respectable fraternity of legs in high life are thrown into a state of extreme consternation by the disappearance of Beau Brummell, a friend of the Prince

Regent, with £40,000, the whole of which he is said to
have fraudulently obtained. He absconded on Saturday
last." (The diarist was two days late in that date). On
May 24 he added: "Beau Brummell's deficiencies amount
to a still greater sum than I mentioned. G—— told me an
hour ago that he borrowed the money in the way of ac-
ceptances from the Duke of Rutland, Lords Charles and
Robert Manners, etc. The Marquis of Worcester stood the
flat for £7,000. Brummell's private debts are very considerable; he has even bilked——. Lord Wellesley says he
is in Picardy." The "£40,000" which this peddler of
scandal pinned upon Brummell was just £1,000, all that
he had saved from the wreck of his patrimony, and it was
this sum to which he referred when he told Charles and
Robert Manners that he had "no means of subsistence beyond the year."

Wherefore it behoved Brummell not to remain at Dessein's, but to move to quarters of more privacy and less expense. Just off the Place d'Armes, at the back of the Hotel
de Ville (a building edified by busts of the Duke de Guise
and of Richelieu) ran the Rue Royale, in which stood a
bookseller's shop at the sign of "Le Pauvre Diable." The
name of it alone was enough to attract the Beau. He went
in and found the proprietor, M. Leleux, an old soldier of
fortune, who wore a cap with a peak. Leleux had been aide
to Francisco Miranda, the dictator of Venezuela, who incidentally only died in July (1816) after four years in
captivity in Spain. As Brummell, much amused, poked
round "Le Pauvre Diable," followed by Leleux who kept

taking large pinches of snuff, he inquired about possible lodgings. While the old soldier had retreated to Calais with enough plunder to live out his days modestly upon a stock of books, he was not averse to increasing his income by giving up a part of his house overhead. They went up to the first floor. Brummell, with little delay, engaged the two front rooms, for a drawing-room and a dining-room; to the rear of the corridor, which extended across the house, he took a bedroom. Already the Beau envisioned for himself surroundings not markedly inferior to those which he had quitted in Chapel Street. To uphold that atmosphere he then engaged a valet, called François Sélègue.

But to furnish his rooms in accordance with his tastes, Brummell had first to establish his credit in Calais. Looking out a banker, he found such an individual in M. Jacques Leveux, and with him left 25,000 francs. Between Leveux and Leleux his life was now established, as if between Tweedledum and Tweedledee; he charmed them both by his manner, which in addition to being regal was original. Soon MM. Leveux and Leleux were saying the same thing round Calais about the Beau. "One would be able," they both said, "to refuse him nothing." And the old bookseller added, "So amusing, so amusing . . . I would keep him without charge . . . certainly a very droll fellow." Under the benignity of these two accommodating Frenchmen, Brummell now set about making his *salon* comfortable with ormolu and buhl. He spent capital, nursing the rather wild idea that other capital would come to him from somewhere, from someone, sometime. He bought furniture in the style of Louis Quatorze, had it fetched down from Paris by a courier well instructed in the tastes of Mr. Brummell in chairs, stools, cabinets, bronzes, pictures and prints. If any of these objects did not suit, it had either to be sent back to Paris, exchanged, or sold in Calais at half its cost, the courier slicing off a little fee for himself each time.

What at first bore the appearance of a warehouse, then, was shortly transformed by this elegant hermit into the drawing-room of an exquisite. A conspicuous feature of it was a large cabinet with brass-wire doors, containing a service of Sèvres, the plates of which were decorated with the beauties of the courts of Louis XIV and Louis XV; it was a sort of buhl seraglio, over which Brummell stood Sultan. To callers at Le Pauvre Diable who gained admission to the first floor overhead, the Beau was occasionally willing to unlock the cabinet, although he assured them that it was "almost profanation even to look" upon the fair frailty therein residing. On a circular card-table, in the centre of the room, lay his toys; gold snuffboxes, enamelled miniatures, mother-of-pearl cardcases, ivory paperweights, tortoiseshell knives, and various knick-knacks in embossed leather or embroidered satin. Some of course he had brought away from London; others he picked up in France; and he was going on accumulating them, like a child with playthings, in response to a craving almost as strong as gambling had once been. There was an ormolu greyhound. There was a paper-press of Siena mar-

ble, surmounted by a little bronze eagle, a thing which
had only lately adorned the desk of Napoleon. But neither
Napoleon nor Beau Brummell any longer had papers to
press. All of these knick-knacks had their quality emphasized by the table-cover upon which they reposed: it
had been embroidered for their owner by his admiring
and still devoted Frederica, Duchess of York.

While the circular table and the cabinet for the Sèvres
dominated the room, Brummell also tricked it out with
japanned screens, books bound in morocco or silk, card-
tables on which no cards were to be played, and paintings
by a young artist of Calais whom he spontaneously determined to patronize and encourage. Likewise he gave work
to a local jeweller, by whom he considered it indispensable
that he should have a snuffbox made of black shell and
gold. Near the fireplace he put his easy-chair, which he
had managed to bring over from England; it was another
gift of the Duchess of York. No stranger could escape the
impression that as old Leleux sold antique books below,
Brummell, above, was prepared to deal in antique furniture. But the difference was that with the Beau everything
on display was a work of art, a thing of beauty, and a
testament of taste.

Now if in consequence of this luxury the funds of Brummell soon began to ebb in startling measure, friends of the
exiled man, as he anticipated, did not forget him. One
morning the clerk of M. de Vos, another banker in Calais,
called to say that a large sum had on the day before been
paid into their bank for him by an anonymous friend; the

amount was said to have been £1,000. His "most affectionate friend and servant," the Duchess of York, not only
sent him purses, card-cases, note-keepers, worked by herself, but a bank-note enclosed in each gift. The old King's
son-in-law, the Duke of Gloucester, who frequently travelled to Paris, stopped off at Le Pauvre Diable to make
sure that the Beau in his solitude lacked no comfort. John
Chamberlayne, never an intimate but an admirer and a
sympathizer, went so far as to say that he designed giving
Brummell a yearly allowance, and so began it. Harriette
Wilson's lover the Marquis of Lorne, now Duke of Argyll,
with whom the exile had for several years been the closest
of friends, tarried in Calais as he passed through and left
money so far as his means permitted. Above all, Alvanley,
who was keeping up his game of hide-and-seek with the
money-lenders, disappeared from London only to reappear
in Calais, there to dine with his brother-dandy at the expense of those moneylenders.

That was the inestimable convenience of Calais; it was
on the road to Paris, and George Brummell stood at the
toll-gate, fastidious as ever in his buff and blue, his shining
boots, and his cravat beyond compare. He went down to
the quay to greet the packet and pick off his friends, and
he went down again to see them embark. Even the Duke
of Beaufort forgave him, calling in the Rue Royale to renew old times. Came Bedford, whose box at the Opera this
exile used to borrow, and Rutland, whose hounds at Belvoir he used to hunt with; came the Earl of Jersey, whom
the Prince made a cuckold, and the Earl of Craven who

had seduced Harriette Wilson; came Lords Sefton, Ward, Willoughby d'Eresby and Stuart de Rothesay. Above all, perhaps, came the amusingly profane Duke of Wellington, as if to make sure that Napoleon was not still prowling about. The financial assistance of this string of luminaries meant much to Brummell, to say nothing of their lively company at an elaborate dinner sent in from Dessein's. But was it well for the Beau that they should thus encourage him to almost as high a degree of prodigality as that which in London had brought him to disaster?

The contrition which had borne Brummell down during the first year of his banishment tended to weaken in the face of these social comings and goings, so repetitious were they of life as it used to be. He was an unstable ascetic. Although he had begun his repentance, as he told Tom Raikes, by getting "off his pillow" at half-past seven, he now advanced that bothersome hour to nine. Then, in his brocade dressing-gown and velvet cap he took his *café-complet,* and read a London paper, brochures, and books until noon. It was on one of these mornings that a representative of certain London solicitors, called Howard and Gibbs, had the temerity to tap, though softly, at Brummell's door. The man had a paper which needed signing or considering. When the Beau bade the caller come in, a head, but no more, appeared, level with the latch, and Brummell instantly recognized it as belonging to a creature who had dunned him in times well past. "Why, you little rascal!" he cried. "Are *you* not hung yet? Begone!" The head obeyed.

At noon Brummell crossed the passage to his bedroom. He was regular in this, so regular that the assistants of M. Leleux kept time by it, and went off to their dinner as soon as they heard their distinguished guest moving above. Then the Beau took two hours to dress. Afterward, always the great courtier, he held his levée, to which came French friends upon whom he practised the language. If the day was fine, he sat at the open window of his drawing-room —exactly as in the old days in the bow window at White's —and allowed his acquaintances to observe him as they passed by. One day a man called up to him that a local banker had absconded, the man having lost by it 1,000 francs. "My good fellow," advised Brummell, "in future take a hint from me, and always overdraw."

As soon as the levée was over—about four o'clock—he went out into the Rue Royale, dressed as if proceeding straight to Devonshire House itself, instead of to the bare ramparts of Calais. But even ramparts help one to maintain a sense of superiority. With the Beau walked his dog Vick, a terrier, so fat that her master had continually to turn round and wait for her to catch up with him. After taking the air for an hour they returned to Le Pauvre Diable. Instead of dining at five, as Brummell had begun by doing, he dressed for dinner, and at six sat down to food sent in from Dessein's, food encouraged by Dorchester ale, a bottle of Bordeaux, and a glass of brandy. "Lying on straw," he described such a repast to Lord Sefton, "and grinning through the bars of a gaol; eating bran bread, my good fellow, eating bran bread." Dinner over, he went to the Théâtre de Calais, where he had a small box. To every aspect of life in which he could recapture a semblance of his old career, his old habits or amusements, he clung with the tenacity of a man who does not intend to let misfortune ruffle him if he can stave off her attack.

Of warm long evenings the Beau stayed away from the theatre, and strolled into the garden behind his rooms. There was at the end of it a summer-house, in which he sat and wrote "memoirs"; to such a task he might well devote many a summer. Sometimes when he stood at his window above, and looked down upon this garden, a lady passed by, smiling; she was Madame la Baronne de Borno, wife of a Russian officer then in England. But Brummell, still too stricken by banishment, by change in his path of life, was unable to return these winsome glances. "Approving and inviting," he confided to Tom Raikes, "are her frequent smiles as she looks into my window from the garden walk. But I have neither spirits nor inclination to improve such flattering overtures." Yet the satisfaction of the experience remained; he was attractive to women even now.

Perhaps the overtures of the Baroness were distasteful to him so long as his mind, not to say his heart, was occupied by Frederica. In the spring (1817) he sent the Duchess a few little presents, bits of French jewellery he had picked up in Calais. As Will Alvanley was going to Paris upon one of his regular "escapes," and on his journey was to see Brummell, Frederica gave him a letter for the Beau. But when the elegant exile went of a certain afternoon down to the quay to meet the incoming packet, and to his delight discerned Alvanley disembarking, that affectionate, good-natured, generous, obliging, but somewhat absent-minded and prodigal friend informed him that he had burnt such a letter from the Duchess. All that Brummell could do was to write to her and beg for another version of it.

"You have lost nothing," the Duchess at length (April 26) replied, "in that letter which was destined for you, and which Lord Alvanley consigned to the flames; it contained only my thanks for the charming gifts which you had the goodness to send me (with which I adorned myself on the evening of my little birthday party), and my regrets that you were no longer one of us. These regrets are renewed daily, and especially the reasons which are the cause of them. Believe that nobody feels the loss of your society more than I do. I shall never forget the agreeable moments that I have owed to it, and the only thing that would compensate me would be the certitude of your happiness, for which I send the most sincere wishes, as for that which can contribute most to it."

Alvanley himself, whether he burned letters or not, could by his very company contribute as much as anyone. His drollery was a perfect foil to the wit of Brummell. But Alvanley noticed that the Beau in exile tended to succumb to hermitage, to the shelter of solitude, to a kind of agora-phobia which frequently besets those upon whom the melancholy of misfortune encroaches. While Brummell would accept any amusement inside the ramparts of Calais, he was reluctant to go away from the town, and quite refused to spend one night under any roof other than that of Le Pauvre Diable. Here was a tendency toward the very opposite extreme of his life in London. Introspective to such a degree he might, in the opinion of Alvanley, lapse into a state of mind that would be bad for him. At length Alvanley prevailed upon his friend to go a journey to Dunkirk, about twenty-five miles distant along the coast, a little change which old Leleux the bookseller heartily supported, for with Alvanley he agreed that his *locataire* would benefit from new scenes. When the two dandies had departed, Leleux thought he had got rid of Brummell for at least one night. He was mistaken. The Beau knocked him up at four o'clock in the morning.

But the boat from England did not always yield such a glorious guest as Will Alvanley. Lest nobody of consequence arrive, the custom of Brummell was to take with him down to the quay a local luminary, a man who assumed that a great figure like the Beau knew everyone in England, and as the passengers came off the packet Brummell quite forgot the monotony which menaced him, let go his imagination, and, identifying each newcomer, filled his companion with awe. This one, said the Beau, had once been butler at Belvoir; that one had sold snuff in a shop in St. James's; a third had kept a lodging-house in Jermyn Street. One day, down the plank stepped a distinguished soldier who had lost his nose in Wellington's wars. "That man," said Brummell, "used to be a hatter."

Someone repeated this observation to the gallant man, who on the following day called at Le Pauvre Diable full of sound and fury. "I am sorry," remarked the Beau with his utmost gravity, "very sorry that anyone should conceive it possible that *I* could be guilty of such a breach of good manners . . . there is not a word of truth in the report." The soldier, quite mollified, was turning to take his leave when Brummell added, as if to himself, "Now I think of it, I never in my life dealt with a hatter without a nose."

Yet the boat from home brought him other things besides curiosities of the passenger-list; it brought him gifts, letters, news, books; he need not be too forlorn. Late in 1817 a friend sent over Scott's *Rob Roy,* newly published; in March of the following year another friend, Colonel Hughes of St. James's, sent a second copy. *"Rob Roy* arrived here," Brummell acknowledged, "in a storm more bleak even than those which usually dwell upon his native hills; I had received and read him before; but that does not in the least diminish my obligation to your good-natured memory." He then went on to comment upon the news, in which he kept up as much interest as an ostracised politician: "The Indemnity Bill makes me sick; so indeed does everything where Castlereagh is concerned . . . they . . . are now anxious to form a new Parliament for the purpose of reviving their first-born hope, the income tax—I hope in God these vampires will not be allowed to pluck its carcass from the grave of corruption. . . . Have you read Horace Walpole's letters to Mr. Montagu? . . . much the most pleasant light reading I have had for an age. . . . The climate of Venice, I fear, has sadly impaired my friend

Byron's imagination, for I never waded through such gali-
matias as 'Beppo'—he had better confine himself to mis-
anthropic lamentation, for he is lost the moment he at-
tempts to cultivate 'Broad Grins' like George Colman."

Not always did these letters dwell upon politics and
poets; he could relate his adventures no less. Writing again
to Hughes, Brummell was able to speak quite dispassion-
ately of what he saw during the course of a walk just outside Calais: "A singular circumstance of mutual suicide
happened here three days since; a pair of young sentimental lovers walked out together, coolly tied themselves round
their waists with a shawl, and more coolly threw themselves into the canal about half a mile from this town, and
were drowned before assistance could be given. . . . I was
myself strolling near the fatal spot, and saw them taken
out of the water . . . much of the interest was diminished
in finding the young lady extremely ill-looking—it has
been ascertained that she was four months gone with child
—this mends the catastrophe, making it a triple murder."

The tragedy of it, so final, so premeditated, so infinitely
more grim than any reversal which beset his own seques-
tered plight, left George Brummell almost in a mood of
self-congratulation. He did not brood upon that scene
alongside the canal, but let his thoughts roam to a certain
high bank of the Thames, where he knew his Duchess of
York was continually thinking of him. What could he do
for her, his "most affectionate friend and servant," to show
that in his mind the memory of her was equally strong?
In order to occupy his indoor hours he decided to make for

the Duchess, in the laborious fashion of the day, a decorated screen. Choosing one of six panels, about five and a
half feet high and twice as long, Brummell set about cover-
ing it with prints. The impulse to this task derived from
the same propensity as that which led him to make a book
out of poems written by his friends, that ornate book of
blue-velvet, paged with vellum, fitted with clasps, and protected with corners of silver gilt. For prints to cover his
screen with, the Beau had only to draw upon his "collection"; prints of all kinds were simply one of the things
which he had for years been given to "collecting."

While such an expanse of scissors and paste may seem a
puerile and trifling occupation of an idle man, even of a
man of shallow mind, it must be remembered that a screen
of this sort was in its day regarded not only an artistic
achievement, but a chronicle of the times in pictures, alle-
gorical as well as actual, that it was much prized as a piece
of furniture, and that in the present case it was above all
to be a testimonial to a friendship which no amount of toil
could overvalue. Brummell's scheme was to paste the print
of an animal on the upper part of each panel except the
sixth and last: he chose an elephant, a hyena, a tiger, a
camel, and a bear; for the sixth, he calmly selected his
running-mates in eminence, Byron and Napoleon. Round
these figures were to be imposed hundreds of pictorial episodes, engravings in line, mezzotint, or lithograph, sketches
in chalk, pastel, or pencil, of every form and colour, each
encircled by garlands of flowers, the rose predominating,
and no edges of drawings to be discernible. There was in

prospect a review of the age; but it was to be also the confessions of George Brummell.

Here was enough work to keep the Beau busy in Calais for some time to come. Perhaps word of it reached someone in London. At all events the Betting Book in White's, under date of 1819, witnessed this entry: "Lord Yarmouth gives Lord Glengall four guineas to receive one hundred guineas if Mr. G. Brummell returns to London before Buonaparte returns to Paris."

CHAPTER XI

THE KING

1819–1821

SINCE BRUMMELL had become virtually one of the family of M. Leleux, he made himself agreeable to each member of that family; but to one of them he was especially drawn for a personal reason; this member was Leleux's green-and-yellow parrot from Havre, called Loro. Studying the bird from every angle, Brummell found he looked exactly like an old acquaintance then in the news, a man who had just been committed (1819) to Newgate for publishing a libel upon one of the Beau's companions at Oatlands—Lord Erskine; the resemblance, so marked in the solemnity of the parrot, was to John Cam Hobhouse, the idolator of Byron. "A traveller, a poet, ay, and a patriot, too," said Brummell with mock gravity; he had no love for obsequious persons. But in view of the beak, the plumage, and the solemnity, he chose to call the parrot Hobhouse. This bird often broke out of his cage, flew up to the Beau's windows, and exercised his beak on the curtains and the

buhl furniture; when Leleux pinioned him, Hobhouse
walked upstairs like any other visitor, knocked at the door
of Mr. Brummell, and was let in. He would not return to
his cage until, again like a visitor, he had received both
wine and biscuit.

But if the Beau regarded the intimacy between Byron
and Hobhouse as something overdeveloped on the part of
the gentleman in Newgate, he was beginning to wonder
a little whether at the other extreme he had not rather
needlessly allowed his own relations to the Prince to evap-
orate. In time, scantiness of funds would not permit him
to live even in Calais in comfort. Why should he not apply
for a post in the foreign service of England? But could he
hope that the Regent, after years of indifference, would
second any such application? Captain Samuel Marshall,
the British Consul in Calais, was in fragile health, and
talked of resigning, or at least of asking to be sent to China.
Marshall himself might recommend Brummell. Yet would
he? Brummell when dining at the consulate had loudly
passed on to his dog Atous (successor to Vick, who had
died of overfeeding) a wing of capon, on the ground that
it was too tough for himself to get his teeth through. But
now, at the end of January (1820) something happened
that caused the hopes of the Beau in this direction to stir
afresh. George III, the "old, mad, blind, deaf, diseased and
dying King," actually did expire at Windsor, and the Regency itself, the uncrowned kingship, ended. Would "Big
Ben," now George IV in fact, be magnanimous enough to
sink old prejudices beneath his throne?

"He is at length King," Brummell a month later wrote in answer to a letter from Tom Raikes. "Will his past resentments still attach themselves to his crown? An indulgent amnesty of former peccadilloes should be the primary grace influencing newly-throned sovereignty; at least toward those who were once distinguished by his more intimate protection. From my experience, however, of the person in question, I must doubt any favourable relaxation of those stubborn prejudices which have during so many years operated to the total exclusion of one of his *élèves* from the royal notice; that unfortunate—I need not particularize."

Nevertheless he thought it wisest to await whatever the event might disclose; nothing could be gained, so early in the new reign, by putting forth requests prematurely. Time hung less heavily upon his mind than financial uncertainty, for by this year he had fairly well mastered the French language, and, dodging the English trippers, he moved with ease amongst the French society topmost in Calais. Its superiorities as a civilizing influence were a revelation to him. Here was a man who knew everything there was to know about manners in England; but in rural Calais he grew aware of a sense of cultivation more advanced than even London could boast. Someone told Brummell that Tom Raikes was considering in this same year (1820) a school abroad for his daughters. On this point the Beau, with his own benefits in mind, hastened to advise his friend:

"I hear you meditate a *petit domicile* at Paris for your

children: you cannot do better. English education may be all very well to instruct the hemming of handkerchiefs and the ungainly romp of a country dance, but nothing else; and it would be a poor consolation to your declining years to see your daughters come into their elbows, and find their accomplishments limited to broad native phraseology in conversation, or thumping the 'woodpecker' upon a discordant spinet. You will do well, then, to provide in time against natural deficiencies by a good French formation of manners as well as talents; and you will not have to complain hereafter of your gouty limbs being excruciated by the uncouth movements of a hoyden, or of your ears being distracted by indigenous vulgarisms."

Chesterfield himself could not have written more authoratively on the advantages of living with the French people; Brummell was that curious exception who could have well got through life on his natural manners without ever leaving England; but he perfectly knew that very few of his compatriots could do as much, and now, his life in Calais, if not productive in any other way, was at least rich in the novel experience it gave him of life amidst the first race of Europe. The society of the more interesting families in Calais filled in his evenings, while Brummell alone gave over his days largely to the assembling of pictures for the Duchess's screen.

To one not sensible of the personalities, the movements, the popular beliefs of the age, this screen might have seemed the patchwork of a lunatic. But every print and symbol pasted on it would convey a meaning to Frederica; the very animals were there because of her zoological interests. A suggestion of the prints now in place on the first panel will illustrate the whole: Napoleon (as on the sixth panel) was the top portrait, beneath the elephant; on the throat of Napoleon, a butterfly; round Napoleon, fruit and flowers; above him, a cannon with a sword in its mouth, and a serpent round the sword; above the sword, a flag with a Russian eagle on it, crossed with a scythe; below all this, General Upton, the Marquess of Hertford, and Lord Sefton, in conversation, but between Sefton and Hertford, the head of a lovely woman (the Duchess herself?) ornamented by ostrich feathers, the whole surrounded by "a swarm of Cupids." The allusions need not be carried clear across the screen; but it may be added that the neck of Byron, on the final panel, was adorned by Brummell with a wasp.

Through the summer of 1820 the Beau pursued this bizarre design of his with great zest, this history, it might be called, of all that he and the Duchess together had known, lived through, or discussed. Then, suddenly on August 6, the Duchess died, aged only fifty-four. When the news reached Calais, Brummell folded up his screen, laid it aside, and resolved never to touch it again. For her death was a distinct shock. To a man already stranded it seemed to leave him more stranded still, isolation accumulating upon the head of isolation, and from a purely material standpoint the worst of it was that the Duchess had been a contributor to his maintenance, not only at Christmas but between times. Yet the thing that counted with

Brummell was the affection of this woman, her loyalty to him, the great friendship itself. "I 'av many dog, as you know," the Duchess used to say in her best Anglo-German, "but dough I vos delight in de attachment and de faith of my dog, I could not say de dog is *virtuous*—still, I velcome de sweet spirit of *affection*—dat it is, vin my regard." But unlike many women who are inordinately fond of dogs, Frederica was capable of extending her own affection to human beings, and of those so favoured, Brummell assuredly stood with the foremost. Fourteen years back, when he lost the Duchess of Devonshire, it was Frederica who came the nearest to replacing her; the charming younger Duchess of Rutland, who at Belvoir drew landscapes whilst the Beau sketched portraits, did much to assuage him, and happily she still survived, and he was still in her thoughts; but Frederica, especially after Brummell had quarrelled with the Prince, was the woman round whom his life had revolved, as well during these four years of his exile as in the four years prior to his flight. So long as Frederica lived to give him cheer, she was present to him; separation was hard, but it was endurable. Now, for the first time since he had left London, there came to George Brummell the twinges of being desolate.

One of those who knew full well what the passing of the Duchess must mean to Brummell was his best friend Alvanley, who in due season went so far as to speak to the afflicted Duke of York on behalf of the unfortunate exile. He did more. Now that the Regent had become King, Alvanley wrote—from his hotel, the Waterloo, in Jermyn

Street—to Earl Bathurst. This man had for eight years been secretary for war and the colonies in the ministry of Lord Liverpool, and was continuing in office.

"I am aware," said Alvanley to Bathurst, "that I have little right to address you on the following subject, but I trust you will forgive my doing so on the score of old family friendship. Poor Brummell has now been four years at Calais. He has lived upon what those who were most intimate with him have been able to do for him. So precarious an existence, however, is hardly worth having. I have been told that you have expressed yourself kindly with regard to him. Perhaps you might be able to give him some small situation abroad, in order to relieve him from the position in which he now is. I say nothing about the circumstances that occurred previous to his departure from England. I cannot excuse them in any way. They, however, are no longer fresh in the memory of those who were not sufferers, and I know that the greatest sufferer is most desirous that something should be done for him. The Duke of York, who has been very kind to him, would gladly assist any effort in his favour. I will not trouble you more on the subject. If you can do anything for him, I am certain you will. If not, I am certain your reasons will be better than any I could give."

So long as the Beau had a friend left like Will Alvanley he need not be too downcast. There were in London many who had not suffered from his debts, but who had profited from his companionship; if they could be found, Alvanley was the man to find them. By the example of Brummell the gentlemen of London had aspired to dress, as Byron put it, with a "certain exquisite propriety"; indeed, upon glancing at the very coat of Brummell, one "might almost say the body thought." If this reformation in costume meant so much, why should not the beneficiaries be willing to assist its inventor in his distress? It was not as if Beau Brummell had never been a man of achievement; on the contrary, he was already a piece of English history. Byron himself, now writing his cantos of *Don Juan* at Ravenna, still liked to remind the forgetful world of the eminence of its Prince of Beaux. When at the turn of this year (1821) Hobhouse acquainted Byron of the flight abroad of Scrope Davies—the gambler-dandy who had refused Brummell a small loan on the eve of Brummell's escape—Byron exclaimed: "Brummell at Calais, Scrope at Bruges, Buonaparte at St. Helena, you in your Newgate apartment, and I at Ravenna, only think! So many great men! There has been nothing like it since Themistocles at Magnesia, and Marius at Carthage."

In fact, Brummell himself remained quite conscious of his own distinction; he was still self-possessed, and that feeling, he was confident, would be the last to fail him. He was now doubly desirous of making a slight change in his surroundings for a way of life somewhat different. He wished to vacate his rooms, not only because they reminded him of his wasted labours for the Duchess of York, but for the reason that under the new reign of George IV he hoped his friends in London might bring it about to have him named consul; in that case, he could in new quarters begin life afresh. As he did not wish to leave M. Leleux, the Beau made an agreement with him for another set of rooms to the left of his old ones, but consisting of a dining-room on the street floor, a drawing-room overhead, and a handsome bedroom to the rear, all accessible by a private entry and staircase. The first thing Brummell did, in the ecstasy of moving, was to redecorate; he laid a floor of black-and-white marble just inside his private door; then he adorned his dining-room with a paper of rich crimson. If he should become consul, and was to entertain visitors at Le Pauvre Diable, the ground-floor at least must present an appearance worthy of the host. This was an expense, perhaps an extravagance; but was he not justified in relying upon a more substantial income before long? It should far exceed any sums he had been accustomed to receive from the Duchess.

No sooner had the Beau moved into these resplendent new rooms than word came, in the summer, that the King was to make a journey to Hanover in September, sailing from Ramsgate and disembarking at Calais. Of this visit Brummell expected nothing; and yet as the time of the royal arrival drew near he could not escape the upsurge of long memories. On the morning the royal yacht came in, the Beau, instead of remaining indoors as usual with his journals and books, had gone out in his immaculate cravat, not to the pier, which was crammed with the curious, but in his customary direction toward the ramparts. He was now returning to Le Pauvre Diable, while the King, in a carriage with the French Ambassador, was proceeding by way of the Rue Royale to Dessein's. Through the crowd Brummell managed to get across the Place d'Armes; but as he turned into the Rue Royale, on the side opposite his lodgings, and struggled toward the curb in order to cross and get out of sight, he was blocked. The carriage with the corpulent King approached, and all hats came off, including that of the Beau. There he stood, unshielded, unmistakable, a man in a thousand. "Good God!" cried the King, almost *vis-à-vis*, "Brummell!" And the carriage passed on.

Just across the street old Leleux was peering from his own door, a keen observer of all this. Brummell, "pale as death," made his way over Rue Royale, did not speak to his landlord, and entered the house by his own private door.

In a sense it was a re-enactment of the recognition scene between Henry V and Falstaff, except that in physical appearance George IV resembled not so much his illustrious ancestor as Falstaff himself.

At Dessein's the Duc d'Angoulême awaited the King. He had been deputed by Louis XVIII to congratulate George upon his arrival in the French dominions. It seemed that everyone in Calais who possessed a uniform, however antiquated, had put it on, and as soon as the King crossed the threshold of the hotel, dignitaries from hither and yon milled in to sign the book. In the course of the day Brummell did likewise. Hearing that an elaborate dinner was to be given the royal guest in the evening, he lent the hotel his valet François, to make the punch according to a recipe which Brummell knew that the King fancied. Before François left for Dessein's, his master also gave him a bottle of rare maraschino, well remembering the King's fondness for it. But Brummell himself remained in solitude at Le Pauvre Diable.

In the morning every one of the King's party, except Sir Benjamin Bloomfield, confidential adviser, called upon the Beau, at the hour of his usual levée. He received them with all his old aplomb, his elegance, his fastidiousness, even as in the opulent days in Chesterfield Street; and he welcomed them as if they were his friends in Calais, or his familiar callers from London. These companions of the King, severally, then tried to persuade Brummell to request an interview with his sovereign. They failed.

Had he not written his name in the book at Dessein's, lent his valet, sent a gift of maraschino? Little did this retinue of gentlemen know their Brummell. It was the King's move.

On the next day George IV drove on to Laeken, the royal palace near Brussels, where he was to stay with the King and Queen of the Netherlands. As he gathered himself into the carriage, he said to Sir Arthur Paget, who had commanded the yacht that brought him over, something that was on his mind: "I leave Calais, and have not seen Brummell."

CHAPTER XII

RETURN AND RETREAT

1821-1829

IF IT WOULD HAVE BEEN a tactful thing for Brummell to bury his pride, and to attend a levée held by the King at Dessein's, and if the King by his parting remark indicated that he himself had rather expected such a call, Brummell, satisfied in having remained true to his own character, still reckoned that he had in London enough friends in power to obtain for him an appointment. So long as Castlereagh was not only the leader of Parliament but was in the Foreign Office as well, the Beau nursed little hope; these two men were by no means friends. As Brummell had said a few years before to Tom Raikes, "The Indemnity Bill makes me sick; so indeed does everything where Castlereagh is concerned." How, then, was the embarrassed exile to circumvent a politician who would be sure to make difficulties? How, with funds evaporating, was Brummell to live until by devious and tedious ways a consulship might be got for him?

Sometimes at Le Pauvre Diable he showed his visitors the memoirs which he had been writing in the summer-house, chapter by chapter. "Here's a chapter on Carlton House," he said. "And here's one on Mrs. Fitzherbert and the Prince." This news got about. A London publisher offered £1,000 for the book.

Badly as the Beau needed the money, he refused it. "I promised the Duchess of York," he explained, "that I would never publish any notes of mine during the lifetime of George IV or his brothers, and I am under so many obligations to her, and have such a deep respect for her generous and amiable conduct to me in our early friendship and since, that I would rather go to gaol than forfeit my word. She is the only link that binds me in this matter."

Instead of fretting about the money sacrificed in respect of these Memoirs, Brummell began in this winter another book, which would do harm to none, which might fetch a tidy penny, and the material for which he knew almost as much about: "Male Costume. Grecian, Roman, and British Costumes from the Roman Invasion to 1822." This title did not explain just how the Greeks got into the Roman invasion, nor just when, nor where, the Greek influence did penetrate; but he knew his subject. The Book of Costumes braced his hopes as he laboured upon it through the dark months, whilst no word came from England about a diplomatic post, and whilst Captain Marshall, the consul in Calais, was now showing no disposition to withdraw. So absorbed, however, was Brummell in his writing that as spring came on he seems to have reached the astonishing conclusion that the readiest way for him to obtain money would be to make a secret journey to London and sell the book. Failing that, he could at least sound his old friends in person about his chances of being accepted into the foreign service. Provided his stay was short enough to enable him to keep clear of unforgiving creditors, who in any case might not recognize him after his absence of six years, the venture was perhaps not too dangerous.

Evidence of this unheralded reappearance of George Brummell, like a ghost, in the scenes which he used to dominate, rests in a *fin-de-saison* entry in the weighing-register at the old wine-shop of Berry Brothers, St. James's Street. On July 26, 1822, the Beau once more sat in the chair of the mammoth T-shaped scales (still to be seen), whilst an attendant piled weights in the pan at the other end. It was a moment to recall memories. In his heyday, as Brummell strolled to and from White's, many a duke and many a dandy, careful of their figure, had stopped in with him at Berry's to test their girth, and to sip a glass abstemiously small of something rare. There were Ester-hazy and York, Bedford and Argyll, Rutland, Portland, Fife, Sefton and Welby, now "in their flowing cups freshly remembered"; Charles James Fox, the friend and patron of his boyhood, had made the scales at Berry's groan; Foley and Alvanley had been there with the Beau; so had Byron, "Birron," as Brummell and his friends always called him. If the Beau himself now seemed an apparition, the room which he came back to haunt was a galaxy of ghosts. For eight years, from 1798, when Brummell left his regiment, until 1806, when Georgiana Devonshire died, he had taken note of his weight at Berry's from once to seven times annually. Then for two years he disregarded it, as he disregarded many things after he lost his first Duchess. When he resumed, once or twice a year, he again left off in 1810, perhaps only accidentally at a time which coincided with the flight of Hester Stanhope from England. So long as Brummell was weighed in either boots or half-boots, his weight in all this time fluctuated less than a stone, from something over twelve stone to something over thirteen; in his great-coat of course he registered more. Only twice after 1810 had he visited Berry's, the first occasion being after his quarrel with the Prince, and then not until four years later, in 1815, when the Beau was worried about his gambling; he turned the scales at half a stone less. But what had exile done to him? Back in the wine-shop for the first time in seven years, again Wellington boots as in 1815, he found that his weight had dropt to 10 st. 13, lighter than he could ever recall. He had lost 26 pounds. If being weighed was a mere incident of George Brummell's return to London, it was also a tragedy of St. James's Street.

He did not find a publisher for "Male Costume." But he seems to have left the manuscript somewhere in town, as if in forlorn hope, since it later turned up in the hands of a bookseller. Nor did the Beau discover any encouragement upon his application for a consular post. To all appearances, he retreated from England as quietly as he came, knowing now that he could only await across the water the results of any efforts which his onetime companions might be willing to prolong on his behalf.

Yet if Brummell had tarried in London a bit over a fortnight after his call at Berry's, he might have seen reason, in a sudden and dramatic change which befell the Government, for expectations, and his presence on the spot would perhaps have enhanced them. On August 12 the overwrought Castlereagh fatally cut his throat with a penknife, and George Canning in the following month returned to great office on his own terms, namely, "the whole inheritance" of Castlereagh.

Here was both a fellow Etonian and a contributor to Brummell's famous Album. While it was true that Canning and Brummell *minor* were together only one year at school, and that Canning was head of the sixth form whereas Brummell was at the bottom of the first, and while the two men had not often met since the days of the Duchess of Devonshire, these two links did exist. Were not all those who had given their verses to the blue-velvet book friends of the Beau? He could think of no exception amongst them. Alvanley had lately ascertained that the bereaved Duke of York would "gladly assist"; at once Brummell petitioned the Duke, as a friend of much more recent intimacy, to speak to Canning about a post.

The Duke did what he could. Unhappily Canning was neither a man of very charitable inclinations nor a man who valued old memories; all he took into consideration in this case was that Brummell had once fled from England owing a lot of money. He answered that if the Duke insisted upon his broaching this matter to the King he would do so, but that upon his own responsibility he could not recommend Mr. Brummell. The Duke, foreseeing failure, did not press the application.

At all events, so far as Calais itself was concerned, Captain Marshall, the consul, was now remaining tighter than ever at his desk, and after Brummell heard unfavourably from the Duke he had no choice but to resume "borrowing" from various friends until he could supplicate the Foreign Office through someone else. In this predicament the Beau in Calais—"King of Calais" the natives were now in the habit of calling him—was not alone; two more of his dandy acquaintance, Berkeley Craven and Henry Baring, having fallen into similar gambling difficulties, came to live there; Craven he had also known, like Canning, from Eton days, and later at Oatlands. But these newcomers were not always good company. Unlike Brummell, Craven kept no valet, no François, but a sort of male housekeeper, who dined with him, and who met his guests as equals. One evening when the Beau was at Craven's table this creature said, "Mr. Brummell, I'll trouble you for a potato." Brummell looked about for a spoon, but found none. "Oh, take your fork," said the fag. "I'm not particular." Later on the Beau took Craven aside. "My dear Berkeley," said he, "how can you ask gentlemen to meet such people at dinner? If your horses are ill, pay the fellow five francs and have done with him."

While Brummell heard no more about his manuscript on Costumes, he did not relinquish his interest in collect-

ing poems for the great Album. A few months after his
return to Calais (1823) he added seven longish stanzas on
the rather lugubrious subject "Weare's Murder," by the
Rev. John Mitford, commemorating the extinction of one
William Weare on the St. Alban's Road; this was something of a lapse from the standard set in the Album by
Byron or Brinsley Sheridan; the significance of the contribution was that Brummell still kept his book going.

It was at about this time that he received a call from his
disreputable old friend Harriette Wilson, who after an un-
prosperous intrigue with the Marquess of Worcester had
been, since the accession of George IV, living in Paris.
Harriette was now thirty-eight, a bit on the down-side for
a courtesan, and, compiling material for her own "Memoirs," could not resist looking in upon the man whom she
used to vilify both to his face and behind his back, almost
like a female Thersites. But Brummell never expected anything else from her. Her inquiry, she said, whether Monsieur Brummell was at home, was answered by his valet—
"just such a valet as one would have given the Beau in the
acme of his glory, well powdered, very ceremonious"—
that Monsieur was shaving, but that he always received
whilst shaving. She found him in a Florentine dressing-
gown, and thought "from his increased *embonpoint* and
freshness, his disgrace had not seriously affected him."
Harriette said Brummell touched "lightly" on the subject,
as he evidently so touched his face, for he continued shaving "with a peculiar grace, and the smallest razor she had
ever seen." She asked him if he did not find Calais melan-

choly; he assured her he had never in his life been in any place where he could not amuse himself. He made his dog do tricks for her; he spoke of a green silk shoe of a Parisian actress which he had. Harriette could make but trivial conversation, and could only marvel at the naturalness of a new French wig which Brummell, now bald, was wearing. She went way disappointed. "From what I had heard of the hero's fall," she lamented, "I fully expected to have found him reclined on a couch, worn down to a skeleton."

When Captain Marshall, the consul, invited the Beau in this same season (1824) to meet Michael Luscombe, whom Canning had just appointed Chaplain to the British Embassy in Paris, Brummell was hardly in the mood to turn from impious company to devout. "My dear Marshall," he replied in a note, "You must excuse me not having the pleasure to dine with you and the Trustees of the Church establishment this day. I do not feel myself sufficiently prepared in spirit to meet a bishop, or in pocket to encounter the plate after dinner; moreover, I should be a fish out of water in such a convocation."

In the world itself he would soon be a fish out of water if his old friends kept dying at the rate they had maintained since his exile. Within a few months after Brummell retreated from Marshall's invitation died the last of his Duchesses—Elizabeth Rutland, like him, still under fifty. The Beau had at the moment a little framed miniature of her which he had started to do, a half-finished crayon, showing her wealth of curls, her headdress, her draped costume; of this miniature he now had no other thought than to leave it unfinished, as she had left her own life.

Member of a family which had been one of the heaviest losers from Brummell's debts, the Duchess, like the Duke and his brothers Charles and Robert Manners, put friendship before finance, and as long as she lived had remained devoted to her old companion in art. What was important to her was that she and the Beau used to draw pictures together at Belvoir. What else remained in her mind was that George Brummell, child of the house, had enlivened many a party in the country, had shot pigeons for pheasants, had hunted in white boot-tops, had forsaken the field for the ladies at luncheon, and without the aid of punctuality had commanded the Belvoir Volunteers. In his exile the Duchess sent him substantial aid, affection, and good cheer. Brummell, under his increased burden of loneliness, treasured her memory.

By way of contrast he was little comforted during this same year (1825) to receive a second call from a woman whom he would have preferred to forget. In the company of Berkeley Craven—she had picked him up somewhere in Calais—Harriette Wilson, having published several volumes of her "Memoirs," and seeking material for still another volume, again interrupted the Beau at his shaving. Making mental note of it she observed, "We found Brummell shaving, just as if he had been shaving ever since my first visit. . . . This time he wore a linen *robe de chambre*. One gets tired of silks and satins after a long residence on the Continent."

Harriette's report of the scene is plausible, though not necessarily accurate.

Brummell, turning up his eyes, told her that her book was infamous. "What," he demanded, "has that truly amiable woman, the Duchess of Beaufort, done, pray?"

"Abused me most shockingly, to begin with," she retorted, "in letters addressed to her son."

"And I?" inquired Brummell. "What have I done?"

"Very little for the State, I believe, at least until you took French leave, and quitted it. True, indeed, your services are appreciated by unanimous consent; excepting only one or two, who would gladly have detained you, for the purpose of justifying their private revenge for having been taken in by you."

"You are the most infamous woman in the world," said Brummell.

"Amen," added Berkeley Craven.

Harriette rather tamely concluded her account by saying that someone told her Brummell had grown a very good man in Calais, lived quietly, and put up for the consulship, "in which case we must let him alone."

But not long after this call a military man who had the honour of keeping Harriette at the moment invaded Le Pauvre Diable and requested Brummell to explain his "insult" to her, which she accused him of making in the course of her morning visit. The Beau ordered this cockalorum to leave the room. The intruder was disinclined to. In the fire, a poker was resting, its tip red-hot; Brummell seized it, and drove the man out.

While it did not appear to Harriette Wilson that the Beau was exactly ground down by poverty—she on the contrary noticed not only the elegance of his valet, but all the old appurtenances to dressing for which Brummell in his London days was renowned—it was true that as the last half of this decade of the twenties advanced, and no consular employment seemed forthcoming, the scale of life to which Brummell was addicted became more and more difficult to sustain. If Harriette had met with him outdoors, her malice would have rejoiced in his altered look. Near this time, for instance, Lord William Lennox turned up in Calais, and asked the Beau to dine at Dessein's. At the sight of him, Lennox was saddened. "Poor Brummell looked pale and emaciated," he soon after informed a friend. "His still well-fitting clothes were what is usually termed seedy; his boots were not so brilliant as they used to be when he lounged up Bond Street . . . his hat, though carefully brushed, showed symptoms of decay, and the only remnants of dandyism left were the well-brushed hair, the snow-white linen, and an exceptional tie."

That Brummell was able to keep himself in linen and muslin was largely due to his friend Tom Raikes, who sent him gifts of the material required; that he could wear clean ties and cravats was owing to the indulgence of his washerwoman, who let her bill run up, knowing that she would be one of the first to be paid whenever "Monsieur" did get money. Funds came in, though at intervals uncomfortably infrequent, from Brummell's brother and sister, and from a few friends who continued endlessly sympathetic; then it was that the tradesmen got first consideration from him. He might put off his draper, his decorator, his upholsterer—those new rooms at Leleux's were a bother to pay for—but his hatter, his bootmaker, his chemist, his tobacconist, above all his tailors, whom he taught how to cut and whose business greatly profited thereby, these men he kept pacified by periodic partial settlements. To this end, Jacques Leveux, the banker, was of infinite help. So sensible was he of the honour of serving such a great client as Mr. Brummell, not to mention the entertainment he extracted from Brummell's drollery, that he made advances of credit a regular practice, on the strength of "prospects" from England; again, Brummell always sent the business of his distinguished British callers to Leveux, annually no small sum. This scheme of keeping up a front was growing progressively more difficult for the Beau; few could have succeeded in it so well and so long as he had; but as time dragged on he found his eminence of the past less easy to recapture and fetch to the aid of his distress of the present.

It is commonly a tendency of men who approach the age of fifty to take uncommon notice of obituaries, though perhaps less because they are thinking of their own extinction than of that of persons whom they have either known or known about. In an impoverished exile, this tendency may well grow acute, because of its possible bearing upon one's personal fortune; it resembles watching the fluctuation of the stock market. Brummell since his flight to Calais had gleaned little solace from the dwindling circle of his acquaintance, whether the deceased were hostile, friendly, or indifferent. When in January (1827) the Duke of York died, he mourned measurably; the Duke, without being in any sense beloved by the Beau as the Duchess had been, was always loyal, generous, and sympathetic, if not too helpful; he had not troubled to press the case of Brummell beyond the frown of Canning. But in the following August a strange consequence occurred. George Canning himself, a man of only fifty-seven, worn out by the antagonism of Wellington, Peel, and other ministers, and weakened, oddly enough, by a racking cold which he had caught at the funeral of that very Duke of York, gave up the ghost —in the same room, incidentally, in which Charles James Fox had died, in Devonshire's house in Chiswick. Brummell could not now avoid a hope reviving within his breast for a consulship.

Not that Lord Goderich, the immediate successor to Canning as Prime Minister, could be expected to take any substantial interest; but the Duke of Wellington, stepping into the post of commander-in-chief, was at once a friend at Court. Wellington, indeed, upon repeated solicitations of both Alvanley and the Marquess of Worcester, proposed the appointment of the Beau to Lord Dudley, the Foreign Minister. Here was a snag. As Foreign Minister, Dudley was a cipher. He would temporize, equivocate, agree to do a thing, and then either forget it or neglect it. He was a scholar of sorts; and he liked to write articles, talk pedantry, and "take an interest" in public education; when people spoke to him about appointments to the foreign service they were discussing the wrong subject. As soon as Wellington mentioned Brummell to him, Dudley demurred, and turned the conversation into another channel. But the Duke kept at him, and Dudley "at last owned" that he was afraid the King might object.

Whereupon Wellington himself went to the King. This errand at best was dubious. While George IV had not seen his exiled companion since 1821, he still remained incurious about the fate of the man who to his sovereign's mind had built for himself a monument only of impudence. So far as the petitioner himself was concerned, the King had no choice but to listen: Wellington stood too firmly within the Government circle to be evaded. But the royal memory of Brummell's misdoings had continued not very forgiving; Dudley's apprehensions were well founded. No sooner had the Duke opened the question of the consulship than the King likewise made objections. He said Brummell was "a damned fellow," that Brummell had "behaved very ill to him." Wellington tactfully let the King run out his spool of abuse. But, no doubt considerably to the surprise of the Duke, before this interview closed he "extracted" the consent of the King to the appointment.

All that now remained to be done was to signify the royal pleasure to Dudley as Foreign Secretary. This Wellington did, and, busy with ministerial duties of his own, gave the matter no further thought.

The great achievement of the Duke's call was that he actually brought George IV round to the point of overlooking the bygones of George Brummell. If the Beau could have known that, he would have experienced not only profound satisfaction, but an immediate rebirth of hope for the future. Unhappily for him, a sudden upheaval in the cabinet took possession of the minds of all the ministers, Goderich's government fell in February (1828), Wellington came in as Prime Minister, and three months later Dudley himself resigned, having failed in the hurly-burly to act upon the appointment of Brummell to a consular post.

Over in Calais, the poor Beau allowed hardly a day to pass without writing to someone in England to intercede with the Duke, and he had to write to fully as many friends for loans to tide him over. He was in debt to tradesmen, to François, to Dessein's for dinners, and to a second banker, Isaac Pecquet, in the sum of nearly 10,000 francs altogether. Letters of appeal to England no longer brought so prompt a response as heretofore, neither from Worcester, nor even from Alvanley.

Summer came on, without any news from Wellington, and at length, in July, faced with a peremptory demand for £73 within six days, the Beau wrote to one Colonel George Dawson to beg him to collect that much from others, who should be given in exchange twice the value in oriental furniture and bijoux now at Le Pauvre Diable. "Would you so essentially oblige me," he asked Dawson, "as to endeavour to gather together a few amiable Samaritans who might so kindly bear me and my actual difficulties in remembrance as to advance £25 each to satisfy this urgent demand? One hundred would relieve me and give me a few pounds over to scramble on with. It would make me happy for the present. You are acquainted with the different things belonging to me in China, Japan, etc. Select what you please to the amount of double the sum ... it shall be faithfully sent ... in payment. I would sell myself if I could raise a shilling upon my worthless body and soul ... I am, as you may have heard, expecting employment through the interference of that best of friends, the Duke of Wellington, but before such expectation may be realized I am sadly alarmed lest some overwhelming disaster should fall upon me."

Dawson, it turned out, was unable to round up any "amiable Samaritans," because he was racked with a fit of the gout. But he was good enough to answer within a few days, and he requested more particulars of Brummell's aspirations for a consulship. Meanwhile Alvanley, the ever-indulgent, sent as much as he could spare of his own against the £73.

"Your kindness to me," replied the Beau (August 2) to Dawson, "gives me good spirits for the moment, and I thank you with all my heart. For a long time past I have been unaccustomed to even friendly acknowledgments. Alvanley has sent me £50 through Drummonds. He does not like making further application to others—for speaking is always more effective than writing—or I might, perhaps, be relieved. ... He is, however, the best judge of the grounds of such disinclination; and I thank him equally as the steadiest friend I possess. There certainly is a vacancy in the Consular Department at Petersburgh, for though

the present incumbent, Sir Something Bailey, is gone back
there, I know he has tendered his resignation, and that
Marshall, the Consul here, has several times written solicit-
ing that preferment. Can you find out *quietly* whether it
is the intention to place me here as Consul, or to send me
elsewhere, of course a vacancy occurring to facilitate the
business."

Leaning upon Dawson, or upon those few whom Dawson could summon to the cause, Brummell managed to
get through the winter, and in January (1829) was able to
welcome in good spirits a "German Prince" who visited
him at Le Pauvre Diable. "I found him," said the Prince in
Letters which he afterwards published, "at his second
toilette, in a flowered chintz dressing-gown, velvet nightcap with gold tassel, and Turkish slippers, shaving, and
rubbing the remains of his teeth with his favourite red
root. .... His air was that of good society, simple and natural, and marked by more urbanity than the dandies of the
present race are capable of. With a smile he showed me
his Paris peruke, which he extolled at the cost of the English ones, and called himself, 'the former *young* man who
passes his life between Paris and London.' " Brummell also
interrogated the Prince, but "without belying his good
breeding by any kind of intrusiveness"; the visitor had
come to him from London, and told him about people and
things there. "I am *au fait* with all of them," exclaimed the
Beau. "But what good does that do me? They let me die of
hunger here. I hope however that my old friend the Duke
of Wellington will one fine day send the consul from here

to China, and that then he will appoint me to his place. Then I shall be saved."

But as the year dragged on, and no assistance from the Duke seemed to be stirring, Brummell was almost at his wits' end. His only remaining device with which to evade the clutches of those who came to collect their bills—the scheme of distracting them from that painful errand— was itself wearing out. Thus he described it to Major Chambre, an acquaintance who dropped in upon him during this year: "Whenever anyone of my creditors calls upon me, the moment he enters the room I commence an amusing conversation, and tell him anecdotes that I think will interest him. This has hitherto succeeded very well, for I divert their attention from the subject that brings them to me. But my stock-in-trade is exhausted, and I am now completely used up. I have nothing left to tell them, and I do not know what to do."

What he did was to fall in love, or to think that he was falling in love with a young English girl in her teens, one of whose irresistible attractions was that she had "lovely eyebrows." She was a devout Catholic, and so eager was the Beau to make himself acceptable in her sight that he proceeded apparently, after only a short acquaintance with her, to abandon his own religion and become a Catholic himself. At this juncture, one of his compatriots in Calais was making the rounds of the British residents to collect funds for building an Episcopal chapel. He knocked at Brummell's private door in Le Pauvre Diable. "I am very sorry," the Beau greeted him, "that you did not call last week, for it was only yesterday that I became a Catholic—but never mind; put my name down for a hundred francs." There was George Brummell. He had not enough money to feed himself with; and he gave away such a sum for a subscription. Perhaps love impelled him to this extravagance; at all events it impelled him to write to his young lady, in the endeavour to capture her approval of his conversion. Her reply was not encouraging; she put him off, upon which he sent her a second letter, and even a third.

"When I wrote to you," he said in his latest, "a century ago in plaintive strains, and 'with all Hackman's sorrows and all Werther's woes,' you told me . . . that I must desist from my vagaries, because I was trespassing on consecrated ground; but you offered me instead your *friendship,* as a relic . . . I kissed the rod, cherished the relic, and enveloping myself in penance inscribed you a missive . . . to mortify you also, as a votary, with a little congenial castigation. I daresay . . . I was excited by the pious enthusiasm of my recent apostasy. . . . You are, it seems, displeased at it, though my heresy from my first delightful faith was your own work. I know not now where to turn for another belief.

"I will tell you the truth in plain, unmystical language, for I have not yet learnt to renounce *that;* I was irritated because I thought you had cut me dead in the morning; and when I was *tête-à-tête* with my solitary lamp in the evening, a thousand threatening phantoms assailed me. I imagined that you had abandoned me; in short, a cohort

of blue devils got the better of me, and I am now all com-
punction and anguish. Pray be once more an amiable and
compassionate being, and do not contract your lovely eyebrows . . . in sullenness at my numberless incongruities and
sins. Be the same Samaritan saint you have already been to
me . . . Whatever I may have said in a frenzical moment of
exasperation was *unsaid* and *unthought* an hour afterwards, when I sought my couch and proffered my honest
prayers for forgiveness . . . I am more than conscious of all
my . . . faults; but indeed they shall be in future corrected,
if you are still a friend to me. I had vaunted in the vanity
of my chivalrous spirit that I had at length proved one in
myself; but it was an empty ostentation, for I find that I
cannot exist but in amity with you."

Nothing like such an outburst had come from the Beau
since the days of his youth in Chesterfield Street, when he
was flirting with all the eligible young Lady Marys and
Lady Janes in Mayfair. But he was never desperate about
those affairs; no sooner had he got involved than one of his
Duchesses lured him away to the country. Alas, even the
Duchesses were now gone, and he was a solitary. Craving
an adventure in affection, Brummell pursued this young
girl, who, for her part, did look over her shoulder as she
ran. Again he addressed her with all his fervour.

"Yesterday morning I was subdued almost to insanity;
but your note in the evening restored me . . . and as if I
had been redeemed from earthly purgatory, placed me in
heaven. Thank you, thank you, dearest of beings; how can
I requite all this benevolent open-heartedness, this delight-

ful proof and avowal of my not being indifferent to you?
. . . By the dim light that was remaining I perceived something white at your *porte-cochère*. It was evident that I was
recognized, and the figure advanced with your *billet*. In an
instant I seized the hand of your faithful and intelligent
messenger, compressing it forcibly . . . I should have
saluted her, if I had not fancied at the instant that I heard
someone coming up the street. We parted, and I returned
to my solitary chamber.

"There I lacerated the letter with impatience, and then
the light of love and joy, and the refreshing breath of evening, stole through the open window over my entranced
senses. After that I sought another stroll on the ramparts,
and again returned home contented with you, with myself, and with the world. I have known few that could
equal, none that could excel you; yet they possessed not
your charms of countenance, your form, your heart, in my
estimation. Certainly they did not possess that unaffected
and fervent homage, which in my constant memory—in
my heart's blood—and in my devoted soul I bear to you."

Not so long before, here in Calais, Brummell would
have nothing to do with Madame la Baronne de Borno,
who had smiled up at him from the garden behind Le
Pauvre Diable; now a young girl, little more than a child,
apparently made him forget he had any other care in the
world. The next thing was that rumour in Calais accused
this Miss of "returning his passion," and further, insinu-
ated that Brummell was planning to abduct her. The
community of English people decided to send one of their

number, an elderly army officer from London, to Le Pauvre Diable to demand an explanation.

Little did they appreciate the compass of Brummell's former acquaintance. Hardly had the old officer worked into the gist of his protest when the Beau interrupted him:

"Why, Vulcan," said he, "what a precious old humbug you must be, to come and lecture me on such a subject—you who were for two years at hide-and-seek to save yourself from being shot by Sir T. S——, for running off with one of his daughters."

CHAPTER.XIII

CAEN VIA PARIS

1829–1830

The belated romance of Brummell soon blew over. Not that the meddlesome officer had anything to do with the end of it. That "precious old humbug," fearing that he himself would be exposed, hurriedly withdrew from the scene, and the Beau heard no more of the alarm which he had wrought upon the moral excitability of his compatriots in Calais. In the meantime, as his acquaintance with his young lady simmered down to the basis of the "friendship" which she had offered him, he found later in this year of 1829 other things which caught his more material interest; he grew absorbed in the news which was coming over to him from England.

The reign of George IV as King had developed on the personal side two new intimates, the Marchioness Conyngham and Sir William Knighton. Lady Conyngham was quite in the tradition of the previous mistresses. Past fifty when George was crowned, she was, if not a grandmother, a plump dame with five children all grown up. Though neither beautiful, witty, nor accomplished, she was yet a soothing companion, who, if not in actuality the mistress of the King, was asked by him at Brighton to do "everything to show that she was mistress there." Down with him to the Royal Lodge at Windsor she went as well—dragging along her whole family including the husband—where the King drove the Marchioness about in a little pony-chaise. If he saw his ministers, Lady Conyngham fortified him prior to their coming, and nursed him from exhaustion after his interview. In this decade no other woman had challenged her dominance.

But Sir William Knighton, the King's physician, had in the same period wormed into a position of comparable power. This ascendancy was owing not so much to his success in curbing the fleshly appetites of his master as to his skill in managing the King's finances. He had the ingratiating bedside manner of a good provincial doctor. When the King dismissed Sir Benjamin Bloomfield—of his entourage in Calais—for presumption and Methodism, he made Knighton keeper of the Privy Purse, and the doctor and Lady Conyngham, so far as they were able to agree in the course of their rivalry, proceeded together to impress upon the King the importance of devotion to the established religion. It became a convenient substitute for a man beyond the reach of therapeutics.

In the early autumn of 1829 it was plain that the King, though well past sixty, would never attain his three-score-and-ten. His hand was so gouty that it was as large as two hands, he had inflammation of the lungs, was going blind in one eye, and was so distressed by a pain in his bladder that he could only relieve it by cups of laudanum. It was no time for him to attend to affairs of state, and yet the ministers, Wellington, Aberdeen (now Foreign Secretary), and the rest, continually journeyed to Windsor and talked to their sovereign, puffed out like a pinchusion, as he sat up in bed in a cotton nightcap and sipped chocolate.

All this time Brummell was wondering why, especially in the midst of all the opportunities for interview that Wellington must be taking, no word had come through. Yet his faith in the Duke remained almost sublime. The fact was that even if the King no longer objected to helping the Beau with a post, Aberdeen did, and Wellington for the sake of peace in the cabinet at a critical hour hesitated to insist upon the appointment. The ministers had their hands full trying to decide the larger issues of government under a King more than half dead.

But when an old friend of Brummell's, General Sir Robert Wilson, advised him at about this time of an impending visit to Calais, the hopes of the Beau for early action pathetically rose once more. Wilson after fighting through the Napoleonic wars had subsequent to Waterloo been imprisoned for contriving the escape of one of Napoleon's supporters, had interposed between the mob and the troops at Queen Caroline's funeral in 1821, and as a member of the Opposition had played a critical part in forming the Canning ministry of 1827. Now, for the first time in years, he was being allowed to travel abroad.

"Most happy shall I be," wrote Brummell (September 11) to Wilson, "to shake you once more by the hand, and I am delighted to hear that the contemptible prohibition against your *passe-partout* in these dominions is at an end. I am still vegetating, for I will not call it living, with the fat weeds that sleep within the stagnant ditches that surround this place. I am indeed comparatively as fat; but that can be accounted for by the windy nature of my nourishment, hope long deferred yet still green and promising in the fancy. My dependance is placed upon the good offices of one great man, who as he has always extended every kindness toward me, will not neglect any favourable opportunity to be of service to me."

Visitors to Calais became the messengers of the Beau upon their return to England. General Wilson was one of them. Word of the plight of Brummell soon reached Charles Greville, who throughout the present reign had been Clerk of the Council, and was therefore in habitual touch with the chiefs of all the parties in the state. Early in December Greville made excuse for a talk with Wellington, and implored that George Brummell be taken care of. The Duke rehearsed what he had already done, explained the mishap of Dudley's dawdling, and said that he was anxious to oblige Alvanley and Worcester, but that Aberdeen still interposed. Whereupon Greville determined to visit the Beau, in order the better to inform himself. In the first week of March he crossed to Calais, and called at Le Pauvre Diable. Like everyone else he discovered Brummell "dressing," and was fascinated by the quiet dignity of

Hobhouse the parrot. The Beau, having no acquaintance with this odd officeholder—who was a sprig of the houses of Warwick and Bentinck, really a minor man of fashion, "well-born, well-bred, handsome, and accomplished"— hardly realized that he was entertaining an angel unawares. He kept Greville in his place, but expanded upon his hardships and his joys, and dwelt upon his indestructible hopes for the morrow. Greville, on leaving, set down these notes in his diary:

"At Calais (March 6) I had a long conversation with Brummell about his consulship, and was moved by his account of his own distresses to write to the Duke of Wellington and ask him to do what he could for him. I found him in his old lodging, dressing—some pretty pieces of old furniture in the room, an entire toilet of silver, and a large green Macaw perched on the back of a tattered silk chair with faded gilding; full of gaiety, impudence and misery."

While at this precise time the King, now in Windsor Castle, seemed to be growing stronger, in April he was attacked with shortness of breath, a consequence of his old lung trouble. Calling for cherry brandy he gulped it down, and panted, "I am very nervous but very brave." Knighton and his assistant doctors came rushing in, to find that the King's heart had weakened from an aggravation of dropsy. When in the middle of May the Duchess of Gloucester, having visited the King, was asked how he looked, she replied, "like a feather bed." He was tapped, he improved, then suffered another relapse. All that Knighton could think of prescribing was a huge Bible, which he placed beside the bed, while Lady Conyngham darted about in the Castle invoking the Deity and scooping up valuable souvenirs. Of her, the vulgar mob outside the walls repeated the jingle:

"First she packed and then she prayed,
And then she packed again."

George Brummell, as these tidings were carried to him across the Channel, only observed, "All the harm I wish the King is, that he would leave me but a small portion of the sums that the Marchioness of Conyngham and Sir William Knighton have already received."

The King, because of his heart, could only sleep sitting up, head in his hands, hands on a table. Early on June 26 he burst a blood vessel in his stomach, clutched his doctor's hand, and said, "My boy, this is death." And it was.

The only thing which it can be said that George IV bequeathed to the man who had once been his most admired intimate was the goodwill of his brother and successor, who now became King William IV. This man, a jolly, erratic, kind-hearted creature, no little a buffoon, with eyes full of merriment and hair rearing up like windswept grass, was far more approachable than his predecessor on the subject of Brummell. None knew this better than Will Alvanley, the man who like Burke had "read the book of life a long time and other books a little." Alvanley had never given over his determination to rescue his friend in Calais, and scarcely had the ceremonies of the accession died down before he beseiged the Prime Minister, still Wellington, to reopen the subject. While the Duke had not forgotten, Alvanley rightly reckoned that it would do no harm to remind him. The appeal was duly made by Wellington, the King gave his consent, and on September 10 (1830) Brummell was appointed consul at a salary of £400, not at Calais, but at Caen, the capital of lower Normandy.

The first thing for Brummell in his good fortune to undertake was to repair the embarrassments created by his ill fortune. He could not otherwise leave Calais. Counting up, he found his total liabilities to be 24,000 francs, half of it owing to tradesmen, and the other half to an overdraft at the bank of the genial Leveux. At Le Pauvre Diable, his new rooms, so ardently fitted out for the house of the Consul, with the crimson wallpaper, the marble floor in the hall, the ornate bedroom, were now a sorry sight; the Beau had not even paid his decorators. The least he could do was to part with his buhl furniture, those rare inlaid pieces sent down from Paris, cumbersome, perhaps, to transport to Caen. But he had lived with it for a dozen years, almost as long as he had owned his things in London, and it was a wrench to let it go. Mournfully he held a sale. The money therefrom was something less than half the sum needed for the tradesmen.

But the other half was owing to François, for house expenses. Why not take François to Caen, and pay him off gradually? To this arrangement François was not too agreeable, although willing to go to Caen; he himself,

however, was liable to the tradesmen. Brummell then set
about an arrangement with the banker Leveux. He still
owed roughly 18,000 francs. His salary was to be 10,000.
By a letter of assignment to the Foreign Office in London,
the Beau made over to Leveux 8,000 francs of this sum per
year, for two and a quarter years, when the entire obligation should be discharged.

In little more than a fortnight after his appointment,
then, Brummell left Calais for Paris, in the company of a
King's messenger provided by Samuel Marshall the con-
sul. He slept the whole way in the coach, but, as the messenger gravely put it, "snored very much like a gentleman." Arrived in Paris, the Beau went to stay at the
British Embassy, where his old friend of better days at
Watier's, Lord Stuart de Rothesay, was ambassador. Lord
Stuart he had of course entertained subsequently in Calais.
The plan of Brummell was to remain in Paris for a week,
long enough, he thought, to seek out between the Palais
Royal and the Rue de la Paix a snuffbox worthy of his
selection.

Paris had just quieted down a bit after the July Revolution, which, having dethroned the elder branch of the
Bourbons in the person of Charles X, the unchastened and
autocratic brother of Louis XVI, acclaimed the accession
of the Duc d'Orleans. The Duc, urged by Prince de
Talleyrand to accept, and having in fact begun to reign as
Louis Philippe, in turn appointed Talleyrand ambassador
to England. But Talleyrand had not yet left Paris. This
veteran statesman, now seventy-four, with a whisk of

straight white hair slanting down upon his shoulders, and limping about on the foot which he had injured in childhood, was for the moment taking his ease after having served both Napoleon and Louis XVIII as Foreign Minister and Grand Chamberlain. He was self-assured, ironical, humorous, and friendly. He met George Brummell—doubtless through de Rothesay—and entertained him as a "fellow-diplomat."

To meet Talleyrand was to meet his shadow, his petted pupil, confidant and companion, Comte Casimir de Montrond, a man twelve years younger than the Prince, but fully as talented in the trickery, the intrigue, the elastic of diplomacy. From such a pair, Brummell might even in the intercourse of a few days imbibe a pretty lesson in the elements of foreign service. Montrond was gay, gallant, fighting, frivolous, gambling, devil-may-care—so far a man well worthy the mettle of the Beau. But he had long trodden the stage of high politics—Napoleon, Metternich, Nesselrode—had been exiled, disgraced, twice imprisoned, and even now was under police supervision. Murat, Napoleon's marshal, had called Talleyrand and Montrond "a couple of dung-heaps in silk stockings." At least they were classed together. When a certain Princess asked Montrond why he was so attached to old Talleyrand, he replied, "Ah, Madame, how can one help loving him? He is so deliciously full of vice!"

To meet Talleyrand, one might say, was to meet everyone who mattered in the government of France. Brummell was next presented to the Foreign Minister, Comte Louis

Mathieu Molé. (This ministry Talleyrand himself had declined, while slyly contriving with Louis Philippe to retain
the real direction of it from London). Yet Molé, though
twenty-five years junior to Talleyrand, was no puppet; he
had spun a remarkable career of his own as councillor to
Napoleon and director of public works, and he was a
national figure. Still another celebrity whom Brummel
encountered in the swath he was cutting was Comte
Horace Sebastiani, the Corsican soldier, lately ambassador
to Turkey, and now a character brilliant in Parisian society. He had fought beside Napoleon to the last. Prominent at present in the Chamber of Deputies, he had been
minister both of Marine and of Foreign Affairs, and whilst
in the Foreign Office had uttered the historic line "Order
prevails in Warsaw." These two men indeed showed
rather more interest in Brummell's new appointment than
the others did; they gave him letters to the Préfet of Caen,
to the General in residence, and to three or four of the
"big-wigs" in the neighbourhood.

In the tortuous game of European diplomacy the Beau
might well conclude, for all his past sophistication, that in
the company of such personages he was a babe. Yet why
should he sit at their feet? His duties in Caen would be
not to plot for stratagems and spoils, but to verify the pass-
ports of voyagers with foreheads high, hair red, eyebrows
the same, eyes greyish, noses *retroussés,* and faces pimply.
The rest was commerce and bills of lading. In Paris,
whithersoever Stuart de Rothesay led him, Brummell
dined at the tables of Talleyrand and Montrond, of Molé

and Sebastiani, but tempered their dizzy politics with one or two evening parties in the house of the Princesse de Bagration. She was the widow of the great Russian general, hero of Austerlitz and Friedland, who in 1812 had been killed at Borodino. With the Princesse, the Beau lived again the sparkling days made memorable to him in the England of his Duchesses.

This one week of the old life was not enough, and yet it was too much. Failing in his important object, to find the snuffbox of his dreams, Brummell left an order at Dabert's for an enamelled gold one, to cost 450 francs, nearly all that was coming to him in salary for his first quarter on duty. On October 2 he quitted Paris in style, though with renunciation; Paris had unhinged him for so abrupt a retreat to rusticity. Accompanied by his valet François, he drove off for lower Normandy, 140 miles away, in a coach and four with two postillions, determined that his entry into Caen, at least, should be one that the natives would remember. Three days later the Beau put down there, at the Hotel de la Victoire, nearly falling into the greasy arms of the cook, whom he mistook for the landlord. "Give me," said he, "the best rooms, the best dinner, and the best Lafitte." As he signed the visitors' book, he added, "His Britannic Majesty's Consul."

In the gathering dusk of an October day Brummell had not much time to look about. But he was soon to find that Caen lay on the bank of the Orne only seven miles in from the English Channel, that it was a bit southwest of Havre, and that it was as far from Calais as it was from Paris.

The population was some 20,000. There were wide streets, shady boulevards—Rue St. Jean the chief one—and public gardens, but no ramparts. In the church of St. Etienne lay buried Matilda, queen of William the Conqueror; more conspicuous were monuments of the conquering Plantagenets, the University of Caen having been founded by Henry VI in 1436 near the close of that 100 years during which the English remained in possession. Another monument, but by and for the French, was that to Malherbe, the waspish critic, who was born in Caen; ever since his death in 1628 French poetry had fallen off in its more poetic qualities, and only now, in 1830, did it show signs of coming back into its own. If George Brummell in Caen was to reopen his Album of verse, he might well inscribe in it a toast to François de Malherbe. But while Caen with its university, its library, its art museum, and its rich museum of antiquities, was a town with obviously more flavour to it than Calais, the prosaic business of the Consul was to lend an eye to its agriculture, its horse-breeding, its cloth, lace, leather, and gloves.

For a week he remained at the Victoire, said to be the best hotel in Caen. But his friends in Paris had spoilt him, he said, "for at least a year to come." It seemed to the Beau that in the Victoire he had to undergo "all the horrors, and all the more horrible cheating, of one of the worst hotels in Europe." Lamenting his plight to his friend Marshall in Calais, Brummell protested, "During seven days I gnawed bones upon unwashed dowlas in this charnel-house ... and during seven nights I thought it necessary to scratch myself without sleeping." Then after diligent but cautious inquiry he came to find that in the Rue des Carmes, a convenient cobbled street nearby, a Madame Guernon de St. Ursain was not using half of her house, and that she might take him in. Proceeding to this address the Beau saw a neat façade of grey stone between two darker houses, three storeys with dormer windows for a fourth, and the middle floors fitted with little iron balconies at each window, within which the lace curtains alone were enough to tempt him to inspect.

Mme St. Ursain, he had heard, was kin to Guernon de Ranville, a former minister of the government; her house was clean; her daughter Ellen, a little girl, aged fourteen with a "snowy complexion" was charming; her two cats from Angola, called Ourika and Angolina, were fascinating; and her parrot Jacko, who performed tricks to get sugar, proved irresistible. Brummell moved in. One week later François the valet, having been paid up, departed to open a café in Boulogne upon his savings. His master thereupon engaged a local man, who complacently bore the name of Isadore.

Brummell then decided upon his costume as consul. In the morning he put on a snuff-coloured coat with a velvet collar a shade darker. His waistcoat, washable, was cashmere on a white ground, made from a shawl, and within that, unrivalled as ever in his heyday in St. James's Street, stood his white neckcloth. He chose dark blue trousers, pointed boots—which he required polished on the soles as well as above—primrose kid gloves, and a high black hat a bit larger at the crown than the circumference of his head. For evening dress, he changed to his Whig colours as in London: blue coat with velvet collar, buff waistcoat, and black trousers; to his lapel he fixed the consular button.

His appointment to the consulate had been heralded weeks before his arrival. This news, the knowledge of who he was and what he had been, his grand entry with the whips of the postillions cracking, and his letters from the redoubtable Molé and Sebastiani, started Brummell off a great man, as he put it, "without a sixpence in his pocket." They dined and fêted him. They elected him without ballot, an honour not before accorded any Englishman, to their Société, or club, a sort of Brooks's, except that, country fashion, it closed at eleven o'clock at night. "All well-educated, well-mannered, and well-conditioned people," the Beau remarked, "no industrious master of arts ... no superannuated imbecile clodhoppers." Indeed his new distinction, for which he had importuned for ten long years, was worth all the anxiety he had spent upon it.

Three weeks after his arrival, on October 26, his new friend the Préfet, M. Target, and the Deputé, M. de la Pommeraye, gave Brummell "a grand to-do" by way of a reception and dinner. He carefully prepared "a neat little extempore," and upon being called on to speak, he not only praised the conduct of Louis Philippe but "let off" upon success to the commerce of the two countries being toasted. He condoled with the outs, agreed with the ins, and said all he could to make all parties satisfied with him. Privately, although content with his staff at the consulate, he believed that his office was not doing much of any importance for the commerce in question. "I forsee," he confided to Marshall in Calais, "that little or nothing is to be made of my department; *n'importe,* I shall try something in the spring to better it. I am perfectly contented with my *Chancellor* Hayter, who is well versed in his business, and from my investigation, I believe to be an honourable *adjoint."*

As for the English in Caen, he called upon "all who were worthy such a compliment." They were very respectable persons, who seemed to be there to educate themselves and their families; more to the point, the leaders of this set, Messrs. Villiers and Burton, were men of independent fortune who maintained mansions like the embassy in Paris, or even like Devonshire House, generally open at half-past five to a well-provided dinner, and always open house in the evening. These compatriots were abundantly hospitable to the Beau, who within their doors got not only good food, but good company and recreation. "The French of the best class," he acknowledged, "mingle much in this society, and there is always a fiddle for the amusement of the young ladies . . . I shake hands and gossip with the fathers and mothers, and pat all their dirty-nosed children upon the head, and tell them that they are beautiful. What can I do more with my scanty means?"

His means were scanty at the moment largely because he had spent all he possessed in Paris. While the uncommonly expensive snuffbox was not paid for, it indicated the scale of his extravagance. He bought *patés* at Chevet's in the

Palais Royal, and took one with him to Caen. Then he thought it was too wonderful to eat. But when a compatriot one day said he intended to dine that evening at the house of another compatriot, one Jones, a retired soap-boiler, Brummell conceived the idea that he might get himself invited too by sending this *paté* to Jones as a present for the party. The idea was the more piquant because Jones, a Radical, had condemned the "profligate appointment of such a man (as Brummell) to superintend the interests of the British nation at Caen." But he could not withstand the *paté*. The Consul was invited. At the dinner, he waited patiently for the appearance of his delicacy; it never came on. As the Beau was leaving, he bade Isadore go round to the kitchen and inquire why; the answer was that Mr. Jones was saving it for his young son's birthday. "Go back to the kitchen," said Brummell, "and say that I particularly desire to see the *paté de foie gras*." When Isadore returned with it, his master reasoned that it would be a sin to leave such a work of art with such people, ordered it put into his carriage, and driven to Mme St. Ursain's. He himself remained to pay his adieux to Mr. and Mrs. Soap-Boiler, then followed on foot.

For his breakfast, straight off, Brummell despatched this *paté*. "I never," said he, "inserted my carving-knife into such another." It was his last Parisian morsel. When a day or two later three young Frenchmen of the Carlist party —who desired to carry out the wishes of the deposed King Charles and enthrone his grandson the Duc de Bordeaux —called and found the Beau in the intricacies of shaving, the memory at least of his titbit was still with him. "Pray stay, messieurs," said he, "I have not yet breakfasted—no excuses; there is a *paté de foie gras,* a *pain de gibier*——" In truth he had not a scrap in the house but a penny roll and a pot of coffee on the hob. One of the young Carlists, on leaving, observed to his friends, "He must live very well."

But they achieved the aim of their visit, which was to enlist the attention of the Consul to the cause of the Carlists, or as they rather liked to be known, the Legitimists. Louis Philippe, the "citizen-king," was to their mind a usurper. For fifteen years after the Restoration, office-holders under the elder branch of the Bourbons had been men of the best families, some of whom had spent their winters in Caen instead of in Paris. The July Revolution overturned this social system. To Brummell, indeed, the new order, ousting the nobility, was somewhat distasteful. On every hand he heard Legitimists bemoaning the degeneracy of modern days, and even upbraiding England for allowing France to do as she pleased. To a reasonable extent, he took sides with these Legitimists. Having paid his respects to Louis Philippe at that public dinner, he did not feel bound to continue voicing such sentiments, especially if amongst his new acquaintance those whose manners, houses, and liqueurs appealed most to him happened to be partisans of the Duc de Bordeaux.

Of these, one who influenced Brummell during his first winter in Caen was the Marquise de Seran, a woman of charm and of polished wit; years before, she had known

him slightly in London, whither she had fled from the
French Revolution. When he was prince of the dandies
the Marquise had huddled in a Soho lodging; now, Fortune had spun the wheel the other way, and as the Beau
sat at her fireside in Caen they exchanged anecdotes of
exile. But the woman from whom Brummell heard most
about the Carlist cause was his landlady, "a most cleanly
devout old lady," as he described her. It was her late husband who was a cousin of Guernon de Ranville, one of the
condemned ministers of Charles X. Mme St. Ursain was
in the best provincial fashion a *salonière,* and to her drawing-room she invited local leaders of the Legitimists, whil-
ing away with them the late winter afternoons in discourse,
very animated, upon a single topic: the succession to the
throne of France. Brummell wished to be well with his
landlady. He agreed with her views.

CHAPTER XIV

THE END OF THE CONSULATE

1831–1832

FOR HIS first six months in Caen, Brummell had enjoyed what amounted almost to a resurrection of his days in London. He was Consul, he was a personage, he was still the autocrat of fashion, he was sought after by everyone, and when he ran up a bill, his creditors felt honoured. Each day the Beau wore three shirts, and each day three neckcloths. At this pace about a third of his income of 2,000 francs was demanded by his washerwoman alone, and even if nothing out of his total salary had been paid over to Leveux of Calais, this unbridled man would yet have been living on a scale beyond his resources by half.

In April (1831) he was obliged to apply to Leveux for relief. He told the good Jacques that he had counted upon his friends for continued donations, but that it would be "another difficult century of four or five months before it pleased them to rescue him." In fact, the men in London, little realizing that four-fifths of Brummell's salary was being allocated to Leveux, thought that after their own long and arduous representations the Beau was at last provided for; after ten years of effort and concern they were rather complimenting themselves upon their release. Brummell did not write to them; but if he had been still in Calais, and had caught some of them passing through, they would have heard no little of his difficulty of trying to live like a Consul on 2,000 francs a year. Until Leveux should be paid off, the entire question of local credit was in jeopardy.

These points also he tried to establish in his letter to the banker. Far from admitting his own possible extravagance Brummell on the contrary observed: "I care nothing for the luxuries nor the pleasures of life; I had to give them up long ago; but it is a question at the moment of my honour, my reputation, and all my interests present and future, since I fear a total lack of means of providing even the official expenses which the obligations of my consulate each day impose, and the scandal of the ignominy which stares me in the face of being continually hounded for little debts may soon cause the loss of my post." He therefore begged Leveux for Leveux's "own good" to send help.

For some time Jacques thought over this eloquent but practical appeal without replying. Then Brummell wrote again: "I have been in hopes, my dear sir, for a month, of hearing from you. Pushed to the last extremity, and to avoid my being chased about by the people of this town, finally to save the shirt on my back, which is truly almost all that I still possess . . ." This was enough. Leveux sent funds for the "difficult century," the four months, after which the Beau had said he believed his friends might step in again.

But if he did write to England, he got no immediate response, and in midsummer he was forced to put his case to a local compatriot, Charles Armstrong, of the Rue St. Jean. This man served the English colony as grocer, tea merchant, packet-agent, house-agent, and dealer in foreign exchange. "For ten days," Brummell implored him in August, "I have actually not had five francs in my possession . . . the means of procuring either wood or peat . . . or of getting my things from the washerwoman. A trifling advance would arrange these difficulties . . . I have not anything to offer you by way of security . . . if it is not my small stock of plate, for which I paid six hundred francs, and my watch and chain, worth as much more: to these you are welcome . . . if you can spare five minutes . . . you will oblige me by coming down here: these matters are better arranged in person than by writing." Armstrong, who had profited somewhat by Brummell's patronage, did as he was bidden, settled with a few of the hungrier creditors, and magnanimously declined to take away the security offered.

Perhaps he did not quite appreciate what he was now in for. Brummell had hardly escaped from this midsummer siege when Isadore the valet, out of patience with having been kept in arrears, announced that he was leaving in a day or two, and refused downright to go without all that was owed him. Again the Beau besought Armstrong for help: "That damned ungrateful brute, Isadore, persecutes me at every instant: the fellow says he is going to Paris on Thursday, and will not depart without being paid, in money or by bill, and I believe him capable of employing a bailiff. I am wretchedly bedevilled, and out of spirits, and hate going out of the house." Once more Armstrong obliged, but this time accepted a gold watch, with chain and seals, for the favour. Then, hot upon the flurry stirred up by Isadore—whom Brummell proceeded to supplant by a woman, at lower wages—came the local bankers, Gilbert and Bellamy, gentlemen not so indulgent as Jacques Leveux; they had to have their bills renewed and fortified by the signature of the magical Armstrong.

One might well wonder how in the course of this alarming indigence Brummell managed to placate his landlady. Mme St. Ursain, in truth, took the same view of this little matter as the landlord of Le Pauvre Diable in Calais. If M. Leleux would have kept the Beau "for nothing" if he had stayed, if he took his rent from the mere entertainment which his guest afforded him, Mme St. Ursain was almost equally indifferent. Her lodger forgot to pay, and Madame pretended to forget that he owed. M. Brummell was a distinguished gentleman. It was an honour to have him under her roof. He was grown so far a Legitimist that on the anniversary of the July Revolution he hung the British flag not from the Consulate, but on an outhouse—upon the pretext, to satisfy the *parvenus,* that he kept his "official papers" there. Above all, Brummell, kind to the point of affection to Madame's daughter Ellen—now a

pupil in the local English school of a Miss Wheatcroft—
had undertaken to teach the young lady of the house how
to write his language. His place in the Rue des Carmes
was secure.

The method of the Beau in giving his lessons was to
write to "Miss Aimable," as he formally called Ellen, at
her school, to correct the replies which she returned, and
to go over with her the exercises which she brought home
from her English teacher, one Miss Davidson. "During the
present week," he informed Ellen in November, "I have
led a most idle and unprofitable life; never in bed before
the moon has retired, and in consequence unable to open
my jaded eyes till the morning has almost vanished. . . . I
shall certainly turn over a new leaf . . . to improve you in
the knowledge of my uncouth native dialect . . . you merit
every commendation for your assiduity. If you were not
influenced by such laudable solicitude, I am sure you
would not voluntarily undertake these constant peregri-
nations to Miss Wheatcroft's in such abominable weather,
for the purpose of conferring in other languages than your
own with Miss Davidson and Signor Matteo . . . Prosecute
your studies . . . you will soon be omniscient."

If Brummell intended these letters to be adventures in
vocabulary, he was a professor. But he clung to his habit
of turning over old leaves, not new ones. Avoiding the
streets by day from fear of creditors, he missed few opportunities of diversion at night, for he was in demand in the
stately houses of the Carlists, and in consequence, his letters to Ellen were somewhat irregular. Perforce they occa-

sionally took the form of notes not so floridly instructive. "It is in vain," he again wrote her, "that I had promised myself a quiet evening at home. I am really beset to attend a stupid *soirée,* and, without being guilty of a palpable excuse, it is impossible for me to send an excuse. I am compelled, then, to defer the pleasure of writing to you more diffusely and more academically until to-morrow morning."

Perhaps this party was one which the Beau attended at about this time at General Corbet's, during which a certain Mademoiselle asked him "who figured" at a "hop" which he had graced not long before. His answer was that the only novelty was a governess, who had played so well on the piano for the quadrilles, and later so outdanced the others herself, that her accomplishments partly made up for her plain figure and face. This conversation then wavered to the brilliancy and comfort of General Corbet's fire, and progressively to one of Brummell's aids to warmth through the winter nights, hot water in an earthen bottle clad in a petticoat of flannel. But Mademoiselle had not stopped thinking of the governess. "Would you not prefer," she asked the Beau, "being married to the governess you have been praising than to the bottle in the bed?"

"The lady in question," he answered, "to whom you so unreservedly return, might indeed prove a preferable substitute for the innocent bottle; but I have much too good an opinion of her to suppose she would entertain such warming-pan ideas."

Mademoiselle exploded into "horse laughter," at which

the whole assemblage turned round. Brummell took a pinch of snuff, withdrew, and made off to his solitary chamber, "painfully ruminating upon the lax morality of society."

For the hostess to whom he related this experience in a letter, the Beau appended a few lines upon the young woman of the conversation, whom he called "Moggy," and of whose *propriete* he had his doubts:

"Fair Moggy, fair Moggy, the morning falls foggy,
And your tears, like the rain, may soon piteously pelt;
Yet my hopes still denote, that at sight of my note,
Your reason, like butter in sunshine, will melt.

'Tis unkind to deceive, in my candour believe,
All the perfumes of Araby will not now plight us;
Shed your skin, like the snake, and perhaps for your sake,
More refreshing *amitie* may *enfin* unite us."

It was a curious thing, this renaissance of his gaieties of the drawing-room, this renewal of applause from both mothers and daughters, all this fresh acclaim, deference, and salute to a figure whose personality had not for a moment sagged with his pocketbook. Once more, as Consul, Brummell enjoyed "position," that imponderable asset which he had known so long ago as a Captain in the Prince's regiment, and which he had thrown away. What matter if Caen was not London? Caen was a microcosm within itself. The women, French and English alike, sought his intimacy; if he reserved that for Ellen St. Ursain, he pretended to give the others as much of himself as was good for them. As long as he had taken up versifying again, he now added a few lines by a lady from England, one of them a bow to the new English King, to his Album, that storehouse of memories which he never tired of looking into. These verses were called "The Contents of a Lady's Toilet-Table Drawer":

"Some ribbon, two combs, and one with a tail:
Soda powders, a compass, and lace for a veil;
Some patterns of *broderie,* relics of hair,
A bow off a cap, a knob off a chair;
A white *pelerine,* and a collar of Tory's,
A muzzle, a hairpin, and Miss Edgeworth's stories;
A piece of the fender all cover'd with rust,
A stay-lace, a pencil, a buckle, a crust;
Some cotton and pens, a shoe and a slipper;
A box with some pills for rousing the liver;
A medal of William the Fourth's coronation,
Black pins and white pins of every gradation;
A shoe-horn of Grenier's he'll never get back;
Some *ecarte* and whist cards, but not a whole pack;
A duster, a bill, a penknife, a whip;
A box with no lid, and some sugar for Gyp;
An almanac, pencil-case, seals and blue wax;
A glass box for *bonbons,* with five or six cracks;
Some needles for darning, curl-papers, and sand;
The *galope* of 'Gustave,' a bodkin and band:
And this and much more, with my own eyes I saw
Taken out of a Tidy and fair lady's drawer!"

Brummell could play with his new friends in this vein, tell them gay tales of the days when he had ruled, and even laugh at the folly of those who had permitted him to be the despot of fashion. This was his evening emancipation from reality. Daytime only landed him once more in the battle of the duns. In December the Beau had again to importune the indispensable Armstrong: "I am positively pressed for 280 francs . . . before four o'clock to-day, or I shall be exposed to the utmost disgrace . . . the plate are in the closet in my room, and you may have them by sending any confidential person . . . I do not like to *trust* my servant . . . as it may be known, or she may be seen with them in the street . . . small difficulties often extend to irreparable destruction of character." Once more Armstrong tided his fellow-countryman over the wearisomely familiar emergency.

On the day before Christmas the Beau reminded Ellen, "my very dear Miss Aimable" that she was to celebrate the next day with him by taking a lesson in English: "All the plagues of Egypt, in the shape of visitors, have obtruded themselves upon me this morning, on purpose, I believe, to interrupt my transcribing verses, or otherwise communing in manuscript with you . . . I am compelled to be brief . . . you have promised to take a lesson with me to-morrow morning, Christmas Day! What a period of rejoicing and *fête,* according to the customs of my native country, this used to be to me . . . while now, of 'joys that are past how painful the remembrance' . . . I have not indeed much to enliven me; but with all my cares, you are always a consolation."

But Brummell presented one front to Ellen, another to

Armstrong, a third to bill-collectors, and still another to the hostesses of Caen. Of these, Ellen St. Ursain probably got nearest to the true state of his feelings; she helped him over the Christmas season, kept him from brooding too much upon the "broken toys of his past days." When early in 1832 one singled him out at an evening party, one would not suspect that the Consul had a care in the world. Nor did he, so far as his office was concerned. Captain Jesse, on a visit to Caen after six years in India, a man who aspired to play Boswell to the Beau, first met him in February in the drawing-room of an English hostess, and noted "the extreme neatness of his person . . . the polished ease of his address . . . the graceful manner in which he made his way through the crowded *salon* up to the lady of the house." It seemed to the Captain that to friends Brummell bowed at an angle of forty-five degrees; to a common acquaintance, at one of five; while a slight relaxation of features was the acknowledgment that a person inhabited the same planet as himself. Beau Brummell, though now virtually a pauper, retained the *bel air,* the *tournure,* the elegance, that no other man in the room possessed, however ancient their Norman lineage.

Captain Jesse, who was in no hurry to leave Caen, resolved to cultivate his hero. After calling formally several times in the Rue des Carmes, Jesse turned up one evening to dine, and clad not in the blue and buff affected by the Beau above the waist, but in black coat and trousers, and white waistcoat. After the Burgundy had circulated adequately, Brummell leaned a trifle toward his visitor and remarked, "My dear Jesse . . . excuse me, you look very much like a magpie."

The abashed Captain made no remonstrance. Invincibly he turned up in the morning to watch Brummell dress, and was dumbfounded to discover that the Beau after shaving devoted two hours to washing himself, enough to gain him "a reputation for sanctity in a Mohammedan country." The door between the drawing-room and the dressing-room stood ajar, so that in a mirror over the mantelpiece Jesse was able to observe each process of what he called "the secrets of his dressing-table." The spectacle of Brummell wielding a flesh-brush, thought the Captain, would have brought tears of joy to a skin specialist, since the Beau kept up this operation until he was scarlet. Then he put on a flannel undershirt. Then he took a dentist's mirror in one hand and a pair of tweezers in the other, and went at his forehead and chin, "till he had drawn," said the fascinated Jesse, "every stray hair."

Putting on the rest of his clothes without unusual deliberation, Brummell gave meticulous care only to his Parisian curled wig, each lock of which was well seen in its right place. The sole jewellery he wore was a plain ring, dug up on the Field of the Cloth of Gold by a labourer, and sold to the Beau in Calais; and a watch-chain of Venetian-ducat gold in massive links, only two of which showed. His hat, worn a bit on one side, he never took off, not even to a lady; he could not have replaced it in the same position, and it might have disturbed his wig. A brown silk umbrella, in a silk case which fitted as perfectly as his own coat, was surmounted by the smiling but not flattering face of George IV in ivory, wearing a curly wig. So Brummell walked tiptoe down the Rue St. Jean, slightly stooping, picking his way along the highest cobblestones to avoid dust or mud, and making Jesse keep his distance, lest that obsequious but careless man splash the boots or trousers of one who was still a Beau.

Perhaps he went out to meet one of his ladies of the *salons,* either French or English. The lady from England, for example, to whom he had sworn "by those humble ancestors who sleep in their parish churchyards" that he would never reveal her as the authoress of the lines on the "toilet-table drawer," was demanding something in return. Brummell at length sent her a sketch of his lamented Duchess of Devonshire, together with a note containing a hint that they should meet on the same day. "I am ashamed," he told her, "to send you so unworthy a sketch of a beautiful woman . . . the miniature, which I afterwards finished, was given to Lady Harriet Cavendish, now Lady Granville. Do not unjustly fancy that you are for a moment forgotten, because I do not immediately remit to you my relics of past times in writing, or *en crayon.* You shall have others as I go on, unwillingly digging in old green boxes. . . . The sun shines bright, and promises me the consolation of meeting you in your morning's whereabouts. Yours forever and ever, Amen!" On the way to find his flirtatious dame Brummell might encounter Mme de Rigny, sister-in-law of the Minister of Marine; or Mme du Lac, who was said to have the "sweetest face and most beautiful foot" in Normandy. It was not only beneath the midnight chandeliers that the Beau dallied with the society of Caen.

Yet he never knew when he would be safe in the streets; if he was not molested, he owed his freedom to the for-bearance of the tradesmen. One April morning of this year (1832) Brummell was startled by his faithful Mme St. Ursain, who in some agitation came up to warn him that bailiffs were at the door of the house, and were threatening to break into his rooms. Hurriedly she piloted him into a spare room, and shut him up in her wardrobe, asking him the while whether he preferred the sanctuary of her bed-room, into which no officers of the law had the right to intrude. The Beau accepted the wardrobe, letting his dear friend bury him amidst the hanging gowns, flounces, and lace. His habitual presence of mind did not desert him. Scarcely had the good lady locked the door than she heard muffled screams from the lodger: "Madame St. Ursain! For mercy's sake, take the key!"

Weary of being harassed by duns, and vexed with the triviality of his duties as Consul in a town so small, Brum-mell began to wonder whether he should put in for trans-fer to a post in which both the pay and the work might be more considerable. Even a marriage ceremony which as Consul he had officially performed in his drawing-room three months before appeared now to have been of little use. Pounding upon his door one morning whilst he was still in bed, the mother of the bride demanded that Brum-mell should come and stop her son-in-law beating her daughter, and from running off with her furniture into the bargain. The Beau, standing drowsily in his nightgown on the other side of the door, shouted through the wood that interference in domestic wrangles were none of his consular business. "Call to-morrow, madam, call to-morrow," he insisted, as the woman went on without ceasing. "I will consult my Chancellor." As the voice finally retreated down the corridor, Brummell summoned his *bonne,* berated her, and ordered that she never let that creature into the house again. This was the high point of his official life in Lower Normandy.

He heard that his colleague Gordon, in Havre, was withdrawing; that sounded attractive; alternatively, he had often wanted to be stationed in Italy, where living was cheaper and climate finer; why not ask for Leghorn? Lord Palmerston, who as a man of fashion like himself the Beau used to see in the drawing-room of Harriette Wilson—strange how many of his old acquaintance he once met with in the house of a harlot—was now in the Foreign Office, and was all-powerful. Brummell had no claim on him, not even that of a schoolmate, for Palmerston was a Harrovian. On the other hand, the Beau in his London days had been thrown with Palmerston much oftener than with Canning, for at that time Palmerston was a figure more familiar in society than in politics. Brummell now wrote to this man who since then had climbed to importance; he suggested to the Foreign Secretary the change which he had in mind, and adverted to the narrowness of the opportunities in his office at Caen.

It was a bad moment to complain to Palmerston of the paucity of work in any consulate. The government were about to send British forces into Afghanistan, an expensive undertaking, and the Foreign Secretary was casting about to see where he could find the funds. If he could close down a few consulates hither and yon, that saving would help a little. Palmerston was all for business, and, no more than Canning, did he allow a thing for past acquaintance with a man now facing hardship. Instead of taking up Brummell's question of a transfer to a post that was busier, the minister in his chilly reply only inquired whether there was, or was not, any necessity for a consulate at Caen.

The Beau in his turn was obliged to deny the need of it, and to say that a vice-consul could do the little required. (Hayter, his own "honourable" chancellor, had in fact taken care of virtually all the work during the two years past.) But Brummell added: "Your Lordship must be aware that by informing the Government of the inutility of a consul at Caen, I am actuated by purely disinterested motives. Your Lordship will also bear in mind that my bread depends upon the trifling emoluments which I receive as consul at Caen. Should Your Lordship, therefore, on my suggestion think fit to abolish the office, I trust some means of subsistence will be provided for me by the Government."

A fortnight later, in May, Palmerston thanked him for the information, terminated his appointment, closed the consulate in Caen, and said nothing about a transference of Brummell elsewhere.

CHAPTER XV

THE STRICKEN MAN

1832–1835

No sooner had Brummell taken down the Lion and Unicorn from over his doorway than his creditors swarmed into the Rue des Carmes. To let the bills of a Consul run was one thing; to let go unpaid the accounts of a common debtor was not to be tolerated. One Longuet, who kept a restaurant and to whom the Beau owed 1,200 francs for meals sent in, vowed he would arrest Monsieur if he stepped out of the house, and would starve him if he stayed in. Immediately a group of young Carlists, hearing of this threat, proceeded to the restaurant and informed Longuet that unless he relented they would never dine again in his house. Brummell, so far as Longuet was concerned, was left at liberty.

Quite become at heart a Carlist himself, the Beau, relieved of official obligations, now professed his sympathies outwardly. He cut the tradesmen at the Prefecture, he withdrew from the houses of nearly all the office-holders

in the Government, and he lived exclusively either with
the Legitimists or with the few English families whom he
recognized. When Louis Philippe passed through Caen on
his way to Cherbourg, the authorities thought fit to give in
his honour a ball, and to it they invited Brummell. He declined the invitation. On the next day, a friend meeting
him asked whether he had attended the ball for the King.
"What King?" inquired the Beau. "Louis Philippe." "Oh,
the Duke of Orleans, you mean; no, I did not go, but sent
my servant."

While this shrinking from the political party in power
because he disliked their manners was quite in character,
it soon alienated from him many people in his hour of
need. In the course of the summer he ran wholly out of
funds, and had to fall back upon Charles Armstrong again.
"Send me seventy-five francs," he begged him, "to pay my
washerwoman; I cannot get a shirt from her, and she is
really starving on my account. I have not actually money
to pay my physician, or for my letters to and from England." Armstrong heroically complied once more. But
Brummell still owed nearly a year's deduction from salary
to Leveux of Calais; as no salary was any longer coming
in, Jacques would probably get nothing more; again, Brummell through all his stay with Mme St. Ursain had never
paid her but 600 francs; the least he could now do would
be to move to a cheaper lodging, and spare her any further
injustice, for she had been so much more than kind.

In September, therefore, the Beau with heavy heart
arranged with a new landlady, Madame Fichet, to let *en*

pension two rooms on the third floor of her Hôtel d'Angle-terre, breakfasting in his sitting-room, and dining at the table d'hôte. It was very hard to leave the Rue des Carmes. He knew he would miss Ourika and Angolina, not to mention Tigre, a tom-cat next door who fancied them; and he would miss Jacko the parrot above all. He promised Ellen to continue his letters to her. But when the time came for him to go, although he had to pass the door of the drawing-room of Mme St. Ursain, he could not bear to say good-bye to her, and he went away from her house in silence.

For the benefit of Armstrong as well as himself, Brummell now conceived the idea of sending the amiable agent to England, since urgent letters to various friends in that country had lately fetched no response. But a letter to one on this subject did bring an answer, an answer which conveyed to the Beau in the narrow dreariness of his hotel room no small cheer. "I really think," wrote the angel in London, "that a personal interview of Mr. Armstrong with the persons you have named would do more good than letters . . . all that I can do to ensure his seeing them I will. I don't know how to get at the Duke of Wellington or Lord Willoughby. I will write to George Anson and his brother Litchfield, Bagot, Alvanley, and . . . old Allen, who, I assure you, spoke of you the other day in the kindest manner, and I tried hard to get a *pony* out of (Lord) Coventry for you when I was in town. Worcester, I fear, is still in the country; otherwise I am sure he would have been more ready to exert himself than anyone."

Upon this assurance, Armstrong embarked for England in mid-autumn. After he had gone, the spirits of Brummell began to droop; he was afraid his one-time friends in St. James's might turn a cold shoulder just the same; he huddled by a little fire in the corner of his room and fancied that the frost of November was settling upon him as upon the leaves and flowers, and that he should like nothing better than to curl up like a bear and sleep until spring. These thoughts he began on a dismal Sunday evening to set down in a letter to Ellen: "I am at the instant subdued by chillness and blue devils, and feel as if I was in my grave, forsaken and forgotten by all those who were once most dear to me. The greatest unhappiness is that of holding to nothing, and being isolated. I am sick of the world and of existence.

> "Whate'er they promised or profess'd
> In disappointment ends;
> In short, there's nothing I detest,
> So much as all my friends."

You must perceive, that is, if you have the patience to read these vague saturnine jeremiads, that——" His right side went numb. His pen dropped from his grasp. As he tried to get up from his chair to call for help his voice—to a servant who by chance had just entered the room—sounded thick and unnatural. Brummell thought this attack was rheumatism, more than ordinarily severe. A doctor, who came quickly and bled and blistered him, made no mention of the nature of it, but knew that the thing was paralysis.

He got better, as paralytics after their first seizure so often do, and by Thursday was again able to take up his pen to reply to ladies both French and English who within twenty-four hours after his attack had made anxious inquiries. "I have risen to-day," said the Beau, "with my head perfectly quiet, my chest and all its vicinity composed, and free from that oppression and those excruciating spasms which I thought, and at one time sacrilegiously prayed, would put an end to my sufferings in this world. Once more, thanks to heaven and a constitution still unshaken, I am returned to my senses and at peace." Indeed within a few days, being invited to assist at a French wedding, he attended in spirits almost as jubilant as when he had been *chevalier d'honneur* at the marriage of the Prince of Wales.

Reasonably convalescent, Brummell therefore awaited in happier mood the return of Charles Armstrong from London, whatever news that obliging messenger might bring. The news was good. Armstrong had proved to be a most persuasive suppliant, and everyone of the friends previously named as potential sympathizers contributed to the fund when visited personally by a man who pictured to them the plight of George Brummell, reduced to two rooms, on the third floor of a cheap hotel in Caen. Not only did Armstrong tap Wellington, d'Eresby, the Anson brothers, Bagot, Alvanley, "King" Allen, Coventry, and Worcester; he added donations from Burlington, Pembroke, Standish, and that kindly itinerant diarist Charles

Greville. It was as if Armstrong had stood cap in hand at the doors of both White's and Almack's, and on behalf of the great Brummell collected a little recognition for favours bestowed many years gone by.

The recipient of this bounty proceeded forthwith to pay off some of his most pressing creditors, as well as some, like Mme St. Ursain, who were not so pressing as deserving. Brummell cherished the fondest regard for his friend in the Rue des Carmes, and for that daughter of hers, to whom he continued to give lessons in English, and latterly in history too. Some of the tradesmen could wait; Mme St. Ursain, who had sheltered him over a year for nothing, must certainly be paid. Soon after the new year (1833) the Beau knocked at her door, and entered her drawing-room quite as familiarly as if he had never left her house. While the good lady cared very little for money, she was sensitive in respect of the things that count, and she did not readily forget what she considered *impolitesse*. She reminded her former guest that he had gone away without bidding her adieu. Brummell, greatly distressed, got up from his chair, took her hand, and said with emotion, "Madame St. Ursain, I would willingly have wished you good-bye; but I was in tears."

He was the more anxious to stand in her good graces, for as the spring of this year brought him returning strength he found himself growing more and more fond of her daughter Ellen, "Miss Aimable," now become a winsome young woman of seventeen. This was no giddy attachment like his adventure in Calais, which had been born of desperation, aimlessness, long emptiness of life; as soon as he got something to do he had dropped that fair lady without a pang. Yet there was always in Brummell a romantic chord which was responsive to femininity regardless of the question of age. For more than one middle-aged hostess of Caen he felt deep affection. If when he was thirty-five he loved Duchesses old enough to be his mother, now at fifty-five he loved a child young enough to be his daughter. To engender in women reciprocal likings toward himself was of course great part of his purpose in dress, in his plumage. In the case of Ellen St. Ursain, he sought her admiration, for it was a prop to his precarious life; but in return for that admiration he gave love.

When in the summer Ellen like many others in Caen went away to the seaside, Brummell could not follow. He could only wander about the deserted town, and look at the houses of his friends boarded up. But he and Ellen exchanged letters, books, confidences. In July she was at Luc-sur-Mer, nine miles away, and he wrote to her. "Why, in the name of common prudence and my own tranquillity, could I not have been contented to restrict my knowledge of you to the worldly etiquette of taking off my hat to you, when we casually met? . . . I have sedulously avoided running my crazy head into what may be termed inconsequent distractions, and now, in spite of all my theoretical circumspection and security, I find myself over head and ears, heart and soul, in love with you . . . I shall put myself into a strait-waistcoat, and be chained to the bedpost . . . I have yet sufficient command over my drooping faculties to restrain any tributary tears . . . we all know that they may be counterfeited upon paper with a sponge and rose-water . . . it was my intention to go to the seaside for a day . . . but you would laugh clandestinely at me in your bustled sleeve . . . and I should only have to "bay the moon" . . . What am I to do for a diurnal matinal correspondent and afternoon gossip, now that you are "over the hills and far away"? I am almost inclined to think that your sensibilities are as cold as your snowy complexion; still I shall ever be immutably yours in this world."

In August, still with his mind upon the education of Ellen which he had undertaken, he tried to get for her *The Betrothed* of Manzoni, in the original Italian. But the "ourang-outang" of a bookseller sent him a miserable French translation. Still he sent it on, and told Ellen to cast it into the sea if it bored her. As a counterpoise the Beau enclosed, without comment, a copy of his own *Butterfly's Funeral,* though hardly expecting her to read between its lines the autobiography of George Brummell. His daily life in Caen had grown "dreary, insipid, and unprofitable." He left his room only to walk along the Cafarelli, a promenade laid out on the banks of the Orne, and approached from one of the quays by a bridge; it was named after a préfet appointed by Napoleon, as that préfet had planted rows of trees there, trees which unhappily refused to put forth very many leaves. "Not a civilized being now there," said the Beau, "to exhilarate my solitary ramble." He had kept looking back, as he walked, in the fancy of seeing Ellen coming over the bridge.

But when this young woman responded with a note in praise of the *Butterfly's Funeral,* Brummell was delighted no end, "contented with himself and all the world," and he sallied forth into the byways of Caen as if he were again walking down St. James's Street, twenty years before, the arbiter of fashion: "I have this morning perambulated over this deserted town, acknowledged everyone whose physiognomy was familiar to me, *lancé* two bad jokes at His Excellency Monsieur le Baron . . . in judgment of his new heathenish mouse-coloured pantaloons, and even disturbed my hat with my best strait-laced salutations to Madame (Countess) d'A——, and her contemptible troop of monkeys in the shape of men." Brummell ended by begging Ellen to write to him and tell him she thought of him, "be it so or not"; and he sent her by courier another packet of books.

When so many were away from Caen, he missed this young girl the most; but when they flocked back in the autumn, he was too occupied in various directions to dedicate his soliloquies to one person. There were Mme de Rigny and Mme du Lac, M. de St. Quentin, Henri de Vauquelin, Henri de Ste. Marie—Carlists, *modérés, juste milieu,* Guizoistes, Molistes, Thieristes, every shade of political colour which provincial France could boast, and they all in turn made great play of converting Brummell to their own views. Society in Caen was a political kaleidoscope symmetrical in only one thing: that it did not like Louis Philippe.

As the Christmas festivities came on, the Beau played his

part like a Frenchman born. On Christmas Day he protested to one of his French hostesses that he was going to
church not because he bore the "cross of Palestine upon his
shoulder," nor because he was a Jesuitical Don Escobar
who justified immoral acts by purity of intention, but
because he must do penance for the trespasses of the evening, when he was to "dine with the Pharisees." In Hôtel
d'Angleterre he was as cold as a homeless dormouse. But
to write to this good lady was always to feel a "thawing of
the heart." He told her he was attending a masque ball at
Mme de Rigny's on New Year's Eve, at which time he
would take off his wooden shoes and *galope* with the rest.

Brummell in truth felt well enough at the turn of the
year 1834 to withstand these holiday gaieties. An aftermath
of the fancy-dress ball, only two nights later, was a party
at the old Countess's, the lady with the troop of "man-
shaped monkeys." She was an octogenarian, a true relic of
the days of Louis XV. She took quantities of snuff, wrote
satirical verses on the manners of the *juste milieu,* and
spat on the parquet floor. Her sonnets she reserved for the
youthful Henri V (Duc de Bordeaux), who she vehe-
mently insisted must be enthroned in order that he might
restore the society of her own early years. "Ah, Monsieur,"
the Countess used to say, "how sad our *salons* are become!
I no longer recognize myself in them. In my youth, a wife
had her men friends, and her husband had his women
friends; each amused oneself in one's own way. Now, we
see married couples always together. That's a fact. Ah!
how obscene are the customs of to-day!" On this evening,

she sat down to five-sous whist with Brummell, and they
played until a "dissipated hour," whilst the Countess, instead of attending to the game, "made half-closed eyes at
him." "This," said the Beau, confiding his experience to
another hostess on the next day, "afflicted me afterwards
with a relative nightmare—I fancied in the dream I was
struggling with my Aunt Margaret's ghost."

But he soon had to pay for these dissipated hours more
than the *sous* which he lost to the Countess. One evening
in April, when he was dining at the table d'hôte in his
hotel, he was startled to feel his soup trickling upon his
chin. Getting up from the table, he went into an adjoining
room and looked in a mirror; it revealed that his mouth
was distorted, drawn up toward his ear; paralysis had
stricken him again. The same doctor came, found Brummell in a high fever, put him to bed and deprived him of
food. For three days he was mildly delirious, asking quix-
otic questions about butterflies. But when the doctor set
about applying a blister to the back of the Beau's head,
and in preparation ordered a few stray hairs to be shaved
off, the patient sternly objected, on the ground that—
despite his wig—a bald neck would make him look older.
(He never owned to more than fifty.) However, the hair
had to come off, the blister went on, and Brummell con-
valesced.

His first thought was of Ellen, who had this year gone
early to Luc-sur-Mer. Just before she left he had made her
a gift of his Album. "You may, perhaps," he told her, "find
something in my old Album to yawn over, if it does not

actually close your eyes; what it contains was written in other and happier days, and most of them were given to me by the authors *themselves,* long before their minor productions had assumed any other form than that of manuscript; such as the Duchess of Devonshire, poor Byron, Sheridan, and Lords Erskine, and John Townshend—all now peacefully sleeping in their graves." He revealed that the verses unsigned were the "namby-pamby compositions of an unfortunate person who should be nameless, but whom she cut dead during the past several evenings." Now, emerging from another bad illness, Brummell took not so casual a view of his historic Album; he reminded Ellen of its deeper import; "it is but a poor old album indeed, and unworthy as a gift to you; but it has been for years the constant companion and friend of more solitary hours, and has often solaced and diverted me through the many vicissitudes, errors, and disappointments of my life." As he wrote, asking her whether she intended to summer among the mermaids, the Beau told her his hand trembled like the rushes that shaded the *Grave of the Butterfly*. He had been in another world, he said, and found it no paradise. But he sent Ellen a sketch that he had promised her, an unfinished portrait of the Marchioness of Worcester, drawn from memory; it was the first thing he had attempted since his "resurrection."

Brummell was now facing another lonesome summer in Caen. One morning as he was at breakfast in his sitting-room a mouse appeared, and seemed interested in crumbs. The Beau gave it some. It came back the next day, and again and again, and it grew tamer; at length it came to run up Brummell's leg, and took its breakfast out of his hand. Having reached this companionable stage, it actually took the place in his sympathies of Ourika and Jacko, until one day the *garçon*, dusting the room, threw a bootjack with deadly aim, and the mouse was done for. Again Brummell was reduced to a solitude which he could ill support.

Notwithstanding his illnesses, he had never quite given over the thought of another post in the consular service. To a friend influential in London he communicated his hope that he would not be allowed to die like William the Conqueror, in Normandy. Palmerston, indeed, was not permitted to forget that Brummell was still eligible, and a ray of light actually seemed to be dawning when in the drabness of this summer in Caen a message came to the Beau from the Government that he should be prepared to leave. He replied that he hoped the direction would be toward Italy. "If what I have solicited in my answer," he informed Ellen St. Ursain, "should be accorded to me, I shall take up my wallet and staff, and seek the auspicious heaven of that country and climate." In anticipation, he went out to a rousing Carlist dinner with Henri de Vauquelin.

The man to whom Brummell wrote was Earl Granville, now British ambassador in Paris in succession to Stuart de Rothesay. In his letter to Granville, the Beau enclosed one to Palmerston. In due course a reply came to say that there was at present no vacancy either in Italy or elsewhere, except one which Brummell was recommended to refuse. Yet this same vacancy was the one which ten days earlier the Beau had been ordered to prepare for. From a Foreign Office come occasional instructions which are difficult to fathom. But the likelihood is that between the issuance of the original order and the official evasion of it, Palmerston got wind of the physical unfitness of the former Consul at Caen. Brummell saw that he could act only according to the recommendation; he declined the appointment. Being in pain, both physical and mental, he took a good dose of laudanum, and three days later went down to Luc-sur-Mer, to recover from his chagrin in the company of Ellen.

It may be said that Ellen St. Ursain virtually pulled her elderly gallant through the summer, for Brummell several times visited the seaside, staying not at the hotel, which he called a "vile caravanserai," but with De Chazot, another friend from Caen. When in the autumn he returned to his rooms at Mme Fichet's to stay, not only his enfeebled health, but money troubles, recurred to bear him down. At the time Armstrong had come back from England, he brought enough funds to clear away all immediate debts; that had been a glorious release. Beyond this sum, the devoted friends of the Beau had also undertaken to contribute steadily £120 a year for his general maintenance, an amount half again as much as his curtailed salary from the consulate. Now, to the embarrassment of both Armstrong and Brummell, this contribution was falling in arrears. To make matters worse, Leveux of Calais was clamouring for 15,000 francs still due him, an account to be added to 5,000 francs owing to Armstrong, not to mention the bill at the Hôtel d'Angleterre which had run for six months unpaid. While Armstrong had now taken over entire charge of collections and disbursements on behalf of Brummell, Brummell himself did not hesitate to despatch letters to England asking for extra allowances. His wardrobe was so threadbare that Armstrong had to make him a gift of half a dozen shirts, and Brummell, in thanking the faithful Alvanley at this time for a special contribution, was moved to say, "My old friend, King Allen, promised . . . to send me some habiliments for my body, denuded like a new-born infant—and what a Beau I once was!" If anybody could and would induce Allen to act, it was Will Alvanley, who, living on a meagre trust fund himself, never swerved from the man who had once been first among his friends.

No doubt these financial anxieties told heavily against the shattered constitution of Brummell as winter came on, for before the end of the year he suffered a third paralytic attack. Happily it was less severe than the others. He put up a brave front, went out as often as he felt able to go, and the gaieties of the season knew no dampening from his being a part of them. Ellen St. Ursain was now a débutante. That was enough for Beau Brummell. From one *salon* to another she drew him with her "snowy complexion and beautiful eyebrows" as if she had been the Duchess of Devonshire in his palmiest days. To Brummell,

in youth, in middle age, in decrepitude, it was very life to
have one woman to admire, and to give her the best of his
heart, his homage, and his courtliness.

It mattered not so much which woman he chose. So long
as Brummell remained in Caen, the object of his affections
could well continue to be Ellen St. Ursain; but if he should
go away, the lady might better be someone who lived in
the town of his destination. And why should he not go
away? Was there not yet a chance of appointment elsewhere as Consul? Suppose he returned to Calais? Marshall, it was repeatedly rumoured, might at any moment
be giving up his consulship there. Then what of women
friends in Calais? Just before he had left that town for
Caen, he thought he was in love; he had even pretended
to turn Catholic for love. If he went back, he might find
the good lady, who had been involved in that episode,
quite as friendly as Ellen.

In January (1835) a letter from François the valet, now
back in Calais, set Brummell's mind still more in this direction. François mingled petitions with news: his old
master's laundress was demanding money for the keep of
a dog that the Beau had entrusted to her; poor Leleux
might have to give up Le Pauvre Diable; François himself
wanted to know why there was so much delay about a post
to which Brummell had promised to recommend *him*.

"I have done," answered the Beau on January 14, "and
shall again do, all that is in my power to obtain for you the
work which you desire. But there must first be a vacancy.
Nobody likes to *delay* anything. Tell the laundress that I

shall have some money sent her by you, for the board of 'Mouton,' as soon as I receive it, so that she may always take care of that poor animal. If the affairs of M. Leleux grow worse, and he has to part with his house, try to get hold of Loro the parrot and keep him for me. I am told that M. Marshall thinks of leaving Calais, having been offered a better consulate. If you hear anything authentic about that, let me know at once. My best remembrances to your wife and to François your father-in-law.

(P.S.) "M. Dabert, of Paris, has written me that he has a bill of 380 francs accepted by me, and due the 18th of this month, which will be presented to me here. Tell Valobra (agent in Calais) that I entrusted to him a little golden box with medallions in enamel, the resale of which should have closed that claim, and that I shall not pay the bill in question before I know what has become of the said box, and another in papier-maché which I gave him for a model."

In this letter neither the question of the snuffbox bought five years before in Paris, nor the question of the dog and the parrot, was as indicative as his tenacious expectancy that Calais might one day see him again. He was as anxious for Marshall the consul to withdraw from that town as when he, Brummell, had been living in Le Pauvre Diable. There was the wretched Beau in Caen, stricken with paralysis thrice, and still believing that he was fit to be a consul, even reckoning, perhaps, that if he was too infirm, Palmerston, busy juggling nations in the Foreign Office, would have no means of knowing about any such infirmity. Was not Beau Brummell still curtsied to, invited, petted by the ladies? Did not even a young girl, Ellen St. Ursain, seek his patronage, accept his gifts, and welcome his affectionate friendship? Why should the celebrated Brummell, a man approved of by the King, still not dignify a consular post?

But early in the spring of 1835 Ellen St. Ursain was setting out for England. The news fell upon Brummell like a blow. It seemed to him that he could bear paralysis, debt, penury, anything but the loss of her. "You are going away," he wrote to her. "It is a melancholy reflection for me that this is probably the last time I shall ever again write to you. Some day, perhaps ere long, you will read more of me, with the rest of the world who may give themselves the trouble." But the Beau was making midnight out of dusk; he was not to lose his much-beloved *protégée* so utterly, so swiftly; he was only in the throes of spontaneous pessimism. Almost before he knew it he was writing Ellen again at twice the length: "Inclosed I send you letters . . . two of my oldest friends, high in their office at Court . . . you will be favourably received in the quarter to which they will present you. . . . My nerves are too shattered, and my rheumatism too inveterate, to enable me to call and take leave." In this last sentiment Brummell did revert to his original gloom, but not so much for reasons of health as for that reason which had prevented him, a few years before, from saying good-bye to Mme St. Ursain in the Rue des Carmes.

After Ellen had arrived across the Channel, and settled

into her new life in Sussex, she sent Brummell a letter in
the care of a naval chaplain who was going to Caen. He
brought back word to the Beau that Ellen was looking
"charmingly well." Brummell was almost disappointed.
He waited a month, and hearing no further from her, sent
a letter in April to say that he was not inquiring after the
cherry-ripe cheeks of a dairy-maid. Ellen had said that she
was rather surfeited with discussions in Sussex upon animals, agriculture, and politics. The Beau sympathized, and
urged her to get in touch, if she could, with his acquaintance in town, who were doubtless held there by the zenith
of the London season. Meantime, she might read a few
English books which he prescribed. "You do not know,"
he concluded, "the good your letter has done me."

It was well that it had. Ten days after he had written this
letter, in the morning, whilst he was still asleep in bed,
Brummell was roughly awakened. A bailiff stood over
him, with a writ of arrest, sworn out by Jacques Leveux
for 15,000 francs. Unless he could pay that sum he must go
to prison forthwith. The Beau, after taking some time to
make sure that this was not a dream, raised indignant and
vociferous protests. That was no use. Then he asked to be
left decently alone for a few minutes, in order to dress.
The bailiff and his guards denied him any such privilege.
For the first time in his life, Beau Brummell had to dress
in a hurry.

While Madame Fichet had kindly dispatched a servant
to a number of his friends, in an effort to raise the money,
the sum was too disconcerting, as Brummell well knew,

and he himself sent out another servant to call a coach, although he had no money to pay for it. Then, taking leave of Mme Fichet as if he were going to the scaffold, the Beau bade her give especial care to his papers. "They are the only things I possess," said he, "to which I attach particular value . . . when I am gone, pray collect them, and lock them up with your own hands."

The fiacre was announced, and the bailiff and his two guards escorted Brummell down the stairs. Outside, the Hôtel d'Angleterre was literally surrounded by gendarmes, lest the rheumatic and paralytic prisoner make a dash for liberty. In the crowd of onlookers, it was said that this ring of police was a compliment to the official dignity which Brummell had once enjoyed as Consul. But all were agreed that no debtor in the history of Caen "had ever been so handsomely arrested."

CHAPTER XVI

A BEAU IN PRISON

1835

AT THE prison, Brummell was pushed into a large cell
which already contained three "common" inmates. These
men slept upon low truckle-beds on wheels, had no chairs,
and were obliged to be content with a stone floor—perhaps
not too severe a hardship in the warm weather now approaching. In honour of a distinguished guest the custo-
dian put a chair in, for the exclusive use of the Beau. But
when in the course of the morning a friend came to con-
dole, he found Brummell depressed beyond measure,
struggling between humiliation and rage, and able to
speak only brokenly: "they have put me with all the *common* people—I am surrounded by the greatest villains—
have nothing but prison fare." Why should he not have a
nice private one-man prison, with meals sent in? His
friend, fearing that poor Brummell in this state of mind
might suffer another stroke, which would finish him, ran
off to see what he could do.

Nor, as in previous troubles, did the ladies forsake their favourite. One of them sent him a comforting note, with a promise of assistance. "In Prison," Brummell agonizedly dated his reply, "6th May, 1835 I still breathe, though I am not of the living—the state of utter abstraction in which I have been during the last thirty hours yet clouds my every sense. . . . Heaven bless you for all your good devotedness in remembering me at such a moment. I have been the victim of a villain, who has closed upon me without giving me the remotest intimation of his designs. I am perfectly innocent of anything bearing the least dishonourable construction in this unhappy affair; and if I was not deserving of the interest you express . . . I would not demand it."

His "demands," expressed likewise to the friend who had called earlier, in due time fortunately reached the ear of those in power, in particular, of a judge who knew him. The prison was full; but this good man freed Brummell from rubbing elbows with the "greatest villains," and arranged for him to share during the day a room occupied by M. Godefroi, editor of *Ami de la Vérité,* a Legitimist paper of Caen. Godefroi had been too truthful in printing his views on behalf of the Carlists. It was great luck for the Beau that he gained a room-mate so in sympathy with his own adopted politics; they would not lack matter for indignant conversation. At night, a bed was placed for Brummell in the narrow corridor of a floor above, rarely used, but up forty stone steps, no small climb for a paralytic. The worst of it, however, was that the barred window of this corridor gave upon the courtyard of the women prisoners, whose ribald cackling soon after sunrise demolished the sleep of the Beau. If he sought relief by descending to the room of Godefroi, and looked through *his* window on the other side, he only heard the pandemonium of the men prisoners who, condemned to the galleys, were roaring about, clanking their fetters, laughing like mad, and singing songs slightly more obscene than those of the women.

In the question of food, Brummell found his new circumstances equally trying. He thought that by managing to have his dinners fetched from the Hôtel d'Angleterre, he could subsist through the day upon coffee and bread at breakfast, omitting lunch, and thus sidestep the grim diet of the prisoners. But the Fichets, despite explicit and repeated commands given them by friends of the Beau, sent him, as late as half-past six, when he was famished, "not sufficient for the poor cat that kept him company." He complained bitterly to Armstrong. "One solitary chop," said Brummell, "about the size of a half-crown, enveloped in a quire of greasy paper, and the skeleton of a pigeon, a bird I could never fancy . . . (and) half a dozen potatoes . . . after a fast of twelve hours. It is not . . . the fault of the son, but the stinginess of the *père et mère*. . . . If they transmit me nothing more solid . . . I shall be reduced to borrow . . . the *soupe maigre* of my neighbours the brigands."

But his very first request, as soon as he had battled with these problems of sleep and food, was for a mirror. Henri de Ste. Marie, the young Carlist, called and showed him the "affection of a brother," partly demonstrated by the gift of means with which to buy this mirror, for Brummell had no money at all. Ste. Marie said that Armstrong had sent also to the prison a bottle of *esprit de savon*. It had not arrived, and the Beau insisted that either the Fichets had intercepted it or the chemist had ignored the order. He asked that Armstrong let him have three towels every six days, "for I cannot procure even a clout to rub myself down in this nauseous place." Again, every three days he required money to pay for breakfast, brandy, and candles. It was furthermore essential that Armstrong proceed to the bedroom of Brummell in the hotel, and send all waistcoats, drawers, and pantaloons, remaining in a chest therein, as well as "a bootjack that shuts up," to be found "under the small commode in the sitting-room." Above all, he missed his tweezers, his silver shaving dish, and his jug and basin. His one luxury was a fire in June, although the weather itself was now hot. Godefroi noticed that after dinner the Beau pulled his chair so close to the fire that he almost sat in it, and there he stayed by the hour, rubbing his legs with his hands, to alleviate his "rheumatism."

One by one the indispensables of his toilet arrived at the prison, despatched by Armstrong, by Henri de Ste. Marie, or by various adoring ladies who knew the fastidiousness of Brummell in dressing. This process the editor Godefroi watched with astonishment and fascination. Within a very few days, Godefroi observed, the Beau had hired one of the prisoners—Paul Lepine, a former drummer in the army, now in gaol for having raised a rumpus in a public-house—to be his *valet de chambre*. In choosing Lepine, who was strong and brisk, Brummell as an old officer himself knew what he was about. Part of this valet's duty was to bring up each day fifteen quarts of water and two of milk, and to mix them for the bath of his master in a "vast washbasin" which had been taken out of an antique washstand and sent to the prison for the Beau soon after his arrival. Alongside this bath Lepine had to put in place not only a shaving-kit but a dressing-case full of phials containing essences and cosmetics. "He shaves himself every day!" exclaimed Godefroi, "every day he washes himself all over, in every part of his body . . . delicacy unheard of in the annals of the prison!"

If it was a problem for Brummell thus to overcome the restrictions and inconveniences of prison, his life within stone walls was at least not monotonous. In the middle of one night he was roused from sleep by a succession of men excitedly edging past his bed, the space between it and the outer wall being so cramped that they could get through only by going sidewise. Outdoors, just beyond the women's court, a great fire was raging in a timber-yard, and these men were the prison guards on their way to take up their stations in the garret. Brummell drowsily drew on his dressing-gown and followed them. Sparks and bits of burning wood kept dropping on the roof of the prison, whilst the women prisoners, terrified in their cells underneath by flakes of falling fire and by the glare of the flames, sent up screams and curses in their fear of being roasted alive. Brummell, crouching in the cold at a loophole, watched the spectacle until after two o'clock, when it subsided. As he tried to make his way back through the dark garret he got entangled in washing-lines which extended across it like a web; trying to wriggle free, he tied himself up all the more; calling out at the top of his lungs for help, he went unheard, because the turnkeys, still on the roof stamping out sparks, were themselves shouting to one another. Poor Brummell sank down upon the floor and resumed his shivering, until at last the men came back on their return and unbound him. On the next day he was not only stiff from rheumatism but sore from the cords which had bound him. Normandy in the Middle Ages had been called "the country of the gibbet." "Sir," said the Beau to Godefroi, "last night George Brummell almost died like a true Norman."

But he did not remain long battered in spirits, whatever the state of his legs. The good hostesses of Caen, in their unflagging sentimental attachment, thought of him in no sense a prisoner, but as an invalid, and they sent him hampers of wine, punch, jellies, and *patés*. Sometimes they all sent the same thing. "You are always good and amiable," he replied to one of them, "but you will be the best of beings if you will have the kindness to renew your benefaction in the form of cake . . . it is my principal nourishment, for the niggardly repast they usually send me from the hotel would not . . . sustain even a *demoiselle* lost in love. I may represent an additional claim upon your bounty . . . my companion Minette, the black cat, who is in the straw at my feet, having produced three hungry kittens—

her delicate state disdains the unleavened bread of the prison. I have another favourite . . . a spider about the size of a bee, which I have so far made sociable that he comes regularly to me from his web every morning to demand his breakfast. You must forgive then my anxiety for the sustenance of these familiar friends, as well as my own."

On the other hand he sometimes grew petulant over the dreariness of his captivity, looked gift-horses in the mouth, and rejected them irritably. One of the things which depressed him was the novels of Bulwer Lytton. "If *The Student* had not belonged to you," Brummell told a kindly English lady who sent in that book, "I should not have been able to wade through ten of its pages; it is equally barren of incident, definition, or plain language. . . . When you have again something more worthy of cheating miserable hours . . . you will send it to me." This good woman the Beau knew well enough to talk to as he liked, honestly and outspokenly, and while he deprecated one thing of hers, he in the same letter was all gratitude for another, such as the fact that she was lending her own servant to fetch Brummell's dinners to him on time, from the hotel. The prisoner, "still sustained with hopes of emancipation from these disgusting regions," took care to make his letters to this gracious person chatty enough, and not all about himself. "My friend Godefroi, the editor," he went on, "from whose table I address you, is looking with anxiety at the ink, to continue paragraphs that will probably prolong his detention here ten years longer. He is really a good-hearted man, and does everything to distract me." It turned out that Godefroi in fact was not the real editor, but a sort of editor's editor, a man hired to go to prison whenever *"L'Ami"* published anything for which the Government demanded a human sacrifice.

When June came, and Brummell had passed an even month in the lock-up without hearing from anyone in England to whom he had appealed, the fears which had swamped him on the day of his arrest engulfed him again: that he "would never leave these abhorred walls alive." He had spent his Saturday morning in a diversion not calculated to encourage him, the "forbidding study" of the human face which infested the court beneath his window. "Groups of these wretches," the Beau informed a certain hostess of Caen (all of his correspondents except Armstrong and one other were women) "condemned of heaven and earth, attracted by the sun, have been sauntering in their chains within ten paces of me; and for want of more palatable resource, I sat contemplating their hideous physiognomies, till I was recalled from my visions of the fabled Rinaldo Rinaldini and his bandits, by one of them exclaiming, 'What's he looking at, that villain of a lord?' " The Beau backed away from the barred opening. The rebuke set him thinking about those friends of his in England, men who indeed might not be found, though they must by this time know of his plight. "I speak," he went on to the hostess to whom he was writing, "only of those who during my more prosperous days were zealously served and assisted by me—to those it was as much, I con-

sidered, a duty as a necessity to appeal, at such an annihi-
lating crisis."

In the morning it was, mainly, that these thoughts over-
came him, for between two and four in the afternoon
Brummell held his levée, when, immaculately dressed
by Lepine the drummer, white neckcloth well tied, hat
smoothed, boots glistening, he descended to the debtors'
courtyard and received in high spirits his numerous visitors
both English and French. This yard was separated from
that of the thieves by a partition so thin that the pic-
turesque chatter on the other side easily came through, and
helped to entertain the callers. These sympathetic individ-
uals might hear from Brummell of "Mazoyer the Bear," an
evil creature with pointed teeth and burly shoulders, condemned for life to the galleys for trying to murder a turnkey. The Beau, on his way to the lavatory of the prison—
which was purposely left open, without a door—might
encounter Mazoyer, who liked to jostle him. So long as
the visitors kept off the subject of Brummell's release, they
were safe; if they unwarily mentioned it, he dropped his
gaiety and wept, from anger, disappointment and chagrin.
Sometimes, then, he found his best moments in the courtyard after the levée, when only the debtors remained. Of
these, Brummell's favourite was M. Bassy, an old butler.
Bassy had been in a great family before the Revolution,
and he seemed as distinguished as the Beau himself both
in conversation and in agreeable manners.

As the dinners from the Hôtel d'Angleterre grew progressively worse, the famished prisoner now decided to order them from a restaurant nearby. In a very few days he found them more meagre still. Instead of the skeleton of a pigeon, they sent him only half the skeleton of one; for a sweet, ten unripe cherries with one pitiful biscuit "that looked like a bad halfpenny." Brummell, using all his residual strength to lift a pen, could only beseech Armstrong once more to intervene. Armstrong again was forgetting the towels, and for two days running the Beau had only soiled shirts to rub himself down with. "I should be loath," said he, "to give up the ghost from famine or filthiness." He begged Armstrong to go back to the vacated rooms in the hotel, fish out more waistcoats and pantaloons, a pair of patched boots, and above all, from the *armoire,* a small glass bottle of Macouba snuff. "Pray tell my friends," he concluded, "that I am very fond of strawberries."

He even dreamed that someone had sent him from England a note of assistance, and that a friend in Caen, having received it, had held it back. "When my Cerberus," he complained to this man, "unbarred my cell at seven this morning, I scrutinized anxiously his iron hand, expecting the cheering sight of a scrap of paper, and even *I* asked him impatiently if no letter had been left at the wicket for me. He shook his gory locks . . . clanked his bouquet of keys in my awakened face, and left me in disappointment. Was my nightly vision merely the effect of a distempered brain . . . or have you really received a word . . . ?" A little later on this same morning his old acquaintance, M. Target, the Préfet, called, and said he had not known Brummell was in the prison, and hoped he was "at his ease." "Oh the Saracen!" exclaimed the distraught Beau. "What reptiles are those who administer the justice and dynasty of this country!"

While he feared they might be as bad in England, he now decided, in July, that his only recourse was to send Armstrong over there a second time on a mission of mercy. For two months Brummell had lived on donations from his compatriots in Caen, together with a gift of 500 francs from Granville, the ambassador in Paris. A number of French friends subscribed still more, which Englishmen of the colony declined on behalf of the Beau, thinking that after his release he ought to feel free of any such obligations. In any case, the total sum would have fallen far short of Leveux's demand. The only hope that remained was for the success of Armstrong, who, early in this month, embarked again for London.

Even during this suspense which wavered toward despair, Brummell found amusement early one morning in a prison episode, when one Auvray, a pickpocket, whom the Beau called "a remarkably good-looking animal, mild, too, in his manners," scaled the twelve-foot wall which separated him from the women's courtyard, and gained the top, although he had fifteen pounds of fetters on his leg. Then, Auvray dropped down on the other side and ran up to the women's common room, where they were all dressing. The women giggled, but too loud, and the turnkeys heard. In a twinkling Auvray was surrounded by six uniforms. When they attempted to clamp fifteen more pounds of iron upon his other leg, he fought, striking out right and left. From across the court, Brummell and Godefroi looked on. "That man is brave," remarked the Beau. "In a siege he would have been a hero. I pity him." Auvray submitted only after a gaoler had hit him with a bunch of keys, and drawn blood. Brummell said later: "I shall remember to my last hour his cries and struggles, to avoid the additional irons that were forced upon his arms and throat . . . he was quieted to insensibility, and conducted to his eternal subterranean cell. And yet I exist in close adjacency to these outcasts!"

But to this existence there was another side as well, the high mark of which occurred not long after, when Baron de Bresmenil, a rich Carlist of the community, was brought in to serve a sentence of five days. Bresmenil had been guilty of treason. Driving down the street in his carriage, he had responded to a clamorous supporter of Louis Philippe with cries of *"Vive Henri Cinq!"* Now, the Baron decided to celebrate his incarceration by ordering a grand dinner from Longuet's for a chosen few, and he allowed Brummell, before all, to select his own favourite delicacies. The chief guest invited from outside was another Carlist, also a close friend of the Beau, Comte de Roncherolles, who brought with him a bottle of cognac d'Andaye, of which he knew Brummell to be extremely fond. As for the food, when the Beau had gathered his recollections of Longuet's successes, he asked for mushrooms, truffles, lobster, and *glacé* fruits, while for wine he stipulated

Chambertin and Lafitte. Three young thieves waited upon the table. When the coffee came on, Brummell, who had been keeping the party in an uproar with his anecdotes, thought of the delicious cognac, and cried to one of the thieves, "Fetch the bottle." Likewise Bassy, the old butler, and Godefroi, who were the other inside guests, equally anticipated this crowning touch.

The young thief went out for the brandy, but did not come back; another was sent after him, and also failed to return; when the third thief disappeared, and seemed unable to produce either the brandy or his comrades, the diners, growing a little annoyed at last, shouted for the lot. They all came in, to announce solemnly that the cognac had vanished. Bresmenil, enraged, got up and threatened to throw the three thieves bodily out of the window, barred though the windows were. Brummell, grievously disappointed and slightly tipsy into the bargain, followed suit, and flung out his arms toward the trembling waiters. "Wretches!" he cried, "have you anything to complain of? We have treated you only too well. Villains, give me back my *pousse-café!*" Tears of anger started from his eyes—the Beau had many tears to shed in this prison—whilst another of the party went out to make a search. Upon returning, this man unfolded tidings which the thieves had been afraid to disclose: the turnkey, one Brillant, to whose care the cognac had been entrusted, had opened the bottle and drunk the whole of it, and was lying dead asleep in a corner, with the precious bottle flat on the floor beside him.

Otherwise this dinner, by the cordial liberality of Baron
de Bresmenil, and the perfect conviviality of all five who
partook of it, was the great event in the prison life of
Brummell, who for days following was sustained upon
the very remembrance of it. So revivified, he was able to
watch with calm the melancholy sight, shortly thereafter,
of the departure of a group of the harder criminals for the
galleys. There were Mazoyer the Bear, Auvray the ladies'
man, Coursiére the celebrated thief from Paris, and Ansieu,
who in a fight with a turnkey had lost part of his nose by
a sabre cut. As the gaolers hammered more irons on to
the legs of these men, the men lyrically cursed judges,
turnkeys, and guards, added a chorus of their own in the
thieves' language and, giving the solo parts to Coursiére,
all joined in the refrain *"C'est au bagne, au bagne, au
bagne, amis, nous y allons."* Brummell and Godefroi looked
on. "I thought," said the Beau, "this morning I was at the
forge of Vulcan: what infernal music! My ears are deaf-
ened with it!" They went down into the prison yard,
where these galley-slaves were leaving from. Brummell
stepped forward to one of them, called Juel, and gave him
two francs, for the manners of Juel had been much superior
to those of any of the others.

With his mind thus occupied not only by the Baron's
party but by the going away of the prisoners, the Beau had
almost forgotten to think about what might be happening
to Charles Armstrong in London. It was now the middle
of July, and Armstrong, pursuing the same methods as he
had used upon his first visit, had in a very business-like

way gone from door to door begging on commission. At every move he was backed up by the Duke of Beaufort and by the ever-reliable Lord Alvanley. General Upton not only contributed again himself, but caused Sir Herbert Taylor, who was close to the royal household, to lay the urgency of Armstrong's errand before the King. Unlike his elder brother the Duke of York, William IV had seen but little of Brummell in England; the King only knew that he had given his consent to the appointment of Brummell as consul; but the King donated £100. This generous act influenced Palmerston, who added £200 from the Treasury, in view of the loss to the Beau when the consulate at Caen was abolished. Armstrong then collected about £250 more, in gifts of £25 each, from a number of men who included the Duke of Devonshire, Lord Sefton, General Grosvenor, Colonel Howard, Colonel Damer, Standish again, and Charles Greville. Also Greville combined with Alvanley, Sefton, and Beaufort to give an undertaking that Brummell should be looked after annually henceforth.

Having now £600 odd in pocket, Armstrong jubilantly recrossed to Caen. This sum was enough to pay off Leveux outright, to the last franc. But Leveux did not get it all. Armstrong speedily made a compromise with the banker of Calais, and used the greater part of the funds remaining to settle the more pressing bills in Caen.

On the morning of July 21st, the solicitor of Jacques Leveux turned up at the prison, and notified Brummell that he was at liberty to leave as soon as he pleased.

CHAPTER XVII

THE LAST RECEPTION

1835-1838

THE NEWS of his freedom fell upon Brummell almost like a shock. For two and a half months he had been shut up, and in that time, seemingly so long drawn out, he had adopted a scheme of life which in spite of his grumbling, his meagre rations, his longing to break away, he had almost got used to. Indeed, membership in a prison was something not without its moments both dramatic and diverting. True, he had written only the other day to one of his dowagers, now at Luc-sur-Mer for the season, of "the death-warrant of his internment" within stone walls. But now that his resurrection had come, what was he to do with it?

To his companions in the prison the Beau on this twenty-first of July betrayed no feeling one way or the other. He appeared to be as calm, as unperturbed, as serene, as on the famous occasion in London of Mrs. Thompson's ball, to which he had not been invited, but having got there, presented a card to Mrs. Johnson's. "Dear me, how very unfortunate!" Brummell had superbly answered on being challenged by the hostess. "But you know, Johnson and Thompson—and Thompson and Johnson—are really so much the same kind of thing." So now, surrounded in the debtors' court by the less fortunate who were congratulating him upon his freedom, the Beau seemed to say, "Release and police—and police and release—what is the difference?" With the utmost leisure he assembled his various belongings, and packed them up, not leaving the prison until five o'clock that afternoon.

Nevertheless it was very pleasant indeed to get back to his sitting-room in the Hôtel d'Angleterre, to come again into possession of his clock, his vases, his brown candlesticks, the brass-ribbed mahogany box with "G.B." on its top, the box with birds under glass worked by the Duchess of York, his own water-jug and ample basin, above all, his old green velvet armchair. It might be a good plan to open his trunks, in the little room adjoining, to see whether everything was there, or to explore the cupboard of his armoire, and certainly the chest of drawers in the bedroom. Brummell, Beau Brummell, must in any case change at once. For he was told of a grand *soireé* this very evening in the house of the General of the Province, that man to whom the great Comte Molé of Paris had presented him. Upon the whole, Brummell thought it desirable to go, and after dressing elegantly, and dining quietly, he set forth.

Seldom, in all the pageant of his career, had the Beau keyed himself up to an entry more gratifying. Far from

being afflicted with any sense of ignominy, he thought he
could feel, and be, quite stately in his reappearance, which
to him was exoneration. The company had not heard of
his release. When he walked regally in through the door
of the ballroom, gasps of surprise greeted him on every
hand, while those who were standing strode toward him,
and those who were sitting rose up to a man. The Beau
advanced into the centre. Complacent, nonchalant, utterly
gracious, he bowed his thanks, and spoke: "Gentlemen, I
am very obliged for your kindness, and charmed to find
myself once more amongst you. I can assure you that to-
day is the happiest day of my life, for I have come out of
prison, and—I have been eating some salmon."

In truth Brummell was at the top of his spirits, a man
new-made, so far as the quality of cheerfulness might carry
him. From this hour the thought of the prison as a shelter,
a refuge, which had perhaps momentarily haunted him,
did not recur. A reunion with his valiant messenger Armstrong, who sang a melody of bills paid and accounts
wiped out, was enough to send the Beau jauntily down
Rue St. Jean to buy partridges for his friends both in gaol
and out. To a hostess of Caen to whom he stood under past
obligations he described himself, a few days after the
soirée, as "in the meridian of sunshiny liberty." The note
to her which accompanied the birds he began, "A little
covey of partridges, living this morning at dawn, take
wing without wind to your kitchen." His own hopes
freshened, he thought that he himself might to his "effec-
tual good" take wing from Caen, and that "time, and

other suns, and other scenes and occupations" would trans-
form him. In this fancy lay yet a fleeting ghost of his desire for a consulate in Italy. Then he gave to Madame a
sprightly account of the fire in the timberyard, which he
had seen burn down whilst in prison; of how in the midst
of the tumult the chief hangman, in a "hoarse bewailing
voice," fearful that the whole prison would catch fire, was
lamenting not the danger to the prisoners, but the loss of
his beloved guillotine, which in his time had presented
him with twenty-three human heads. Brummell, after thus
expanding upon dead partridges and dead men, implored
Madame to come that evening "for a charitable hour" to
another party; the General, festive soul that he was, had
announced a reception at the barracks.

More partridges the Beau sent to the good Godefroi,
who unhappily lay still in chains. And he sent his amiable
remembrances to his other friends in the prison, together
with news of one released at the same time as himself:
Paul Lepine, his late valet. Not often had Brummell written in more ebullient vein: "Blame, my dear Monsieur
Godefroi, the rascally chef, and not my faithful memory,
for having so long delayed my gift of a little covey of partridges, nested within their wall of crust. The jackanapes
told me they were too young to be stuffed into a *paté*, and
not worthy of meriting the attention of a cultivated ap-
petite. . . . Have the goodness to pay my respects to the gallant father Bassy, and make him partake at least of a
thigh; that will be perhaps the only feminine charm that
he can caress in his retreat.

"I had, I assure you, the praiseworthy intention of visiting you these last few days—but a judgment quite unexpected of my former creditor rheumatism prevented me from taking a step toward your house. I beg you to prostrate myself, I and my tender regards, to the velvet pads of Mademoiselle Minette; she is among my dearest acquaintance in that terrestrial pandemonium. Give my respects also to . . . Adolph Lavigne, and his twin Baptiste; do not forget Nestor Frémont, nor Brillant, that spoiled child of spirituous drink.

"You will be pleased to hear that we have recently seen perched upon the coach, en route to Honfleur, our late staff, the marshal Paul Lepine, gay as the carriage which was transporting him, the Swallow! clasping in his arm of Achilles the beautiful waist of a Princess of his own kind and capture, whose august head was crowned with three feathers, red as her glorious bashful cheeks. Thus, from the mire, rise progressively, the heroes of your country!"

Here was a lively inaugural to freedom regained. The Beau celebrated with a benign salute to friends both new and old. Nor did he stop there. Any passing traveller who came to dine at the Hôtel d'Angleterre could draw from Brummell a succession of stories in exchange for a bottle of champagne, and many a bottle, which the Beau himself could not pay for, but still coveted, was passed across the table d'hôte in this fashion. The more renowned for his late imprisonment, Brummell was one of the "sights" of the neighbourhood, to be gazed at by trippers, like the

Cafarelli, the tapestry of Bayeux, or the tomb of Matilda. It might be said that during the rest of the summer he lived upon his notoriety. Now that the Beau was back upon the premises of the hotel, the Fichets could no longer feed him with the "skeleton of a pigeon," but had to let him choose like the others from a very good menu of twenty dishes. Indeed when a rich tripper came in, the Beau lived twice as well as that, drawing as it were a royalty from his great work: personal history. Where was his old exclusiveness, so formidable in London? At the Hôtel d'Angleterre he gave it all, for as long and as often as he could, to his palate.

If in resuming cordialities with friends in Caen whom he had not seen since May he encountered no difficulty of moment, Brummell now began to wonder how he would fare with Ellen St. Ursain, who was still in England. It had been a matter of pride with him not to write her whilst he was in prison, although by neglecting her for so long he risked her resentment. At last he heard indirectly that she was not only "in dudgeon" for this neglect, but that she was returning to Caen within a month's time. The Beau then sent a letter to Sussex. It was a flowery elaboration of this line: "I have not possessed a stray sentence of interest to impart to you." Anything he might have told her, he said, would have been as monotonous as the Sorrows of Werther, and it was much more important for her to believe, now, that for all his silence her "lamented absence" had never for an hour escaped his "best thoughts."

However Ellen may have received this explanation,

Brummell found, as soon as she came back in the autumn, that he had something still to do to regain her amiability. Busily he began to make sketches for her. He drew three, disliked them, tore them up, and began again on another kind of paper. Then he had to write to her about his efforts. "Let me but still have health," he declared, "and you shall, without vanity, be contented with me." Searching in his portfolio for old pieces more worthy, he took out a crayon of the Duchess of Rutland. "Pray have a respect for her," he asked Ellen, "and protect her, now she is no more . . . do not let her be approached by sacrilegious eyes and hands." Some of Ellen's friends he had confidence in. "But there are others who sometimes surround you, and I can assure you, when the original was living, she was never profaned by the familiar contact of people of that temper."

But it was inevitable that Ellen St. Ursain, now a young woman of nineteen, should have come back from England in a frame of mind not altogether the same as that in which she left Caen. She was not quite so yielding to the didactics of a man nearly forty years her senior. Her friends were her friends. When the Beau went to visit her a few nights later he thought the antics of the young people in her company resembled a circus. "Were you," he later inquired, "during your absence in England exposed to the intercourse of any compeers resembling it?" The spectacle of these creatures drove him to his laudanum bottle, after which, he said, he intended to surpass the "prolonged doze of the Seven Sleepers." But he sent her a new drawing just the same, an "original," told her he was going on with two others "in all the colours of the rainbow," and begged her to be "the same amiable creature that she used to be," that their friendship might continue always.

As winter came on, Brummell reverted to his usual daily course: two hours in the tub, two hours at his mirror, reading, drawing, notes to the ladies, dinner, either a *soirée*, a whist-party, or evening tea with a friend, and to bed. His hostesses kept beseeching him for relics of his days in England. While it was not an agreeable task to him to "disturb the dormant remembrance" of those days, he did find pleasure in making the gifts. Upon one dowager and her daughter he bestowed two note-keepers, a green one embroidered by that early love of his, Lady Sarah Savile, and a dove-coloured one, like the eyes of her whose work it was, Lady Foley, the Duke of Leinster's daughter. What else could he do with these things? Who else wanted them? They were keepsakes, but often only sad reminders. He let them go, in exchange for hospitality received.

But this hospitality, luncheons, dinners, or what not, had no bearing upon the income of the Beau. The arrangement which Armstrong had made with Brummell's friends in London was that they were to remit to Armstrong himself £120 a year, half of which he was to pay to M. Fichet as annual maintenance, at the hotel; the rest was for wine, fires, laundry, clothes, illnesses, and whatever else Brummell might within reason require. It made no financial difference to him whether he took meals at the Angleterre or accepted invitations outside. Now if he had had any capacity whatever for economy he might have managed, in a country like France, on the £60 each year at his disposal; during his consulship, after Leveux of Calais had taken his share of the salary, the Beau had only £80 for the whole of his expenses, out of which he had to defray his subsistence. That is, the £120 now provided for him was half again as much more than he had tried to live upon when he was consul. Even so, Brummell as he neared the age of fifty-eight was almost impermeable to the idea of subjecting himself to experiments in thrift. But as an act of heroic renunciation—after disciplinary talks by Armstrong full of warning—the Beau had reduced the magnitude of his laundry to one complete change of linen a day. Other luxuries of dress—scent, Parisian blacking, oil for his wigs, primrose gloves, he declined to give over; they were his life.

Without them, how could he make himself presentable at the *soirées* of the Marquise de Serans? A man in society either gets the essential cosmetics to use or stays at home; for evening parties, which run on for five or six hours, one must dress not only fitly but durably. "To-day I am too much subdued," Brummell on the morning after one of them wrote to a lady, "by the shadows of Vallombrosa at Madame de Serans' last night, to hold up my head if I saw you. I shall take to rouge if this goes on." Again, after a New Year's Eve party which brought in the year 1836, he wrote the next morning to another lady admirer: "Mine was 'The Rake's Progress' last night; and I have but this instant escaped from sepulchre, while the sexton was asleep. I am still in my shroud, and incapacitated of writing to the living in this twilight." It was a pace which he had to dress up to.

For a year after the Beau left prison his credit was good, and to obtain the requisites of dress in the amount that he used he ran up bills with never a thought. Tradesmen extracted what they could from Armstrong. But by summer Brummell could count on his fingers the francs which he could find in his own pockets. In November, Mulet, the bootmaker, tried to collect of Armstrong something more than half of an enormous bill for the Beau's blacking, and, being refused, he stormed in upon his debtor "in an insolent manner" and threatened suit. "Send me the money," implored Brummell of Armstrong, "on *my own account* ... it will utterly destroy me to see a bailiff enter my room, or assault me in the street. I will enter into any promise with you upon the subject of this damned polish ... if you will instantly enable me to pay this scoundrel."

Armstrong demanded that his troublesome client give up that blacking once and for all, and when Brummell agreed, the banker sent him a "reward" of twenty francs and also silenced Mulet. But in a twinkling the Beau, while foregoing his polish, was down again to two *sous,* and in more distress because of a claim lodged against him in December by the lottery-office of Caen. A further pathetic appeal to Armstrong fetched from that gentleman an answer that could only be called stern and uncompromising. The Beau responded, "You have hurt me more than I can express by your note to me this morning. I put down this infernal debt to the lottery-office because I would conceal nothing from you . . . if you overlook it, and still promise me your services, both here and in England, I give you my sacred word of honour I will never again commit such an extravagant and senseless error. I will endeavour to write, the instant I am restored to calmness, to the Duke of Devonshire. . . . It would afflict me to suppose that my immediate unfortunate affairs interfered with your better interests in other quarters." These "interests"—which Brummell in exchange for the continuous indulgence of Armstrong was trying to forward by way of the Duke—were an appointment for Armstrong to a vice-consulship in Caen.

But the agent, holding the whip-hand, insisted upon yet further economies; he thought a clean shirt and neckcloth every day the maddest prodigality. The Beau was horrified. But at this very moment one of the ladies of Caen happened to suggest to him that his looks would be improved if he wore a black cravat. When Brummell asked Armstrong about that, the worried agent was only too enthusiastic in furnishing the means to buy one, and on the next day the Beau instituted, as his permanent neckwear for promenading Rue St. Jean, a black silk handkerchief. His great invention, his starched cravat, white, spotless, and exquisitely folded, was henceforth bequeathed to his imitators.

Having made this concession, the Beau early in 1837 thought he was in order in asking for a shawl dressing-gown, suitable for wearing in the winter. Armstrong sent him an ordinary cotton one. Upon opening the parcel in his hotel, Brummell was enraged, and strode to the window and flung the thing out; it landed like a parachute on the passengers and horses of the Bayeux coach waiting below. What good was a thin cotton gown when all his linen was itself wearing out? "Don't Armstrong," he protested. "It is . . . with the greatest reluctance I am compelled to solicit occasional assistance . . . I told you the truth yesterday, when I represented the abject condition of my linen . . . I have not a single shirt that will hang on my back, nor are my socks and drawers in a better state . . . I would rather be damned than ask for anything that was not readily accorded . . . and yet, during the last two months, I have not possessed five francs for the most indispensable purposes. I am in ignorance as to those who, through your mediation, have befriended me on the other side of the water . . . therefore I am unable . . . to make them acquainted with my continued destitute situation—the belly indeed is filled, but the hand is empty, and the back and limbs unprovided for. I have not heard from any one of them, excepting as you know from my sister; and I could almost suppose she was laughing at me . . . 'she hopes that I have everything comfortable about me.' Surely . . . I had better immediately write to her, to Alvanley, and to others; they may imagine I am living comparatively in comfort, if not at ease, and the positive reverse is the case; and I see it cannot last long with me." Little enough had been the help which Maria Brummell, long the well-to-do wife of Captain Blackshaw, had sent to her celebrated but penniless brother. Maria, free from anxiety,

still lived with her two daughters in a house near The
Grove, the old country place of the Brummells in Berkshire. And yet, what had George Brummell in his own
prosperous days done for his sister? He had let himself
grow estranged both from her and from William. Neither
William nor Maria was inclined, even now, to overlook
that neglect altogether.

Their brother spoke with deep foreboding when he finished his letter to Armstrong with "I see it cannot last
long with me." While he had come out of prison bravely,
and with stout heart and warmth of spirit gone back to
his frivolities of an evening, Brummell had faced his imprisonment only after three paralytic seizures, and any
good which an enforced regularity of hours might have
done him was in his weakened state more than under-
mined by worry whilst he longed for release. That first
impetus to give full rein to his liberty, to accept every invitation, to go to bed at any hour whatever between dark-
ness and dawn, took far too small account of the strain to
which he had in both mind and body been so lately subjected. In this year of 1837 his memory began to go. The
Beau slipped into the habit of repeating stories, long stories, some of them not very good, to the same person. If
this weakness is common enough in people aged seventy-
five, it is not characteristic of those who have barely reached
their sixtieth year; and yet, Brummell assuredly did look
older by fifteen years. It was as if, now that the starch had
vanished from his cravat, to be replaced only by a black

silk scarf that sagged, his face too had sagged, that face already askew, mottled, creased, almost wizened. With his chin sunk in the folds of his black neckcloth, the Beau of St. James's, the pet of duchesses, the idol of princes, had become a creature of reverie.

While the impudence for which Brummell was notable in his great days had subsided under the double blow of exile and poverty, it now curiously emerged. It was like a reassertion of personality, a sudden flare from embers of the past. One evening when he was dozing in the company of two ladies, one of whom had left her daughter alone at the seaside, and the other was chiding her for it, the Beau suddenly looked up and remarked, "She is too plain for anybody to dream of running off with her." It was an echo of the day when he asked a duchess to back out of the room because he could not bear her figure the other way round. Again, at an elaborate dinner-party given by an English hostess, to whom he sat next, Brummell criticized every dish set before him. "What is that?" he pointed to the *filet*. "How tough!" and he sent his plate away. Looking at the bottom of the table, he observed, "What a half-starved turkey!" The hostess wept; but the Beau sat still, and in time consumed a huge meal. Likewise, at his hotel, he indulged the habit of condemning every dish on the table d'hôte. He would raise a slice of veal on his fork, stare at it, shake his head, and exclaim, "Bah!" Nevertheless he proceeded to devour everything that the menu offered. It was perhaps well for Brummell

263

that the good folk of Caen attributed these little dramas of fault-finding to the decay of a mind which had hitherto seemed normally restrained.

But the sad evidence of his infirmity was most noticeable in his dress—the last thing which he in a sane state would have let go unheeded. For some time he had mended his own clothes—his linen, his coat, his trousers; but now he began to disregard their tatters, frayed elbows, torn knees. When he went out—which time was the most important to him—he covered up most of the holes with his old green cloak, holding its fur collar high about his shoulders. Fortunately there was in Caen a tailor who had well profited from the Beau in the past, and who now felt as benevolently toward him as old Leleux of Le Pauvre Diable in Calais; as Leleux at the end would have kept Brummell for nothing, so this tailor now offered to mend his clothes for nothing. "I was ashamed," said the good man, "to see one so celebrated and so distinguished, one who had made a place in history, in a state so unhappy." So the Beau, now down to one pair of trousers, sent his trousers to be mended, and had to stay in bed until they were returned to the hotel.

If he had given up two or three of the luxuries to which he so stubbornly clung, he could have readily bought a change of clothes. But since all his life he had identified luxuries with necessities, in his present processes of thought he slighted the necessities and attached importance only to scent, to oil for his everlasting wig, to *biscuits de Rheims* for a post-luncheon titbit. Armstrong refused downright to pay for such things. Whereupon Brummell began to beg them. Everyday at two o'clock he stepped into Magdelaine's, a confectionery shop in front of the hotel, for two Rheims biscuits with a glass of either curaçoa or maraschino. He paid for them with a bow, a bow so perfect that it would be a sin for anyone to whom it was addressed to give utterance to questions of money. But at long last even Magdelaine could no longer allow this appreciation of courtliness to stifle his sense of economy. As soon as he protested, the Beau accommodatingly began to sell his trinkets, things which in the full strength of his mind he would have regarded it as a degradation to part with: porcelain vases, seals, chains, his last silver snuffbox; a gold repeater-watch for which he had once paid eighty guineas went for a song. In disposing of these articles the only reservation Brummell made was that he would let none of them go to his equals. When a covetous friend offered to buy that familiar bauble of his sitting-room, the ormolu greyhound, the Beau austerely answered: "If you are interested about it, pray accept it; but I don't *sell* it."

In July (1837) Tom Moore, one of the three poet-members of Watier's, himself now fifty-eight, came to Caen and called at the Hôtel d'Angleterre. This visit, this resurrection from a past which had enveloped Brummell with so much of both glitter and grief, was in the main a heartening thing. Then he was not utterly forgotten? Then there were in London those who still recalled his sartorial tyranny? How foolish they were, poets, hostesses, princes, to let him tell them what they must wear! Moore, unlike

Byron, had never been admitted to the highest niche in either the esteem or the intimacy of this potentate of fashion, now so forlornly exiled, and dying. Yet Brummell welcomed him with a glad face, invited him to dine, and talked at great length. Moore was shaken with pity. Returning home, he told the surviving men of Mayfair what he had seen: "The poor Beau's head was gone, and his whole looks so changed that I should never have recognized him. Got wandering in his conversation more than once during dinner."

This news found some exaggeration before long. Even Alvanley, himself now in a declining way, was without seeing his dearest friend disposed to accept the hearsay that the Beau was about nine toes in the grave. "Poor Brummell is become imbecile," Alvanley informed Tom Raikes no later than September. "He saw ——, and knew him; but a few minutes afterwards forgot him, and said that his friends had been kind to him, with the exception of ——, who was a shabby fellow, and had done nothing for him, after having promised everything. He is grown slovenly and dirty; is, however, otherwise well, and lives on what we subscribe for him."

But he was not yet so slovenly that he was excluded from the *soirées* of Caen. As of an evening he now set out for houses still friendly he tottered as he walked, now and again touching a wall for support; and the merciless children of the town mimicked him. Yet the Burton family, one of the very few English families in Caen whom he had taken up at the start, left their door constantly open to him, unkempt, toothless and tiresome as he had now become. Nor did all of his hostesses shrink away; in their recollecting eyes he remained a conqueror. Of one of these more charitable ladies a younger person inquired, "How can you admit such a driveller?" The answer was a simple tribute to an elegant shred of manner that still shone through: "I like to see him take his seat before my fire." Seated, Brummell gently fell asleep, and only stirred to sip a proffered nightcap.

Rather, it was the company of Ellen St. Ursain to which he was now a total stranger, Ellen and her somewhat boisterous young friends. But, if the Beau was an acceptable admirer so long as Ellen was of an age to give heed to his teaching, or to care about collecting his sketches and his verses, she had outgrown him. To that, Brummell was now resigned. As long as his affection for Ellen had been moderately returned, he was very happy in it. Now, he was past brooding. When he criticized her friends, she would have none of his maundering; she fell away, and he let her go. Perhaps it was one of those young men who circulated these satirical verses about him:

"Keen blows the wind, and piercing is the cold;
  My pins are weak, and I am growing old;
  Around my shoulders this worn cloak I spread,
  With an umbrella, to protect the head
  Which once had wit enough to astound the world;
  But now, possesses nought but wig well-curl'd.
  Alas! alas! while wind and rain do beat,
  That great Beau Brummell thus should walk the street!"

It was a picture of him, early in 1838, when at the age of sixty he was doddering into senility like an octogenarian. One gloomy morning before this year had escaped from the clutch of winter a certain English lady, actually not much younger than Brummell himself, a lady distinguished in manner but plain in dress, moved past the window of the *bureau* of M. Fichet. The landlord bustled out into the courtyard of the hotel. "Is Mr. Brummell," inquired the stranger, "still living here?" When Fichet bowed, she said, "I am most anxious to see him. Can you put me in the way of doing so, without the chance of his seeing me?" Fichet, with Gallic acquiescence in the faintest suggestion of romance, assured her of his help. He led her to a private room, which she engaged. "At five o'clock," said the landlord, "Monsieur Brummell always comes down from his room to the table d'hôte. His room is on this very staircase, and he must pass yours. I shall therefore with your permission come back to you at that hour, and when I hear him coming down, I shall go out and meet him. If you stand by your own door, you will see him clearly, for he always carries a light in his hand." This plan being agreed on, the landlord withdrew.

At the hour named, Fichet reappeared in the corridor, off which opened the room whose door was only a few steps beyond the bottom of the staircase. As Brummell slowly staggered down, the landlord started up the steps toward him, and at a level distinctly visible from a narrow aperture in the door of the guest on watch, talked to him for several minutes, by candlelight. Then Fichet returned to the room of the unknown lady. He found her in tears. She could not speak, and it was some time before she could put down her sobs enough to thank him. Then, straight-way paying her bill, the afflicted lady took coach that same evening for Paris. She may have been Sarah Savile, later Lady Monson, and now the Countess of Warwick; at least she was a woman who had loved Brummell equally well, in the heyday of them both, when neither bore a thought, a care, or a wisp of anxiety beyond the dallying hours of youth.

As the Beau lived on in the minds of the women who used to know him, so were the women ever in his own mind, fast ebbing though it was. Out of delicacy for their feelings, he now ceased going to their houses, and passed his evenings, instead, in a café off the Place Royale. There he took his second cup of coffee, which at the Angleterre was denied him, as not being stipulated in the agreement for his board. This second cup, like his curaçoa, Brummell paid for by the very grace of his manners, which to an extraordinary degree were outlasting his mentality. If the woman of the café hinted at payment, the Beau always made a bow which was the perfection of politeness, looked up at the sky, and lyrically responded, *"Oui, Madame, à la pleine lune, à la pleine lune."*

But if he decided that it was time for him to give a party, he stayed away from the café, and directed his attendant in his sitting-room at the hotel to light the candles and to set out a whist-table. The man being provided with a list of the guests expected, mostly ladies, Brummell sat awaiting them in his easy-chair by the fire. At eight o'clock the attendant, always following the same instructions, opened wide the door and announced, "the Duchess of Devonshire." The Beau arose, advanced to the door, and with the utmost courtliness shook hands with the cold air as if it were his own Georgiana. "Ah, my dear Duchess! how rejoiced I am to see you! so very amiable of you at this short notice! Pray bury yourself in this arm-chair; do you know, it was a gift to me from the Duchess of York ... but, poor thing, you know, she is now no more." Weeping, he then sank into the chair himself, and gazed into the fire until the next friends came. "Lord Alvanley! The Marquess of Worcester!" Again Brummell got up, and earnestly went through the same pantomime. At ten o'clock the man announced the carriages, and one by one the phantom guests departed.

CHAPTER XVIII

BON SAUVEUR

1838–1840

THE MORE Brummell's mind gave way, it seemed, the more oil the poor man poured over his wig. When he put it on, sometimes wrong end in front, the oil often dripped upon his dressing-gown. Now and again he could not find the wig, and as he wandered bald about the room, seeking it everywhere, he loudly accused the hairdresser of stealing it, until a servant came in, helped in the search, and generally discovered the wig carefully tucked away between the mattresses. But once this wig was properly on, the Beau liked to cross the street to his perfumer's, and try to get more oil. Upon this errand, one evening in the summer of 1838, he fell down heavily in the mud; as he was brought into the hotel, bleeding and bruised, a waiter discovered that one of his boots was only half pulled on. A few days later, whilst he was again poking about in his sitting-room, there was a great crash of glass; a servant running in saw that Brummell, though not injured, had fallen once more, and this time with the back of his head against a window.

It was obvious not only that the wretched man must no longer go outdoors, but that even indoors he must have someone always with him. An old woman was engaged. The Beau resented this move as an intrusion upon his privacy, but, forced to put up with her, he decided to hate her with politeness. If the creature interfered, he should exact revenge, one of his most dire penalties being to refuse to go to bed. In a high-pitched argument which one day arose, neighbours clear across the street could hear Brummell scream, "Ah! are you then my mistress?" Finally the old woman had to call in the waiter's brother, a corporal from the army. The dispute proceeded along the same lines, until the Beau cried, "Ah! are you then my master?" "Yes," retorted the corporal. "I am your master. Go to bed immediately." Then he took Brummell gently by the arm, led him to the bed, and saw that he lay down in comfort.

Subjected again to confinement, the patient grew worse, for the psychological effect of this restraint was almost as if he had been taken to prison a second time, and in one respect it proved more injurious; in prison he had at least enjoyed the freedom of the debtors' courtyard; now, he was even deprived of a walk in the garden back of the hotel. He began to let his beard grow for three days at a time, a negligence unheard of. When he did shave, Brummell not only wiped his razor on notes from Madame de Stael—that might have been understandable—but upon pages which he tore out of priceless editions of Shakespeare and Sheridan. After breastfast, he took to looking long and earnestly into his fire, his one remaining solace, whilst the hag who kept watch over him sat making lace in a corner opposite. When two compatriots, hearing that the poor Beau was in want of fuel, stepped in to see for themselves, they could draw no complaint from him on that score, nor any conversation at all, except this remark: "What a cursed old woman that is!" He was still hating politely, and enjoying it. No longer did he go down to the table d'hôte, but devoured enormous meals in his room, fifteen dishes at a time, eating meat like bread, until his doctor, summoned for an alarming attack of gastritis, prescribed a measured quantity of food for each time.

With all his encroaching slovenliness, which nothing but imbecility, not even the wretchedest poverty, would have induced him to yield to, it was as remarkable as it was pathetic that Brummell still displayed vestiges of his primary passion, his sense of neatness. One day a certain lord, an old clubmate from London, turned up and asked Fichet, like the mysterious woman caller, if he could see the Beau without being seen. Fichet led the way to the sitting-room of his guest, and entering, left the door open, outside which the lord stood close. Brummell, standing by the fire, was busily dusting his mantelpiece, and a few shells which he kept upon it. "Good day, Monsieur Brummell," said Fichet. "How is your health?" "Very good, I thank you," responded the Beau, still plying the duster. "Have you heard the news?" queried the landlord. "No." "George the Fourth is dead." To this, the only rejoinder was, "Ah! is he?" and Brummell, not even looking up, went on with his dusting. If he found Fichet tedious, he was probably still more annoyed, whether he was for the moment mad or sane, by any mention of the late glorious George. When the Beau was in Calais, and got that news at the time it was news, he betrayed hardly any greater concern. The point of this incident in the sitting-room was not the conversation, but the dusting, the persistence of a life-long impulse in a man who had almost if not utterly lost his reason. The lord who had remained just outside sadly withdrew, to call upon Charles Armstrong and offer help. "I can scarcely believe," said he, "that I have seen George Brummell."

If he had remained until the end of November he would not have believed it at all, for in that month the miserable Beau suffered an attack of abdominal paralysis, his fourth stroke. He then lost control of his bodily functions. When his room at times suggested a sty, Brummell in tones of horrified confidence blamed the condition upon either Fichet's dog or an Englishman who lodged underneath, but who never came near him. There were now left in Caen only two people who did call: Armstrong's servant Auguste, and the English vicar. Auguste, upon the wild protests of Fichet and his wife, arranged for the helpless lodger to lie upon a straw mattress, which was changed every day. But Fichet soon came to insist that Brummell must be taken away from the Angleterre.

At this crisis, the faithful Armstrong energetically made the rounds of public institutions in the neighbourhood, and of possible private houses within an equal radius. But the word of Brummell's multiplication of ailments had got bruited about, and nobody would admit such a patient. In despair, Armstrong wrote to one of the London subscribers to the maintenance fund. "I should think that some of his old friends in England would be able to get him into some hospital, where he could be taken care of for the rest of his days. I beg and entreat you to get something done for him, for it is quite out of the question that he can remain where he is. The clergyman and physician here can bear testimony to the melancholy state of idiocy he is in."

Whether influence from England was exerted upon the case or not, Brummell, though perhaps past consciousness of suffering, had to endure in the hotel six months more of living death, shunned, forgotten, meagrely attended to. Then, in May, 1839, an application for his admission into the Bon Sauveur, a large general asylum in the suburbs, near the Bayeux Road, was after long delay favourably acted upon. This hospital, occupying with gardens and orchards about fifteen acres, was in charge of 75 nuns, Sisters of Charity, assisted by 50 novices, and an army of servants. Of patients, at this time, there were about 150 men and 180 women, insane; but there were large numbers of others about, such as the deaf and dumb, the temporarily ailing, and children in convent; the total, including staff, was over a thousand persons. While the largest building was reserved for the insane, smaller houses sheltered separately the various other classes of inmates, who enjoyed the run of numerous gardens.

When the day came for Brummell to go, Fichet ordered

a carriage to be drawn up at the door nearest to the staircase which led to the Beau's rooms. Then the landlord,
accompanied by Armstrong and Auguste, tapped on the
door of their patient. On entering, they discovered Brummell in his easy-chair beside the fire, with his cherished
wig on one knee, this knee being raised by his having set
his foot on the rail of a smaller chair in front of him. An
old pewter shaving-mug stood on a little table close by; into
this mug Brummell was dipping his brush, and making a
lather, with which he was adorning his wig, most thoroughly, as if to make every hair lie flat. Engrossed in his
work, he never noticed that callers had come. "Good day,
Monsieur Brummell," said Fichet. If his lodger remembered anything at all, he need not have been surprised, for
only a day or two before, the landlord had invited him to
go for a drive on the Cours at this hour, and Brummell
had accepted. But now, contrary to his courteous manner,
which had wonderfully persisted until this day, the man
not only kept on with his brush, but declined to turn his
head, and said simply, "Let me alone." Whereat Fichet
continued: "But I have ordered a carriage for you, to take
a drive with me; you promised me that you would go, and
the carriage is now at the door." Brummell excused himself, saying that he was not well, that he would go another
time. All three men then spoke of the fine day, of a garden
that they were taking him to see, a garden in the lovely
month of May. Brummell, lathering away, would not
budge.

Then Fichet stepped forward, snatched the wig from

his knee, and threw it on the table. His lodger, enraged as only a madman can be, ordered the men to leave his room at once, failing which, he would hurl them out. But six arms, like the arms of a sudden monster, seized the fuming Brummell and bore him struggling and sputtering down the stairs. It was then that he fancied they were arresting him again, and though his legs were swollen and his arms emaciated, he kicked, fought, screamed and shouted. "You are taking me to prison—loose me, scoundrels! I owe nothing." In vain Armstrong tried to assure him he was going to a far happier home. A shriek from Brummell filled the courtyard to its very end. Then suddenly, as he was deposited in the carriage, it seemed to dawn upon him that it was no good resisting, and he sank back in a calm as complete as his outcry had been. As they drove across the Place Royale, they met Henri de Ste. Marie, whom Brummell had not seen for two years. To the astonishment of his captors, the poor man instantly recognized his one-time intimate friend, but drew back from the window of the carriage. "That," said Brummell, "is Monsieur de Ste. Marie." He looked down at his tattered dressing-gown. "I did not bow to him, for I am not fit to be seen in such a *déshabillé* as this."

Nor did he fail to show signs of sanity as the coach drove up to the gates of Bon Sauveur. The gates were closed. As the keeper loudly shot back their bolts, the dread which had overcome Brummell as he was borne down the staircase of the hotel seized upon him again, and he wept, and muttered, "A prison—a prison." Only when the horses stopped in the courtyard, and the sick man got down to be welcomed by a cluster of nuns, did this dread subside, sensing in the gentle manners of these young women a safer atmosphere. The Abbess, a well-fed rosy dame, came up and took George Brummell by the hand. He was delighted. He was quite ready to allow one of the younger nuns to escort him into the house, while Auguste supported him on the other side, and in the maze of this novel cordiality he fancied he was come to be the guest of Auguste's family. "This is Madame, isn't it?" he said to that somewhat embarrassed man. "Ah! you are married! Well, I congratulate you, for"—he turned to the little nun —"you are indeed a pretty woman." So they led Brummell to his own sitting-room, where he was greeted by the two things which his remnant of life craved: an arm-chair and a good fire with flames dancing above it.

After what he had left, this house was a paradise. On the very first day his manservant, a man detailed to attend him continuously, and him only, came to take the new guest out into the garden in a bathchair. The garden was full of roses. Its gravelled walks were edged with box. The Beau—for he was now in surroundings the like of which had known him as a Beau in his prime—could have been no happier in the gardens of Oatlands, wheeled by the Duchess of York.

When the manservant was off duty, a nun replaced him. To every one of the sisters who ministered to his needs he was infinitely polite, grateful, and considerate, almost gallant, as if he were again making his bows in the drawing-rooms of Mayfair. By the time summer had run through, and the cooler weather came, the chivalrous manners of Monsieur Brummell were the talk of the hospital. While he could hardly distinguish one nun from another, the word of appreciation was always upon his lips: "Ah, madame, you are too good to me; I am very thankful."

A few old acquaintances came to call. The patient recognized hardly any of them thoroughly. Yet he seldom failed to pay a tribute to the nun who stood by during the visit. To a certain caller one day he said, taking the hand of the nun at his side, "This excellent nurse of mine is so kind to me that she refuses me nothing . . . I never was so comfortable." But if usually he did not know who his visitors were, he did identify one whose face he had seen day after day: Fichet, the landlord. This man, who had snatched that precious wig from Brummell's knee, was so well remembered that the poor Beau upon seeing him thought himself back in the Hôtel d'Angleterre:" Good day, Fichet; table d'hôte at five o'clock?" "Oui, monsieur." "Very good, very good. I shall come down."

Thus he got through the winter, relinquishing his hold upon life perhaps more slowly than if he had been left to die upon straw in the hotel. He never grew so helpless that he could not answer questions about his wants; personal wants, as a matter of personal architecture, had been his very profession. But in the early spring of 1840 the debility which had so long corroded him seemed to hasten in its course, and the English clergyman of Caen, who had visited Brummell in the hotel at the time of his last stroke, but had subsequently done nothing to help him get into the Bon Sauveur, was sent for. During the month of March this gentleman made several calls at the hospital. In the course of conversations which he attempted with the dying man he found that Brummell was unable to remember any occurrence for five minutes. When the clergyman tried to talk on religion, Brummell told funny stories of his old days in England. "I never," said this spiritual adviser later, ". . . came in contact with so painful an exhibition of human vanity and apparent ignorance."

To this baffled though well-meaning man, two possible explanations of such behaviour did not occur: first, that his personality may have struck Brummell as slightly humorous, and again, that talks leading to the subject of death and the hereafter may have been distasteful to a man who for all his imminent dissolution was very happy in his life at the Bon Sauveur. "With him," observed the clergyman, "there was some response when sounded on worldly subjects; none on religious." The obvious comment is that Brummell to the last was a man of the world.

On the 30th of March it seemed to all that the end was only a matter of hours. Brummell was too weak to make any sort of fight, and he realized it himself. No longer talkative, he grew apprehensive. In the afternoon the English parson came again, and at a glance he fancied that this visit was to be his final one. But his conversation with the patient did not make much headway, since the answers he got seemed to him scarcely intelligible. Yet why should the man have insisted upon answers? Over and over he besought the expiring figure before him to try and pray.

"I *do try*," said Brummell pitiably.

But at twilight the clergyman went away, with serious doubts about the salvation of one so reticent.

It was about eight o'clock when the nun who was attending Brummell noticed on his face a look of "intense anxiety and fear." Fixing his eyes upon her, with an expression of entreaty, but not speaking a word, he raised his hands toward her, as if imploring her to come to his help. The nun asked him to repeat after her an act of contrition, according to the Roman ritual. Brummell obeyed, earnestly. This seemed to soothe him, and as he finished, he turned his head quietly away. About an hour afterwards he rolled completely over, again facing the room—where there were now gathered several of the hospital staff—and as he turned he cried out in pain. Soon, he put his eyes once more to the wall, as if unwilling to let the watchers see him go. In this wise the life went out of Beau Brummell moment by moment, and the final moment was at a quarter past nine.

They took him to the Protestant Cemetery, none of the English colony attending, nor any of his young Carlist friends, neither young men nor young women. The cemetery itself was a tangle of weeds.

Finis

READING FOR THE
REIGN OF BEAU BRUMMELL

READING FOR THE
REIGN OF BEAU BRUMMELL

I. Books, Chapters, and Articles Dealing Mainly
with Brummell

The Life of Beau Brummell, William Jesse. 2 vols. 1844.

Memorandum. (Brummell in Caen). J. A. Barbey d'Aurevilly.
1856.

Du Dandysme et de George Brummell. Ibid. 1845.

Le Fin d'un Dandy, G. Comte de Contades. 1898.

Beau Brummell and His Times, R. Boutet de Monvel. 1908.

Beau Brummell, L. S. Benjamin. ("Lewis Melville"). 1924.

The Beaux and the Dandies, Clare Jerrold. 1910. (pp. 192-297).

Originaux et Beaux Esprits de l'Angleterre Contemporaine,
E. D. Forgues. 1860.

The Wits and Beaux of Society, Grace and Philip Wharton.
1860.

Sous Louis-Philippe: Les Dandys, Jacques Boulenger. 1907.

Moniteur Universel, 7 juin 1880. 'Brummel.' Paul de St. Victor.

Gazette de France, 3 juillet 1885. 'Brummel.' Dancourt.

Edinburgh Review. February, 1843. Beau Brummell.

Beau Brummell, Virginia Woolf. (essay). 1930.

In the Days of the Dandies, Lord Lamington (A. D. R. Coch-
rane). 1906.

II. Books and Articles Bearing Upon Brummell's Family and Upon his Early Life

Notes and Queries. Series I, 2; VI, 11; IX, 1, 2, 9; X, 7.

Historical Memoirs of My Own Time, Sir N. W. Wraxall. (ed. 1904).

Eton Lists.

Annals of Eton, Wasey Sterry. 1898.

Fasti Etonenses, A. C. Benson. 1899.

History of Eton College, Lionel Cust. 1899.

Eton College Register, R. A. Austen Leigh. 1907.

History of Eton, Sir H. C. Maxwell-Lyte. 1911.

Floreat Etona, Ralph Neville.

Eton Portrait, Bernard Fergusson. 1938.

Oriel College Buttery Books.

Oriel College, D. W. Rannie. 1900.

Registrum Orielense, C. L. Shadwell. 2 vols.

Temple Bar, XXXV, 231.

Cornhill, New Series, i, 769.

All the Year Round, 2nd Series, 26, 106.

III. Memoirs, Letters, and Contemporary Books in Which Brummell Plays a Part

Satirical View of London Men and Manners, John Corry. 1802.

Galerie Anglaise. Anon. 1802.

Life of Fox, B. C. Walpole. 1806.

Christie's Sale Catalogue. May 22, 1816.

Memoirs of George IV, Robert Huish. 1831.

Letters (1810-45). Lady Harriet Granville. 2 vols. ed. Gower. 1894.

Memoirs, Harriette Wilson. 1825. ed. 1909, 2 vols.

Memoirs, Journals and Correspondence, Tom Moore. 8 vols. 1853-6.

Journals, Thomas Raikes. (1831-47). 4 vols. 1856.

Personal Correspondence. Ibid. 1861.

Recollections of West End Life, Major Alan Chambre. 2 vols. 1858.

Reminiscences, Capt. R. H. Gronow. 1862.

Recollections and Anecdotes, Ibid. 1863.

Celebrities of London and Paris, Ibid. 1865.

Fifty Years Biographical Reminiscences, Lord William Pitt Lennox. 2 vols. 1863.

Life and Recollections, Grantley Berkeley. 4 vols. 1865.

Anecdotes of the Upper Ten Thousand, Ibid. 2 vols. 1867.

Memoirs, Charles Greville. 8 vols. Ed. Lytton Strachey and Roger Fulford, 1939.

Historical Manuscripts Commission, Bathurst Papers. 1923. (Letter from Lord Alvanley to Earl Bathurst, 1820).

Life and Letters of Lady Hester Stanhope, ed. Baroness Dalmeny, 1914.

Memoires d'un Journaliste, J. Hippolyte A. D. de Villemessant. 1872-8.

Memoires d'Outre-Tombe, F. R. Vicomte de Chateaubriand. 1849-50. Ed. Maurice Levaillant. 2 vols. 1936.

IV. LATER BOOKS IN WHICH MENTION OF BRUMMELL MAY BE FOUND

Round About Piccadilly and Pall Mall, H. B. Wheatley. 1870.
George IV, P. H. Fitzgerald. 1881.
History of English Literature, Taine (trans.). Vol. IV. 1890.
History of White's, Hon. A. B. Bourke. 2 vols. 1892.

Memorials of Brooks's, V. A. Williamson. 1907.

La Caricature en Angleterre, P. M. Augustin Filon. 1902.

Life in Regency and Early Victorian Times, E. Beresford Chancellor. 1926.

Byron, A. Maurois. 1930.

Byron: the Years of Fame, Peter Quennell. 1935.

The Pageantry of Life, Charles Whibley. 1900.

Early Victorian England, ed. G. M. Young. Section by R. H. Mottram. 2 vols. 1934.

George the Fourth, Roger Fulford. 1935.

———

NOVELS CONTEMPORARY WITH BEAU BRUMMELL AND BASED UPON INTIMATE KNOWLEDGE OF HIS PERSONALITY

Granby, T. H. Lister. 1826.

Pelham, or, The Adventures of a Gentleman, E. G. Bulwer-Lytton. 1828.

PLAY

Beau Brummell. A Play in Four Acts, written for Richard Mansfield by Clyde Fitch. (New York). 1890.

INDEX

INDEX

boxes, 56; commands Belvoir Volunteers, 57; dictates fashion, 62-63; makes the Album, 64 et seq.; more love affairs, 69; *bon mots,* 71; meets Harriette Wilson, 73 et seq.; and Julia Storer, *ibid;* visits the Musters, 75; grief at death of Duchess of Devonshire, 77; writes "Butterfly's Funeral," *ibid;* at Watier's, 79; gambling, 80; arbiter of fashion, 82 et seq.; connoisseur of snuff, 85; friendship with Duke of York, 88; Lady H. Stanhope goes away, 89; his supremacy at White's, 90; reputation at its height, 91; at Almack's, *ibid;* attitude to Prince Regent, 93 et seq.; his snuffboxes, 93; rudeness to Mrs. Fitzherbert, 94; snubbed by Prince Regent, 96; joins the York party, 97; friendship with Duchess, 98 et seq.; at Oatlands, 99; jest about old King and Prince Regent, 100; cut by Prince in Bond Street, 103; his retort, *ibid;* cool insolence towards him, 104; says he "made the Prince and could unmake him," 106; friendship with Byron, 109, 114 et seq.; the "Dandy Club," 110; meets Madame de Stael, 110; cut by Prince at the Dandies' Ball, 112; heavy gambling, 115; losses, 116; moves to smaller house in Chapel Street, 119; his furniture, 119 et seq.; continued difficulties, 121; tries to raise money, 122 et seq.; leaves England, 124 et seq.; sale of his effects, 126; settles at Calais, 131; meets old friends,

132, 139; letters to England, 132, 133, 145; discussed in London, 134; settles at Le Pauvre Diable, 135; furnishes, 137; life at Calais, 140 et seq.; writes to Duchess of York, 142; makes a screen for her, 147, 152; hears of Prince's accession to throne, 150; affected by death of Duchess of York, 153; Alvanley intercedes for him at Court, 154; moves his rooms, 156; ignored by King at Calais, 158; his memoirs, 161; writes on "Male Costumes," *ibid;* in London, 162; life in Calais, 165 et seq.; applications for him in England, 172; appeals for money, 174; for appointment as consul, 175; in love with girl in Calais, 177; visited by C. Greville, 185; hears of George IV's death, 187; appointed consul at Caen, 188; in Paris, 189 et seq.; goes to Caen, 192; life there, 193 et seq.; costume, 194; becomes Carlist in sympathy, 198; financial difficulties, 200 et seq.; friendship with Ellen de St. Ursain, 203 et seq.; Caen society, 205 et seq.; description of his toilet, 210; vexed with duns, 212; applies for transfer, 213; loses his post, 214; desperate condition, 215 et seq.; Carlist attitude, 216; changes apartment, 217; sends Armstrong to London, *ibid;* first paralytic stroke, 218; receives money from London, 219; affection for Ellen de St. Ursain, 220 et seq.; social festivities, 223; second stroke, 225; gives Ellen The Album, *ibid;* con-